YEARBOOK 2010

CHILDREN AND YOUTH IN THE DIGITAL MEDIA CULTURE

FROM A NORDIC HORIZON

Editor: Ulla Carlsson

The International Clearinghouse
on Children, Youth and Media

NORDICOM
University of Gothenburg

Yearbook 2010

Children and Youth in the Digital Media Culture

From a Nordic Horizon

Editor:
Ulla Carlsson

ISSN 1651-6028
ISBN 978-91-86523-04-6

Published by:
The International Clearinghouse on Children, Youth and Media
Series editor: Ulla Carlsson

Nordicom
University of Gothenburg
Box 713
SE 405 30 GÖTEBORG
Sweden

Cover by:
Daniel Zachrisson

Printed by:
Litorapid Media AB, Göteborg, Sweden, 2010
Environmental certification according to ISO 14001

CHILDREN AND YOUTH
IN THE DIGITAL MEDIA CULTURE

Contents

Foreword

The Clearinghouse on Children Youth and Media at Nordicom, University of Gothenburg, has published eleven yearbooks to date. In them, researchers and experts from all the corners of the world have treated a wide variety of issues from many different perspectives.

It is the mission of the Clearinghouse to cast light on what is currently known about children, youth and media. One might say that we also help to bring order to a complex subject area, where many diverse views and interests converge and consensus in the research community is lacking. It is our hope that bringing together a disparate body of research findings and ideas about young people and the media will contribute to further knowledge in the field.

In recent years we have especially focused on media literacy and the demands that the new digital media landscape poses – on children and adults alike. A familiarity with the media and an understanding of their logic has become essential. The Clearinghouse addresses and serves a variety of professional and other user groups around the word. These include research communities, policy-makers at various levels, media practitioners, teachers, interest organizations, civil society organizations and other interested groups and individuals. Our guiding vision is to build and maintain a worldwide network. Today that network has more than one thousand members in more than 150 countries. Clearinghouse services reach users in practically every country of the world.

The global dimension is a core principle in the work of the Clearinghouse with respect to both the content we publish and distribute and the contributors who produce it. This, the twelfth Yearbook, represents a departure from that hallowed principle of global representation. That we depart from it this year has to do with the fact that the World Summit on Media for Children and Youth 2010 is being held in Sweden in the Nordic region. In conjunction with the Summit the Clearinghouse and Nordicom are arranging a global Research Forum with participants from all continents. The contributions presented in the Research Forum and the results of that meeting will fill our Yearbook 2011.

But, the present Yearbook showcases the Nordic countries and the work being done in the research communities of Denmark, Finland, Iceland, Norway and Sweden. The focus rests on children, youth and media in a digitized media culture, and media literacy – importance and challenges. We believe that the issues treated here will interest a broad range of readers all over the world.

In addition to the selection of articles, the volume offers a statistical overview of young people's media use in the Nordic countries. It is produced by Catharina Bucht, Coordinator of the Clearinghouse.

I wish to thank each and everyone who has contributed to this volume. It is our hope that it will make a fruitful contribution to our collective knowledge of children, youth and media in the digital age.

Göteborg in May 2010

Ulla Carlsson, Professor
Director
Nordicom

Young People in the Digital Media Culture
Global and Nordic Perspectives – An Introduction

Ulla Carlsson

Young people today face a paradox. On the one hand, globalization, coupled with technological development, has undoubtedly increased cultural output. But on the other hand, it is equally true that, for some, the possibility of access is reduced or restricted. In that sense, the thinking and analysis regarding the relationship between youth, communication and social change must be located precisely in the field of tension generated by this paradox. That is to say, more and better means for communication, increasingly powerful technological devices and the "availability" of enormous resources for information and knowledge exist alongside the increasing impoverishment of large areas of the planet, aggravated conditions of exclusion, and the so-called "digital divide". The divide condemns millions of young people to new forms of communicational "illiteracy", or to put it in other terms, to the emergence of two categories of youth, to paraphrase García Canclini (2004). The one is "disconnected and unequal", with limited or no access to the instruments of the net and technology, and even more serious, to health services and job security. Informalized, their demands and needs belong to a fully structural logic: employment, education, housing – or, in other words, basic aspirations of social justice and wellbeing. The other is well situated, connected and globalized, with access to technology and fundamental amenities such as education, employment and health.

Rossana Reguillo 2009

New media landscapes have transformed both the structure of governance and the social functions of media and communication. In the midst of this development are our young. Young people of today share ideas, thoughts and values through mass media, music and a variety of internet platforms. All over the world they are organizing themselves and networking in many different ways – formal and informal. But opportunity is not equal for all.

Children and youth represent more than one-third of the world population. The ratio varies, however, between regions. In the least developed countries young people account for nearly 70 percent, whereas in the industrialized regions of the world the figure is less than 25 percent (UN Population Division 2009). More than half of the young people live in poverty – on less than $2 per day (ICPD 2009). Many of them lack access to media, information and knowledge. It is a world of poverty with social and economic exclusion, poor schools, gender discrimination, unemployment and inadequate health systems. How long must we wait before we have a world where young people, not least girls, have good opportunities to express their own views and have their opinions respected – to live free from poverty, discrimination, intolerance and violence?

Many researchers and international organizations, such as the UN, UNESCO and the World Bank, and several NGOs underline the nexus between freedom of expression, human rights and poverty eradication. Access to a variety of media, telephony and online services is a vital factor for political, economic, social and cultural development. Independent and pluralistic media is crucial to good governance and strengthening political, and social development, thereby alleviating poverty. Freedom of expression and freedom of information are as effective as education and investments are for development (Novel 2006).

By identifying problems and instigating public discussion of them, the media can raise people's awareness and make them more active. Critical scrutiny, information and public education through the media can improve health, raise the level of formal education, reduce corruption and more – each an important step in poverty eradication. Radio especially plays an important role. Unparallelled in many parts of the world, radio is effective and cheap, yet far-reaching.

It is here that we find the groups that Reguillo characterizes as "disconnected" and "unequal". The Nordic countries are reckoned among the other, "well situated" parts of the world, where education and health care are universal and the prospects of gainful employment are good.

The planet is shrinking – we gain access to cultures and knowledge that used to be beyond our horizons. The communication society of today has enormous potential, not least for those who are young today. But in many parts of the world, there are fears that globalization poses a mortal threat to uniqueness, that media are in control of the globalized cultural sphere. At the same time the world seems to retreat further from us. People defend their identities, and when common culture can no longer be maintained as it once could be, stockades are raised around local cultures, religious beliefs and communities. Transcendance of boundaries and defense of boundaries are twin aspects of the globalization process. More than ever we need mutual understanding of both local and global media cultures to find new ways to reduce the gaps between rich and poor countries – and between rich and poor within every country.

Issues of democracy and development are central, and once again, technological advances are a prime motor force in this connection – not least the questions, how to bridge the knowledge divides in the world, and how to use media and communication both as tools and as a way of articulating processes of development and social change. Globalization processes force us not only to focus more on transnational phenomena in general, but also to highlight social change and difference. We have to argue for a stronger focus on global and regional inequalities and social transformation. About 60-70 percent of the inequality that exists today is inequality between nations; two hundred years ago 90 percent of the inequality was within countries. Thus, the gap between wealthy and poor countries has increased dramatically over the past two hundred years (Bourguignon and Morrisson 2002).

Research communities need to create platforms to achieve long-term goals through national, regional and international collaboration. And, not least, we need comparative studies in order to shed light on important issues. We have to build on past work, but break new ground. We need fresh, unexpected insights and new comparative research questions. We need to develop analytical frameworks that will guide comparative analysis of media cultures. Without comparative perspectives we run an obvious risk that certain factors will grow out of proportion.

The "digital divide", as it is sometimes called, is often a reflection of other divides: of class, gender and ethnicity. So, we should not lose sight of the fact that, *power– and powerlessness, identity* and *inequality* are still concepts of vital relevance when discussing young people in the global digital media landscape (Golding 2005), and we should neither lose sight of the fact that the 'arteries' in the media landscape – not least the routes that communication takes – are creations of political will (McChesney 2008). This is true of internet and mobile telephones as well as television and, even earlier, radio. Without a political will, there will be no development. These truths lie at the core of how we treat the most important issues regarding children, youth and media all over the world.

Young people in the digital media culture.
From a Nordic horizon

The five Nordic countries, Denmark, Finland, Iceland, Norway and Sweden, with a combined population of some 25 million people, are a very small region in the global media landscape. The region today is one of the wealthiest regions in the world, and the Nordic countries rank generally high up in indexes measuring democracy, prosperity, freedom of expression, absence of corruption and similar indicators.

The countries are kindred in many respects, including their media systems. People in Denmark, Norway and Sweden share the same linguistic roots, whereas Finnish belongs to an entirely different family of languages. All share long traditions of public service broadcasting; strong newspaper industries at regional and local levels; long traditions of protecting freedom of expression and freedom of the press in law; early development of ICT. Nearly everyone has access to mobile telephony, and 90 percent have internet access at home; newspaper reading continues to be widespread and frequent; a handful of large media companies dominate television, newspaper publishing and book publishing. Media companies from outside the region have yet to establish a major presence in the Nordic countries. Media ownership is largely in Nordic hands. (Nordicom 2009)

When those who are young today were infants in the early 1990s, neither Internet nor mobile telephones were known for people in general. Today, two decades later, we see how an interactive and mobile communication society is growing up alongside traditional mass media. Passive observers are becoming active participants.

In the Nordic countries people devote more than half of their leisure time to media use, and television viewing remains the single most dominant leisure activity. Among young people, however, internet tends to occupy that principal role. More than 95 percent of youth in the region have access to internet in their homes, and a majority use the web daily. (Nordicom 2009)

We have witnessed the dawning of a new media society with new patterns of communication. Our perceptions of time and space, of the bounds between private and public, have changed. And so have the functions of media. Diversification, fragmentation and individualization are frequently recurring themes in analyses of contemporary media culture.

The boundaries between private and public, between real and virtual are becoming ever more fluid. Definitions of knowledge and information are being revised. Concepts of personal integrity are changing. And, given the rampant consumerism that imbues society today, children and adolescents are a group that attracts companies' interest.

Media are among the most powerful social forces of our time, and whether we are talking about the political, economic or cultural sphere, we cannot avoid taking the media into account. Our attempts to understand mass media have tended to treat the media as being apart from other social institutions – we have asked how the media influence society and culture; what effects mediated messages have on individuals and society, how advertising influences our purchases; how newspaper content influences our political preferences, and so forth. Today, such questions have to be answered in a new context, one that is characterized by the mediatization of societies and cultures (Hjarvard 2008). It is no longer solely a matter of what the media do to us; there is also the question of what we do with the media.

Young people's use of media and Internet

Young people devote an increasing amount of their daily lives to a variety of activities online, but that does not mean that they have quit watching television. Old, conventional mass media like television radio, newspapers, books and magazines continue to occupy a good share of people's days, and young people are no exception. Despite print media's having been pronounced dead some 10-15 years ago by a seemingly unanimous corps of consultants, reading of hard-copy books rests on roughly the same level today as back then in the

Nordic countries – which have a long tradition of reading, thanks to the early introduction of obligatory primary education. In our studies we have found that young internet users, not least heavy internet users, also are heavy users of traditional media.

Figure 1. Internet users' use of traditional media the average day in 2009 (percent)

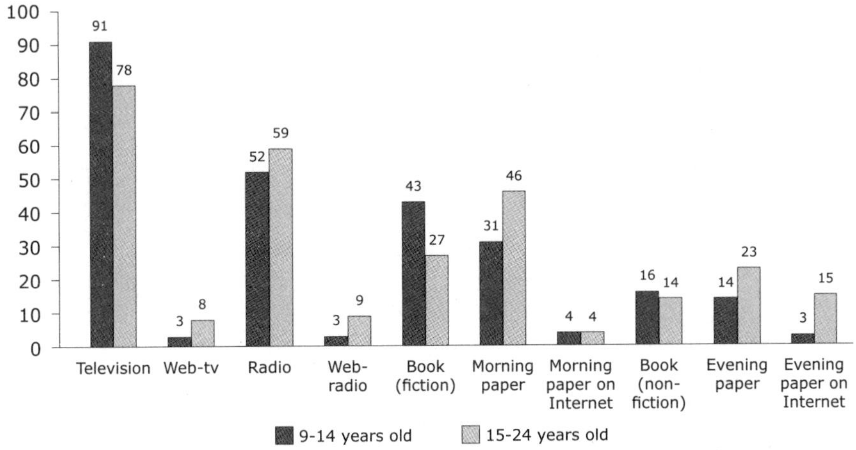

Source: Nordicoms Mediebarometer 2009.

But Internet is much more than what we generally have in mind when we speak of more traditional media. Internet offers arenas for communication, information, knowledge, shopping, entertainment, games, opinion-formation, creativity, artistry – and much, much more. The worldwide web offers media that we know well – we can partake of radio, television, film, music, newspapers on a variety of platforms on the web – to some extent in new forms including interactivity. But what we call 'social media' are something entirely different, enabling activities that combine technology, social interaction and user-generated content. They include different kinds of fora for discussion: communities, blogs and other sources of comment. The web-based activities that show the strongest growth among young people are those that make possible individual interaction, not least what we call 'social networking', as Facebook and Myspace – that is, media of conversation and interplay.

But, many media companies, broadcasters and newspapers, too, are spending a lot of resources on 'social media' – as are several organizations and institutions – in order to capture young audiences. And in these rooms it is not so easy to distinguish media professionals from others. At the same time, we know from recent studies that young people's use is primarily focused on social networking – on contacts with others who share their interests.

Figure 2. Common online activities among young people using internet in their homes the average day (percent)

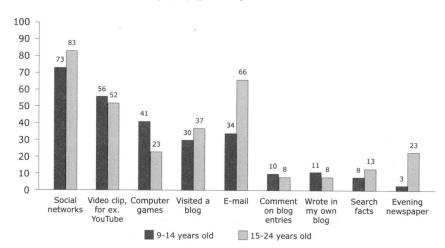

Source: Nordicoms Mediebarometer 2009.

Studies have found that young people are relatively ignorant of the full array of possibilities the web affords in the way, for example, of acquiring information and knowledge. Swedish anthropologist Katarina Graffman, for example, speaks of a "Generation Clueless". "Young people today", she writes, "know very little about being a citizen, but they know all about being a consumer" (Graffman 2008).

A recent study conducted by Pew Research Center in the USA found internet users aged 18-24 to be the age group that was least inclined to send an e-mail to a public official, or to make a political donation online. On the other hand, when it comes to sharing political news or joining a social network that has a political agenda, they are far ahead of all other age groups. They appear to be more interested in communicating political views to like-minded friends than in getting involved in politics. (Pew Research Center 2010)

But, is it really that simple? American researcher Lance Bennet explains young people's seeming lack of interest in social issues in terms of a change in paradigms of citizenship – from a traditional model that he calls Dutiful Citizen (DC), based on a sense of obligation to political participation as one of the cornerstones of democracy, where mass media are the prime source of information, to the Actualizing Citizen (AC), which would seem to characterize young people, who have a "diminishing sense of obligation". They are not convinced of the value of political elections, and they do not follow media coverage of politics, but prefer instead to take part in interactive networks on the web. As Bennet sees it, this gap between the generations has to be bridged. No less than the future of democracy is at stake. (Bennet 2007)

Studies of "Young Election", a Swedish website that addressed young voters in the campaign leading up to general elections in 2006, note that the site "was presented as an effort by the producers to incorporate the AC-oriented young people within DC-like politics. But as the ACs reached the website, they were instantly, almost literally, pushed to go into a DC direction of established party politics. They were basically invited as ACs, but – immediately, once they entered the website – asked to think and behave like DCs. ...This is what happens as the adult world tries to approach adolescents by talking their language and imitating their moods – they cannot really get it right: They talk AC talk, but are too stuck within DC modes of thinking to be able to communicate successfully." (Miegel and Olsson 2010)

Nowadays it is quite impossible to draw a firm line between online reality and "real life". Internet mirrors physical reality and makes the same kind of demands on us as are made in our lives offline, whether it is about political participation or gross violations of our personal integrity. The question is whether we have grasped the full implications of this change.

Regulation, self-regulation, co-regulation and awareness

Some applaud the young people's mastery of the media, while others worry about their inexperience and vulnerability.

Unknown properties of new media technologies have always tended to arouse fears, and, indeed, many parents, teachers and politicians have expressed concern regarding the negative influences of media on children and youth. As long as modern mass media have existed there have been waves of 'moral panic' concerning how the media influence our young. These concerns have increased as media technology has advanced.

Today there is particular concern about what we call 'harm and offence' in media content that can be distributed ever more widely via the internet, computer games, mobile telephones and satellite/cable television; we are talking about violent and pornographic fiction and non-fiction, offensive advertisements, stereotypical and disrespectful depictions of young people, women and minorities, hate-mongering messages, and so forth (Millwood Hargrave and Livingstone 2006).

And there are widespread fears regarding the risks young people expose themselves to on the web through anonymous encounters in the context of social networking – meeting strangers, being groomed, stalked, etc. Other new risks are self-harm, suicide, drugs, gambling, addiction, and commercial risks. On another front, we have issues relating to illegal downloading and the ramifications of the apparently crumbling institutions surrounding intellectual property rights.

For decades different actors have proposed and debated different means to limit the spread of content that may be considered harmful to young people, including laws, self-regulation and co-regulation.

The UN Convention on the Rights of the Child, which celebrated its twentieth anniversary in November 2009, provides an international framework for these efforts in two key articles. Article 13 states that every child "shall have the right to freedom of expression; this right shall include freedom to seek, receive and impart information and ideas of all kinds, regardless of frontiers, either orally, in writing or in print, in the form of art, or through any other media of the child's choice". Article 17 calls upon the signatory countries to "ensure that the child has access to information and material from a diversity of national and international sources, especially those aimed at the promotion of his or her social, spiritual and moral well-being and physical and mental health". Toward these ends the convention encourages governments and civil society institutions to "develop appropriate guidelines for the protection of the child from information and material injurious to his or her well-being".

The question of media and young people has occupied the European Union for a long time, as well. In the EU instruments, responsibility rests first and foremost with the adults – parents, teachers and others, but these adults need help in the form of both political decisions and initiatives on the part of the media industry, e.g., codes of ethics and rules that require the industry to assume its share of responsibility vis-à-vis children and youth.

We know today that it is not enough to use one or the other instrument if we are to achieve our goals. Instead, we need to achieve effective interaction between legislation, co-regulation and self-regulation. All parties – government, the media industries, not least, and civil society – need to develop effective modes of collaboration.

But, in the digitized media landscape and media culture of today we face new challenges – we need policies that balance the goals of maximizing opportunities and minimizing risks (Livingstone and Haddon 2009). So, to approach issues relating to young people and media solely in a regulation perspective is too limited, and limiting. In order to attain an all-round framework, viewers' and users' perspectives, too, need to be taken into account. A better knowledge and understanding of media is needed throughout society.

The importance of media and information literacy

> A responsible and accountable media can be encouraged and regulated, however imperfectly and however vulnerably. A responsible and accountable media culture is another matter entirely, for it depends on a critical and literate citizenry, a citizenry, above all, which is critical with respect to, and literate in the ways of, mass mediation and media representation. (Silverstone 2007, p 165)

Media, and not least internet, can represent social and cultural resources that can empower young people, in both their personal development and their development as members of society, as citizens. These developmental processes involve imagination and creativity as well as learning and knowledge. This is about media and information literacy – better and more widespread knowledge of the media will be a stimulus to participation, active citizenship, competence development and lifelong learning. In this way media and information literacy becomes crucial to ensuring a democratic society. Greater, more widespread competence with regard to media, so-called media literacy, is of the essence. Competence among children and young people is naturally very important, but it is important among parents, teachers and other adults need to be media literate, as well.

It is recognized that media and information literacy consists of a number of kinds of knowledge and proficiencies. In addition to the essential precondition, namely, access to media, young people need an understanding of how the media work, how they create meaning, how the media industries are organized, how they make money, and the goals toward which they work. Not least they need to understand the importance of a critical treatment of sources. The importance of an awareness of, and sensitivity to political censorship and commercial barriers cannot be overstated. Media literacy also means knowing how media can be used and being able to express oneself or express one's creativity using them, i.e., to produce media content of one's own.

The ability to sift through and sort out information from the tremendous flood of data and images in our digital information and communication society is a key skill. As is the capability to analyze and evaluate the information made available by media and via various platforms.

Users also need to be able to avoid and manage the risks media, especially internet, imply. We know from the results of the project EU Kids Online, led by Professor Sonia Livingstone, that there is a positive correlation between use and risk: "Northern European countries tend to be 'high use, high risk'; Southern European countries tend to be 'low use, low risk'; and Eastern European countries tend to be 'new use, new risk'". We also know that children from lower status homes are more exposed to risk online. There are also gender differences. "Boys are more likely to encounter (or create) conduct risks and girls more affected by content and contact risks". (Livingstone and Haddon 2009)

So, there is – once and for all – a need for more knowledge and new skills in the area of privacy, integrity and data security, and copyright aspects of media use. And we all have to understand connectivity.

But, as concluded in the report from EU Kids Online – balancing empowerment and protection is crucial and will require a mix of media literacy and regulation – by law enforcement, content and service providers, interface design, online safety resources, etc (Livingstone and Haddon 2009). The strivings at national level must be strengthened, and all the components and practices must be integrated into national media and education strategies and plans. The importance of media education cannot be exaggerated. Schools must recognize their responsibility to include young people's media culture in curricula at all levels. Success on this front will, however, depend on the formulation by regional and international organizations of a foundation for a more comprehensive and unified framework that encompasses media and information literacy as well as regulation, co-regulation and self-regulation. All in order to be able to identify existing needs and to ensure positive results at both regional and national levels. A knowledge society needs media and information literates.

Public service media can empower young people

The role of public service media in facilitating democratic development is often recognized, as the following statement from UNESCO illustrates: "Through PSB [public service broadcasting], citizens are informed, educated and also entertained. When provided with pluralism, programming diversity, editorial independence, appropriate funding, accountability and transparency, public service broadcasting can serve as a cornerstone of democracy." (UNESCO 2010)

Researchers and policy-makers in different parts of the world are trying to formulate new frameworks for public service media, both the conceptual frameworks and their operational practicalities. The points of departure for these efforts are theories of democratic development, the public sphere, media pluralism, cultural diversity and tolerance. In focus are media audiences, who are the citizens – and particularly the younger generation.

The Nordic countries have long traditions of commitment to public service broadcasting, and the countries have developed public service models that include both regulatory frameworks and financing mechanisms. These models have emerged in response to the fact that the countries are relatively small and sparsely populated. The public service broadcasters in the region also have long traditions of cooperation, particularly with regard to co-production of programs.

Public service broadcasters in the Nordic countries have received recognition for the quality of their programs for children. Indeed, they have an international reputation of long standing for what they offer young audiences. Deregulation of broadcasting markets around the world in the 1980s and 1990s led to fewer in-house productions for young viewers and listeners in most countries' national broadcasting services, but the decline was less in the Nordic countries, thanks to the strength of their public service broadcasters (Blumler and Biltereyst 1998). The same period saw a major expansion of "global" television channels devoted to young audiences – in the Nordic countries, as well – with content that is calculated to attract young viewers in as many cultures as possible.

Young people's importance as actors on the market has grown successively the past four to five decades. Young people are of great interest to commercial enterprises of many kinds. These companies are aware of the young people as consumers in their own right, persons who influence consumption in the family, and not least as future consumers – children hold the key to future markets. Nowadays, young people are exposed to a steady stream of commercial messages directed specifically to them – in the Nordic countries, too. This is despite the fact that advertising that targets children under the age of twelve is forbidden in programs distributed from Sweden. Many television programs, web sites, computer games and cartoons are a form of advertising in themselves inasmuch as they are the vehicles for 'merchandising', i.e., the marketing of toys, dolls, clothing, accessories, etc., to youthful viewers. Product trademarks and logotypes are a nearly universal lingua franca today, a vocabulary shared by young in a good part of the world. (Ekström and Tufte 2008)

In his recent report, *The Impact of the Commercial World on Children's Wellbeing*, David Buckingham observes, "The increasing ubiquity of commercial messages in public space, the privatisation of public services and the introduction of market-based modes of provision, all have potentially far-reaching consequences for children's wellbeing..." (Buckingham 2009).

In a situation like this quality programming for juvenile audiences is important – particularly programs that involve young people themselves (Rydin 2000). Research has shown that audiences – both young and older – prefer to watch television programs produced in their own country and in their own language (Feilitzen 2002). Quality production is relatively expensive, and small countries with "small" languages have little opportunity to recoup the expenses through exports to other countries. The Nordic broadcasters have resolved this dilemma through extensive co-production.

Ultimately it is a question of defending the public sphere. As Brian O'Neill och Cliona Barnesdrar, having completed their comprehensive study of media literacy and the public sphere in Ireland, observe: "Against a background of increasing marketisation and erosion of the public sphere through fragmentation, institutions such as public service broadcasting and the underpinning regulatory frameworks now play a central role in defining that public space in which rights for information, communication and expression are exercised and enjoyed" (O'Neill and Barnes 2008).

In this context it is interesting to note the findings of a study by Shanto Iyengar and James Curran on "the impact of public service requirements on the delivery of news and citizens' knowledge of current affairs" in four countries: the USA, Great Britain, Denmark and Finland. They found that in Denmark and Finland, where news is broadcast in fixed slots during prime time, a relatively large share of the population watch the news, whether or not they are interested in politics or world affairs. As a consequence, they are better informed than viewers in countries where newscasts are not accorded the same prominence in program schedules, e.g., the USA and Great Britain. Newscasts aired in prime time make an important contribution to citizens' "civic competence", these researchers conclude, and children and youth make up a good share of the viewing audiences he is talking about. (Iyengar and Curran 2009)

When models for public service media are discussed, the paragon most often held forth is BBC (the British Broadcasting Corporation). But the BBC – a central institution in a populous country, producing programs in a language that has become a worldwide lingua franca – is a model few countries can realistically hope to copy. Consequently, many countries' interest has shifted to models that have proven viable in smaller countries, and in this context the Nordic broadcasting regimes have attracted considerable interest. With eight decades of experience behind them, Nordic broadcasters have collaborated, mainly in radio, with countries in the southern hemisphere, supporting the development of free media, based on the ideals of freedom of information, freedom of speech and independent, reliable journalism as a necessary tool in a democratic society.

Maximizing opportunities and minimizing risk.
A global challenge

The challenge today is to develop policies that balance two somewhat conflicting goals: maximizing the potential of new information technologies and minimizing the risks they entail (Livingstone and Haddon 2009). This is a challenge facing many different actors – policy-makers, media companies, internet content providers, the schools, the research community, and so forth, civil society organizations, as well as young people, their parents and other adults. It is particularly important that young people themselves be engaged in this work.

We should do well to recall that throughout history, young people have often been active participants in the manifestation of social change, and most times their creative uses of media and innovative practices of communication have been crucial in the process. Consider, for example, the key roles young people play in citizen media, or in campaigning for political freedom, freedom of expression, fair trade, HIV/AIDS prevention, etc. (Tufte and Enghel 2009).

Time and again young people have manifested an ability to use media, to produce content, to understand and interact with a variety of internet platforms like Facebook, YouTube and myriad blogs, as well as traditional media formats and technologies in many different contexts. Their competence can make a crucial contribution to the effort to find fruitful paths forward, toward the satisfaction of the two overrriding goals.

Research can also play an important part in policy processes regarding children, youth and media. Meaningful strategy documents and goal-oriented programs need to be based on knowledge from both research and experience. Often, however, we lack the knowledge, indicators and measuring tools that would help us to explore the insights we need to reach these goals. And that is a fundamental problem, even when we are discussing the media culture of our young.

In order to shed light on important issues we need comparative projects much more open to holistic perspectives and cross-cultural approaches to a much higher degree than is the case at present. Much too often the frame of reference is the media culture of the Western world. There is an urgent need for the agenda to become open to non-Western thoughts and intercultural approaches to a much higher degree than has been the case to date. We need to learn more from one another, to share knowledge and context.

But, we also need indicators, statistics and other tools that document trends in a long-term perspective. The development of such resources allows us to follow developments in the rapidly changing media field, nationally, regionally and internationally, and to bring the emergence of new phenomena and relationships to light. We do indeed need these statistical overviews. Without fruitful statistical tools, no substantial indicators!

Such measures on an international basis will be crucial to our ability to deal adequately with the difficult media issues regarding young people and media on the global arena in the future.

To conclude...

Many pressing issues facing politicians and policy-makers today have to do with digital media and phenomena in cyberspace. International and regional organizations as well as national parliaments and governments have to debate the internet of the future – issues relating to whose terms shall constitute the norm, who shall own and whose needs shall be satisfied, cannot be avoided. These issues touch on vital democratic values – what kind of society do we want, and who is this 'we'? (Mansell 2009). The protection of human rights and freedom of expression, ensuring universal access to the internet as a public service, and promoting media literacy are key priorities.

From that point of view we should recognize that good governance and global leadership are more essential than ever in the age of rapid globalization and digitization. There is a need for multilateral solutions to vital global issues, and several of these have a strong media and communication component – not least issues regarding young people and internet, and media literacy.

References

Bennet, L.: 'Changing Citizenship in the Digital Age', in Bennet, L: *Civic Life Online: Learning How Digital Media Can Engage Youth*. MIT Press, Cambridge 2007.

Banerjee, I. & K. Seneviratne: *Public Service Broadcasting: A best practices sourcebook*, UNESCO, Paris 2005.

Blumler, J.G. & Biltereyst, D.: *The Integrity and Erosion of Public Television for Children*, European Institute for the Media, EBU, 1998.

Bourguignon, F. & Morrisson, C.: Inequality among World Citizens: 1820-1992. *The American Economic Review*, 92(2002)4.

Buckingham, D: *The Impact of the Commercial World on Children's Wellbeing*. Report of an Independent Assessment, Department for Children, Schools and Families, DCMS, London 2009.

Carlsson, U.; Tayie, S.; Jacquinot-Delaunay, G. & Pérez-Tornero, J.M. (eds.) *Empowerment Through Media Education. An Intercultural Dialogue*, International Clearinghouse on Children, Youth and Media, Nordicom, University of Gothenburg, 2008.

Carlsson. U: Why Regional and International Cooperation? Reflections from a Nordic Horizon. *Global Media and Communication* (2007)3.

Carlsson, U (ed.) *Regulation, Awareness, Empowerment. Young People and Harmful Media Content*. The International Clearinghouse on Children, Youth and Media, Nordicom, University of Gothenburg, 2006.

Castells, M.: *Communication Power*. Oxford University Press, Oxford 2009.

Ekström, K. & Tufte, B. (eds.) Children, *Media and Consumption. On the Front Edge*. The International Clearinghouse on Children, Youth and Media, Nordicom, University of Gothenburg, 2007 (Yearbook 2007).

von Feilitzen, C. & Carlsson, U. (eds.) *Children, Young People and Media Globalisation*. The International Clearinghouse on Children, Youth and Media, Nordicom, University of Gothenburg 2002 (Yearbook 2002).

Flash Eurobarometer 248 '*Towards a Safer Use of the Internet for Children in the EU: A Parents' Perspective*'. European Commission, Luxembourg, 2008

Golding, P.: Looking Back and Looking Forward: The Risks and Prospects of a Not-So-Young Field. *Gazette* 67(2005)6.

Graffman, K.: "Mamma vet bäst" ["Mama knows best"]. Intervju i *InternetWorld* 2008-05-28.

Harrie, E., (ed.) *The Nordic Media Market 2009. Media Companies and Business Activities.* Nordicom, University of Gothenburg, 2009.

Hjarvard, S.: The Mediatization of Society. A Theory of the Media as Agents of Social and Cultural Change. *Nordicom Review* 29(2008)2.

Iyengar, S. & Curran, J.: Media *Systems, News Delivery and Citizen's Knowledge of Current Affairs.* SSRC 2009 (http://publicsphere.ssrc.org/iyengar-curran-media-systems-news-delivery-and-citizens-knowledge-of-current-affairs/)

Livingstone, S: *Children and the Internet.* Polity Press, Cambridge 2009

Livingstone, S & Haddon, L: *EU Kids Online: Final Report.* LSE, London: EU Kids Online. (EC Safer Internet Plus Programme Deliverable D6.5), 2009 (http://www.lse.ac.uk/collections/EUKidsOnline/" www.lse.ac.uk/collections/EUKidsOnline/)

Mansell, R: *Power, Media Culture and New Media.* London School of Economics and Political Science, 2009, LSE Research Online (http://eprints.lse.ac.uk).

McChesney, R.W.: *The Political Economy of Media.* Monthly Review Press, New York 2008.

Millwood Hargrave, A. & Livingstone, S.: *Harm and Offence in Media Content. A Review of the Evidence.* Intellect, Bristol 2006.

Millennials. A Portrait of Generation Next. Confident. Connected. Open to Change. PewResearchCenter February 2010 (www.pewresearchcenter.org/millennials).

Nordicom-Sveriges Mediebarometer 2009 [Nordicom-Sweden's Media Barometer 2008] Nordicom, University of Gothenburg, Göteborg, 2010 (This annual survey covers penetration and use of a wide range of mass media among the population 9-79 years).

Novel, A-S: 'Study Probes Correlation Between Press Freedom and Poverty Reduction', in: *Media Development and Poverty Eradication.* UNESCO, Paris 2006 (World Press Freedom Day on May 3, 2006).

O'Neill, B. & Barnes, C.: *Media Literacy and the Public Sphere: A Contextual Study for Public Media Literacy Promotion in Ireland*, Centre for Social and Educational Research, Dublin Institute of Technology 2008.

Reguillo, R.: 'The Warrior's Code? Youth, Communication, and Social Change' In: Tufte, T. & Enghel, F. (eds.) *Youth Engaging with the World. Media, Communication and Social Change.* The International Clearinghouse on Children, Youth and Media, Nordicom, University of Gothenburg (Yearbook 2009).

Rydin, I.: Barnens röster. Program för barn i Sveriges radio och television 1925-1999 [Children's Voices. Programs for children in Swedish public service radio and television 1925-1999], Stiftelsen Etermedierna i Sverige, Stockholm 2000 (nr 15).

Silverstone, R.: *Media and Morality: On the Rise of the Mediapolis.* Polity Press, Cambridge 2007.

Tufte, T. & Enghel, F. (eds.) *Youth Engaging with the World. Media, Communication and Social Change.* The International Clearinghouse on Children, Youth and Media, Nordicom, University of Gothenburg 2009 (Yearbook 2009).

Young People in the European Digital Media Landscape. A Statistical Overview with an Introduction by Sonia Livingstone & Leslie Haddon. The International Clearinghouse on Children, Youth and Media, Nordicom, University of Gothenburg, 2009.

Part I.

Media Literacy: Importance and Challenges

Democratic Digital Literacies
Three Obstacles in Search of a Solution

Kirsten Drotner

The Nordic countries of Europe – Denmark, Finland, Iceland, Norway and Sweden – display a paradox when it comes to children's digital media cultures. These countries are some of the most advanced in terms of the takeup of digital media technologies and infrastructure. At the same time, major differences remain also in these countries in the uses made of these technologies. Why does this paradox exist? What are the obstacles to diverse and democratic appropriations of the options that seem so easy at hand? This chapter explores three of these obstacles, to do with policy, pedagogy, and spatial positions, respectively; and it provides some tentative answers to their existence in the hope that these answers may offer some guidance for action in countries with different social, political and technological structures. Focus will be on children and young people who are vital for shaping future forms of mediated collaboration, communication and participation. On a wider canvas, "child sensitive" answers are therefore likely to be more viable and long-lasting.

The main argument, to be substantiated in the following, is this: indicators of access and uptake of ict and media technologies are a poor basis of action if the aim is to further children's lasting empowerment in a global environment in which complex digital media are formative features. We need to look more closely into matters of use, to the diverse ways in which children shape, share and and store mediated forms of communication, if we are to facilitate children's economic, social and cultural participation. More specifically, I argue that to-day's global interconnectedness in terms of finance, employment and cultural exchange enforces virtual forms of collaboration that can only be developed in a sustained way if people possess digital literacies harnessing and developing their existing resources of use.

It should be noted that I take an inclusive approach to children's digital cultures, since they operate at the intersections of ict, broadcast media and telecommunications, all of which technological convergence is bringing into, often conflictual, re-alignments. This approach is reflected in the data, on which my arguments are based, and in my take on the resources needed in order to further digital literacies.

Assessing access and use

Access to media and ict is a necessary, if not sufficient, prerequisite for sustaining equitable forms of communication. Assessments of people's access to these means of communication are therefore at the core of international benchmarkings of information societies and of media distribution. For example, the Digital Opportunity Index, published by the UN based International Telecommunication Union, ranks countries according to their ict infrastructure, and their access to and uptake of these means. Indicators are, for example, the percentage of broadband and mobile subscribers and the percentage of households equipped with radios, tv sets and computers. In 2007, the Nordic countries were all among the top 15 of 181 countries listed in the index, with Denmark ranked number three, Iceland number four, Sweden number nine, Finland number 11 and Norway number 12. The Republic of Korea and Japan were ranked at the very top as number one and two respectively (*Digital Opportunity Index,* 2007).

Children's ict and media access and uses have been measured more recently in a pan-European comparative study, EU Kids Online, funded by the European Commission. Again, the Nordic countries appear in the top bracket. In 2008, more than 80 per cent of young Danes, Fins and Swedes had broadband web access in the home against an EU mean of 60.7 per cent (Livingstone & Haddon 2009: 31).

When it comes to use, this is measured by frequency of reach or by time spent with the activity. More European children use the internet or their mobiles than television and, not surprisingly, this trend is most pronounced in countries with a wide takeup of web and mobile devices (Livingstone & Haddon 2009: 35, 43). While the comparative EU survey has no means of assessing what users do with the various media devices, statistics from individual countries offer more detail in this respect.

In the Nordic countries, the most sustained quantitative study over time of children's media uses is found in Sweden. In 2008, the top-ranked media activities for young Swedes aged 9-14 were computer gaming (48 per cent) and book reading (47 per cent) closely followed by texting and phone conversation (both 46 per cent). Watching clips on YouTube accounts for 37 per cent while drama series are the most popular pastime when it comes to television (35 per cent). For the elder age band, 15-24, mediated forms of communicaction take priority with texting at the top (83 per cent) followed by telephone conversation (70 per cent) and with gaming at the bottom (28 per cent). Young adult Swedes (aged 17-25) are the most avid media multi-taskers with 56 per cent operating the internet at the same time as other media (Livingstone & Haddon 2009: 56, 57).

The recent expansion of socalled social media, or web 2.0 services, that allow for more user interaction and content creation and sharing hold the potential to widen children's engagement with what the American media scholar, Henry Jenkins, terms a participatory culture (Jenkins et al. 2006). Still, even with wide access to these services, few children in the Nordic countries realise their potentials to the full. For example, many young Danes have an internet profile, ranging from 26 per cent of nine-ten-year-olds to 86 per cent of 14-16-year olds, with Facebook being by far the most popular site. However, far fewer comment often on other people's profiles – one per cent of nine-ten-year-olds and 34 per cent of 14-16-year olds; while a minority, eight per cent in the age band 9-16, often participate in virtual group interactions (Livingstone & Haddon 2009: 60, 61). The discrepancy between potentials and practices, here, is a clear indication that more is needed than technological options and leisured explorations in order for children to harness and develop the entire range of digital options. A key driver of transformation is policy-making in the domains of media and ict literacy.

The policy obstacle:
developing knowledge societies by industrial means

Since the inauguration in 1989 of the UN Declaration of the Rights of the Child, children's access to a diverse range of media has been seen as an integral part of their civic inclusion and democratic participation. In addition, a growing body of policy-makers today claim ict or media literacies as key competences. The UN-based Alliance of Civilizations has as its key priority areas youth, education, media and migration, all of which involve media education as a lever of user-led media and ict literacies. In the USA, the trend is seen in the discourse on so-called 21st century skills (see, for example, Partnership 2002); and in Europe it features in OECD's widely used Definition and Selection of Competences (DeSeCo). Here, the key elements are using tools interactively, interacting in heterogeneous groups and acting autonomously, all of which are facilitated through the use of digital media (OECD 2005: 7). While important tensions remain concerning the precise alignment of ict and media literacies, the discourses illuminate new claims to the central importance played by mediated forms of communication in children's present lives and future prospects.

Irrespective of conceptual differences, the underlying rationale behind these claims is that societies on a global scale are turning towards immaterial forms of production as key drivers of economic and social development. These assumed transformations take different names such as information societies, learning societies, knowledge societies and network societies (Masuda 1980; Husén 1986; Stehr 1994; Castells 1996), and their empirical validity is contested. Still, the widespread policy acceptance of their existence have a reality effect in that they form the basis of financial, political and social priorities. Knowledge society claims are routinely underpinned by arguments that new sets of competences are needed in order to foster and further the new social formations. Key among these competences are media or ict literacies, i.e. those kinds of competences to do with the shaping, sharing and handling of mediated signs, such as text, sound, numbers, still and live images – and mixtures of these.

After nearly a decade of negotiations, the European Commission in 2009 proposed to its 27 member states a Recommendation to advance media literacy with a particular focus on education (European Commission 2009). However, the Recommendation is a far cry from the realities found in most European schools, a situation that is evident also from the comprehensive background overviews and reports on EU level (e.g. European Commission 2007, Celot 2009). What are the issues of constraint?

In its 2009 Recommendation, the Commission lists as particular barriers "lack of shared vision, lack of European visibility of national, regional and local initiatives, lack of European networks and of co-ordination between stakeholders" (European Commission 2009: 3). Perhaps a more deep-seated reason for the scant implementation of media literacy (or even ict literacy) as an acknowledged and important educational competence is that its underlying rationale is at odds with the principles structuring mainstream traditions of education in the global north, including most Nordic countries. These traditions are shaped by the societal needs of industrial societies for specialised, effective and dependable employees for which finely graded and test-based schooling seems to work as an admirable preparation.

Hence, the Nordic countries today display conflictual educational trends. In tune with the principles of industrial societies, standardisation of national curricula, a strengthening of traditional core disciplines, such as mother-tongue and math education, and evidence-based assessments of selected skills take increasing policy importance. At the same time, initiatives are taken to galvanise students' technology-enabled interdisciplinary collaboration and innovation capacities, not least in vocational streams of education, all of which resonate with claims to further knowledge societies.

Norway offers a particularly interesting demonstration of how these conflictual educational trends play out in terms of digital literacies. It is one of the only countries in the world in which these are defined as one of five core competences, and massive investments have been made to integrate digital learning resources into schools. In the biannual surveys conducted to monitor young Norwegians' digital competences, a useful division is made between digital appropriation, integration and production. Although there is a general increase in educational ict use, it is mostly in terms of digital appropriation (information search, software use); and students' explorations of digital forms of production and communication are chiefly a leisure pursuit (Arnseth et al. 2007).

Based on his long-term studies of media and ict literacy practices in Norwegian schools, the educational scholar Svein Østerud sees a deep division in domestic, educational policies between discipline-based and child-based visions as one of the key obstacles to educational innovation, including a more thorough integration of digital literacies (Østerud 2004). These divisions resonate with similar trends in other Nordic countries, where children's needs and rights hold an important position within welfarist developments, thus facilitating child-centred forms of education. At the same time standardised tests serve to boost discipline-based teaching through their selective focus of particular, testable skills. On a wider canvas, the policy divisions, defined by Østerrud, may be seen as welfarist and liberal inflections of the "industrial" tradition of educating effective employees, mentioned above.

The pedagogical obstacle: hierarchies of literacy

While national and trans-national policies serve to delimit enabling conditions and constraints for the advancement of digital literacies, more mundane choices are made in schools as a means of this advancement. Here, the learning resources made available is a key factor. What is the relative composition of books, computer software, film and multimedia at various school levels? An answer to this question was provided by a national survey conducted in 2009 amongst mother-tongue and math teachers in lower- and upper-secondary schools in Denmark. For both groups and across educational levels, the textbook holds unrivalled prominence, with an average of 89 per cent of teachers choosing this as a learning resource. Next came photocopies which were chosen by nearly 70 per cent. Less than a third opted for audiovisual materials, while web-based tools were put into practice by nearly a quarter of the respondents. Very little was made of engaging pupils through web 2.0 services such as blogs or wikis or through mobile devices that are formative in challenging the physical classroom and the fixed timetable as pivotal forms of spatial and temporal organisation of schooling (*Digitale læringsressourcer* [Digital learning resources] 2009: 31).

As in other Nordic countries, Danmark has made heavy investments in educational hardware and smart boards. But these options are put to relatively limited pedagogical uses. Lack of resources to purchase learning resources is part of the problem. But to this may be added that digital literacies are not mainstreamed into pedagogical guidelines, teacher training and assessment goals. So there are few incentives for instructors to verge beyond the portable, versatile and familiar print materials.

Behind these practical choices may be seen a more general reticence to practice modes of literacy that go beyond the traditional three Rs, reading, writing and arithmetic, with which print media are associated for obvious historical reasons. Educational competences, including modes of literacy, are ranked within a cultural hierarchy which puts a premium on knowledge formations that require formal training. Very few children learn the codes of reading, writing and numerical calculation without sustained teaching; while the codes of viewing, listening and speaking can be broken, if not mastered, as integral dimensions of early childhood. To introduce new, multimedia, or digital literacies, as key competences into schools seems to challenge this hierarchy of formal training because pupils come with some sense of what it takes to listen to music, watch tv or comprehend what appears on computer and mobile screens. That these resources are by no means fully-fledged literacies is well-documented in the research literature which time and again has illuminated existing digital divides that follow familiar fault lines of class, gender, age and ethnicity (e.g. Peter & Valkenburg 2006). These obstacles seem particularly pronounced when digital literacies are defined in terms of knowing how to handle the complexities of media in ways that children, themselves, relevant to their current lives and future situation (Warschauer 2004).

While illumination and coordination of national policies are important to galvanise an educational integration of media literacy, as noted by the European Commission, these lofty ideals should not obfuscate the very real, if less ac-knowledged, pedagogical challenges involved in putting new modes of literacy into practice. Educational structures are, and perhaps should be, relatively stable. Not surprisingly, therefore, a number of scholars, regulators and policy-makers venture beyond the confines of school to study and impact innovative forms of media appropriations.

The contextual obstacle: public and private positions

In the Nordic countries, as elsewhere, a number of studies have documented that children's leisured media culture is more diverse, and often more advanced, than are their educational media and ict uses. For example, an inter-Nordic study, conducted in 2006, notes that pupils primarily use ict in school for calculation, word processing and information search, uses that informants perceive to be less diverse and advanced than their out-of-school appropriations. Interestingly, the divide seems more pronounced for boys than for girls and for ethnic minorities irrespective of gender (Pedersen et al. 2006: 36-39). In other words, girls and ethnic minorities benefit the most by sustained ict training in schools.

The discrepancy between educational and leisured ict and media uses have led some scholars and critics to downplay the importance played by schooling as an arena for the training of digital literacy and to celebrate informal modes of peer learning. Young media users have been idealised and defined in terms of generation or technology through phrases such as the net generation (Tapscott 1998), the digital generation (Papert 1996), cyberkids (Holloway & Valentine 2003) and thumb tribes (Rheingold 2002). Such celebratory simplicities serve to obfuscate the uneven takeup and use of digital media and to underestimate very real structural barriers in terms of media ownership, organisation and power (Buckingham 2007, Drotner 2009a).

Particularly when digital uses are seen as levers of learning, the discrepancy between school and leisure arenas play into wider issues concerning civic partici-pation. Since the 19th century, the concept of informal learning has been defined as an alternative to, or supplement of, the formal learning framed by schooling (for an overview, see Drotner 2008). In recent years, the concept has gained increasing currency as part of the policy needs for more flexible and continuous competence formation, needs that are also known as lifelong learning. From a focus on ad-hoc and on-the-job training, lifelong learning now involves a wider set of social skills, such as social inclusion and civic participation, to be developed and practiced in a variety of contexts, including those defined in terms of informal learning (Singh 2005). Thus, the very concept of learning is currently spreading across a range of contexts and dimensions of individual biographies.

The key importance played by digital media for democratic governance, deliberation and civic participation offers new ways in which the nexus between media, literacy and children is being analysed and understood. Most recent studies of this nexus are at pains to extend established notions of politics and participation (e.g. Buckingham 2000, Bennett 2007, Olsson & Dahlgren 2010). Less is made of the enabling spatial conditions on which young people may capitalise in developing their cyber citizenship. In the Nordic countries, public libraries are of particular relevance in this context. Since the interwar years, the formation of local libraries have been among the socio-cultural mainstays of Nordic welfare states, and through the years their rationale of existence has shifted from democratising Culture (with a capital C) unto cultural democratisation. In terms of children, this has implied a shift from their being offered quality fiction for free as a lever of personal betterment for them as adults-to-be on to a situation in which they may appropriate a range of media both in the physical and virtual library as everyday resources, even if books are still the key media in many places.

Young people primarily use the virtual library for specific purposes such as information search and retrieval as preparation for school assignments, and users are primarily from well-educated families. Conversely, local, physical libraries, particularly for girls aged 10-13 and for ethnic minorities, operate as important semi-public arenas that combine the safety of (limited) adult supervision with social networking and socio-cultural engagement (Drotner 2009b). Since many libraries offer access to broadband computers and digital games, young users jointly explore gaming, digital content creation and social interaction on social media such as Facebook and Lunarstorm, thus extending their traditional library uses as resources for cultural reception. This extension raises important policy issues for libraries in terms of their role as informal, or semi-formal, sites of learning and catalysts of civic inclusion and participation. It equally raises important issues for scholars interested in defining and (re-)locating resources of future social engagement.

Search for solutions?

The importance played by complex media environments in the formation of knowledge societies serve to illuminate, and perhaps radicalise, existing tensions concerning social development. Since children and young people, as all adults know, hold the keys to the future, it is no wonder that youthful media and ict appropriations assume an increasingly central role in the attempts to approach these tensions. As this chapter has hopefully demonstrated, the tensions and unresolved dilemmas remain even in societies which, at first glance, seem to possess the requisite technological and financial tools of resolution. More than money and hardware is at stake when children's communicative inclusion and social participation is changing. This chapter has focused on dimensions of trans-national policy-making, on pedagogical priorities and contexts of engagement in an attempt to go beyond familiar scholarly issues of political economy in media studies. While important issues of money, power and institutional organisation do, of course, play into a full understanding of the tensions mobilized by digital cultures, they should not blind us to more bottom-up and user-sensitive perspectives which, at the end of the day, may prove at least as effective as lead-ins to constructive action.

References

Arnseth, Hans Christian et al. (2007) *ITU monitor 2007: skolens digitale tilstand* [ITU monitor 2007: The digital state of schools]. Oslo: University Press.

Bennet, Lance (2007) *Civic Life Online: Learning how Digital Media Can Engage Youth*. Cambridge, MA: MIT Press.

Buckingham, David (2000) *The Making of Citizens: Young People, News and Politics*. London: Routledge.

Buckingham, David (2007) *Beyond Technology: Children's Learning in the Age of Digital Culture*. Cambridge: Polity press.

Castells, Manuel (1996) *The Rise of the Network Society. Vol. 1: The Information Age: Economy, Society and Culture*. Oxford: Blackwell.

Celot, Paolo (ed.) (2009) *Study on Assessment Criteria for Media Literacy Levels: A Comprehensive View of the Concept of Media Literacy and an Understanding of How Media Literacy Level in Europe Should be Assessed*. Brussels: The European Commission. Consulted 10 January 2010 at http://ec.europa.eu/avpolicy/media_literacy/docs/studies/eavi_study_assess_crit_media_lit_levels_europe_finrep.pdf

Digitale læringsressourcer i folkeskolen og de gymnasiale ungdomsuddannelser (2009) Odense, Denmark: DREAM/Læremiddel.dk. Consulted 10 January 2010 at http://www.dream.dk/files/pdf/Rapport-laeringsressourcer.pdf

Drotner, Kirsten (2008) Informal Learning and Digital Media: Perceptions, Practices and Perspectives. In Kirsten Drotner, Hans S. Jensen & Kim C. Schrøder (eds) *Informal Learning and Digital Media* (pp. 10-28) Cambridge: Cambridge Scholars' Publishing.

Drotner, Kirsten (2009a) Children and Digital Media: Online, on Site, on the Go. In Jens Qvortrup et al (eds.) *Handbook of Childhood Studies* (pp. 360-373) London: Palgrave Macmillan.

Drotner, Kirsten (2009b) Children's Media Culture: A Key to Libraries of the Future? Keynote address presented at the World Library and Information Congress, Libraries for Children and Young Adults Section, Milan August. Consulted 10 January 2010 at http://www.ifla.org/files/hq/papers/ifla75/103-drotner-en.pdf

European Commission (2007) Study on the current trends and approaches to media literacy in Europe. Consulted 10 January 2010 at http://ec.europa.eu/avpolicy/media_literacy/docs/studies/study.pdf

European Commission (2009) *Commission recommendation on media literacy in the digital environment for a more competitive audiovisual and content industry and an inclusive knowledge society*. Consulted 10 January 2010 at http://ec.europa.eu/avpolicy/media_literacy/docs/recom/c_2009_6464_en.pdf

Holloway, Sarah L. & Gill Valentine (2003) *Cyberkids: Children in the Information Age*. London: Routledge Falmer.

Husén, T. (1986) *The Learning Society Revisited*. Oxford: Pergamon Press.

International Telecommunication Union (2007) *Digital opportunity index*. Consulted 10 January 2010 at http://www.itu.int/ITU-D/ict/doi/index.html

Jenkins, Henry, Katie Clinton, Ravi Purushotma, Alice J. Robinson, & Margaret Weigel (2006) *Confronting the Challenges of Participatory Culture: Media Education for the 21st Century*. Building the field of digital media and learning. The John D. and Catherine T. MacArthur Foundation. Consulted 10 January 2010 at http://digitallearning.macfound.org/atf/cf/%7B7E45C7E0-A3E0-4B89-AC9C-E807E1B0AE4E%7D/JENKINS_WHITE_PAPER.PDF

Livingstone, Sonia & Leslie Haddon (2009) Young People in the European Digital Media Landscape. Gothenburg: Nordicom, The International Clearinghouse on Children, Youth and Media.

Masuda, Y. (1980) *The Information Society*. Tokyo: Institute for the Information Society.

OECD (2005) *The Definition and Selection of Key Competences*. Consulted 10 January 2010 at http://www.oecd.org/dataoecd/47/61/35070367.pdf

Olsson, Tobias & Peter Dahlgren (eds.) (2010) *Young People, ICTs and Democracy*. Gothenburg: Nordicom.

Papert, Seymour (1996) *The Connected Family: Bridging the Digital Generation Gap*. Atlanta, GA: Longstreet Press.

Partnership for 21st Century Skills (2002) *Learning for the 21st Century*. Consulted 10 Janurary 2010 at http://www.21stcenturyskills.org/images/stories/otherdocs/p21up_Report.pdf

Pedersen, Sanya G. et al. (eds) (2006) *E-learning Nordic: Impact of ICT on Education*. Copenhagen: Ramboll Management. Consulted 10 Janurary 2010 at http://www.elearningeuropa.info/files/media/media10111.pdf

Peter, Jochen, & Patti M. Valkenburg (2006) 'Adolescents' Internet Use: Testing the 'Disappearing Digital Divide' versus the 'Emerging Differentiation' Approach', *Poetics,* vol. 34, no. 4-5, pp. 293-305.

Rheingold, Howard (2002) *Smart Mobs: The New Social Revolution*. Cambridge, MA: Perseus Publishing.

Singh, M. (2005) *Meeting Basic Learning Needs in the Informal Sector: Integrating Education and Training for Decent Work, Empowerment and Citizenship*. Berlin: Springer.

Stehr, N. (1994) *Knowledge Societies*. London: Sage.

Tapscott, Don (1998) *Growing up Digital: The Rise of the Net Generation*. New York: McGraw-Hill.

Warschauer, Mark (2004) *Technology and Social Inclusion: Rethinking the Digital Divide*. MIT Press, Cambridge, MA.

Østerud, Svein (2004) *Utdanning for informasjonssamfunnet: Den tredje vei* [Education for the information society: The third way]. Oslo: University Press.

Paths Towards Digital Competencies
Naïve Participation or Civic Engagement?

Ola Erstad

Much research during the past decade has shown how young people today constitute what has been termed a 'digital generation' simply because they are the first generation to grow up in a culture dominated by digital media (Buckingham & Willett 2006). However, how they participate in this culture and what competencies are implied are open questions. The issue of digital competencies in particular marks a key challenge in the transition of media use and learning from the 20th to the 21st Century.

The question posed in the title is an intentional polarization. In practice, there is a blend of both positions among different groups of young people. Being a citizen in our digital culture involves both consuming entertainment and information, and participating in productive practices. An important democratic issue is how these practices vary among young people and how they are constituted (Bennett 2008; Rheingold 2008). Do the digital media represent changes in participation structures in our society (Levine 2008), and what competencies are needed for citizenship in the 21st Century? Of special concern are the educational implications of such developments, and the role of education in enhancing and further developing the competencies needed.

Not all young people are digital competent, nor are they all interested in every aspect of using new media (Livingstone 2009). They are also largely unreflective regarding the broader implications of such media on our culture, as are most adults. Much of the research today celebrates the creative and communicative practices young people are involved in. However, these practices do not include all, or even most, of young people today. Still, digital media are all around us, and something we relate to in different contexts. In this sense, education and learning are of key importance in a digital culture. Digital competency becomes the term that bridges the gap between what young people know or do not know when using digital media, and how education will create a context that develops such skills, knowledge and attitudes further. 21st century skills are something more than just skills in handling the technology. In broader terms, digital competency raises issues about what it means to be literate in our culture today, and how we must redefine the ways we organize learning to create optimal conditions for education.

Developments in the Nordic countries are interesting in relation to the developments mentioned above, both in relation to media use and developments of digital competence/literacy in school curricula. In the Nordic countries, the term competence is most often used instead of literacy. The objective of the present article is to raise some theoretical and conceptual considerations regarding digital competencies, and to question some of the assumptions of participation and engagement by young people in the digital culture, using in particular some examples of civic engagement and democratic participation. Further, some dimensions concerning how to work on digital competencies in schools will be presented, and some concerns about social inclusion and exclusion in our digital culture will be raised.

Contextual framing

Although media literacy has a long tradition in the Nordic countries, defined at the intersection of our evolving media culture and the education system, such initiatives have never had a stronghold within the school systems in these countries. So, why should we think that the impact might be different now with regard to digital media? Let me first refer to some socio-historical developments in this part of the world that are important in understanding the present initiatives.

An important aspect is, of course, that the educational systems in the Nordic countries are different from educational systems in other parts of the world. There has been a much stronger tradition of project-based learning, a strong emphasis on equal opportunity and high access to media within the schools, more so than in most other countries. Also, the broader social structure and the welfare society model, which are similar in all the Nordic countries, have created a different framework for how people become engaged in their own societies. All these factors make it interesting to look more closely at developments in the Nordic countries. At the same time, children and youth in the Nordic countries are at the forefront internationally as heavy users of new technologies (Brandtzæg & Heim 2007).

Also, social networking sites have existed in Scandinavian countries for some time. Some examples are 'LunarStorm' in Sweden, 'mPetreklanen' in Norway, and 'Skum.dk' in Denmark. Development of these sites started around 1999-2000 and has since then gained increasing popularity among the young population. In a Scandinavian context, this development is partly explained by the high access to technology among young people (Drotner 2001).

For many years, media production has had a strong position in media education practices in grades K-12 (Erstad, Gilje & de Lange 2008). The position of project-based learning, especially in Denmark, has helped to make this possible in the schools (Tufte 1995). Perhaps more so than in many other countries, the production part, in comparison with the emphasis on critique (Burn & Durran 2007: 13), has always been very strong in the Nordic countries.

Another aspect is how researchers like Drotner (1991), Thavenius (1995) and others have related their analysis of media pedagogy closely to the German tradition of 'bildung'. A similar concept does not exist in the English language, but it is indicative of being or becoming 'literate'. Their arguments are that media pedagogy and the growth of media culture as resources for identity formation and learning must break away from the elitist conception of 'bildung', in which the role of education is to introduce the young to some pre-specified books so they will possess what is defined as necessary for becoming 'literate'. The ways in which young people use media culture today create a new way of conceptualizing what it means to become 'literate' or competent in our culture.

The technology push in the education systems in the Nordic countries has been central from the mid-1990s onwards. The main focus has been on the technology itself, and on getting access to computers and the Internet in schools. It is only in recent years that issues of critique, reflection, production, and creativity have begun to come up concerning the ways in which digital media are used in the schools.

The development of digital technologies, increased access to such technologies among the population, especially in the Nordic countries, and efforts in many countries to ensure that school curricula reflect technological developments have only increased during the past decade. We might describe this as a digital turn, from a culture of mass media towards personalized media, and from an education system where mass media like TV, radio and newspapers are defined as marginal towards a situation in which new media like computers and the Internet have a central position in the way learning is defined – all of this happening within a period of 15 years.

Implementation of digital media within the education system has been a priority in all the Nordic countries during the past decade. In Norway, these developments can be divided into three main phases, which together indicate the overall national agenda for scaling up activities using digital media in Norwegian schools. The first phase, from 1996 until 1999, was mainly concerned with the implementation of computers in the Norwegian schools (Ministry of Education, Research, and Church Affairs 1994). There was less interest in the educational context. In the next phase, from 2000 until 2003, the focus was more on whole school development through the use of ICT and changes in learning environments (Ministry of Education, Research, and Church Affairs 2000). The phase from 2004 until 2008 puts more emphasis on ensuring that students acquire digital skills and competencies, and on what learners do with technology, which opens future perspectives on technology and education (Ministry of Education and Research 2004).

Digital competencies as 'equipments for living'

The main objective of what is often called a cultural-historic or socio-cultural approach to the mind is to explicate the relationships between human mental functioning, on the one hand, and the cultural, institutional, and historical situations in which this functioning occurs, on the other (Wertsch, del Rio & Alvarez 1995: 3). The central task is to understand how individual functioning is shaped by and related to the socio-cultural setting within which it exists. This has been an important perspective throughout the Nordic countries in a great deal of research on new media and learning related to the works of Rommetveit (Norway), Säljö, Linnell (Sweden) and Engeström (Finland), in their reinterpretations of the works of Vygotsky, Leontiev and Bakhtin.

Human action is closely linked to communication processes and the use of cultural tools, both material and abstract, for example language, for the meaning-making practices of individuals and groups. Mediated action (Wertsch 1998) as an analytic approach to the study of mind is thereby seen both on the microgenetic level of agents and instruments, and in terms of broader issues of socio-cultural history and issues of cultural struggle, like in power relationships. When studying digital competencies, we have to take these broader perspectives on culture, communication and cognition into consideration as a way of connecting inter- and intra-personal processes.

One point with regard to mediated action is that it involves constraints as well as empowerment (Wertsch et al. 1995, pp. 24-25). Any form of mediation involves some form of limitation. It frees us from some earlier limitations, while at the same time introducing new ones. Our emphasis of course is often on the new possibilities that new media represent for empowerment and new actions. However, we need to keep a focus on the limitations at the same time, on how tools shape our action in an inherently limiting way.

The important point here – and again, a point that is often missed in sociological and psychological studies – is that when a new tool, a new medium, is introduced into the flow of action, it does not simply facilitate or make an existing form of action more efficient. The emphasis is on how it transforms the form of action, on the qualitative transformative, as opposed to facilitative, role of cultural tools.

So when we move from memorizing long stretches of poetry to just saying it is good enough to read the lines out of a textbook with feeling or find them on the Internet, using such external symbolic storage, there is more than just a change in the efficiency of a mode of action and the mental processes that go with it. Such a change imposes search strategies, new storage strategies, new memory access routes, new options in both the control and analysis of one's own thinking, all of which represents a qualitative transformation in mediated action.

This can be related to different mediated texts, as stated by Cole and Keyssar in what they describe as 'equipments for living';

For the richness of our lives depends not only on how much equipment we carry with us, but how we use that equipment and in what context it is relevant. The chisel in the hands of a sculptor is different than the chisel in the hands of a brick-layer, but it is not clear that one uses the tool better than the other. The first step, and one that continues to meet with resistance, is to recognize and work with films such as 'Romeo and Juliet' and 'Nashville', as well as printed books, as equipments for living. This is not to reduce meaning to usefulness, but to enlarge our concept of 'meaning' and 'usefulness'. (1985, p. 69)

Further, this leads us to the importance of literacy in our culture, and how conceptions and practices of literacy change over time. The key issue in trying to understand the implications of new digital technologies for children and young people, therefore, concerns the issue of literacy, or literacies in plural (Cope & Kalantzis 2000, 2009).

This conception of literacy builds on the research tradition that defines literacy as embedded in specific social practices (Scribner & Cole 1981; Heath 1984; Street 1984; Barton 1994). A definition of literacy made by Lankshear and Knobel (2006) encompasses social practices that change over time. They define literacy as: *"Socially recognized ways of generating, communicating and negotiating meaningful content through the medium of encoded texts within contexts of participation in Discourses (or, as members of Discourses)."* This definition is not bound by certain technologies. It proposes to study literacies in practice (what people do with technologies and digital texts), and not as something predescribed, indicating that we need to understand what people are already practising concerning technological literacies and the role of education in employing such literacies to achieve new knowledge levels. The important message is that digital competence among young people today is of direct relevance to discussions about learning in schools, and it seriously confronts earlier conceptions of literacy and learning.

Some literacy theorists have sought to hold together the many new literacies under umbrella concepts that stress the plurality of literacies, such as 'multiliteracies' (Cope & Kalantzis 2000, Snyder 2002) and 'metamedia literacy' (Lemke 1998). According to Kellner (2002: 163), "The term 'multiple literacies' points to the many different kinds of literacies needed to access, interpret, criticise, and participate in the emergent new forms of culture and society." Kress (2003), however, argues against the multiplicity of literacies, suggesting that it leads to serious conceptual confusion. He believes that, instead of taking this path, it is necessary to develop a new theoretical framework for literacy that can use a single set of concepts to address the various aspects of literacy.

In addition, it is important to stress that digital competence is related to *situational embedding*, that is, the use of technology within life situations. To understand such processes, we have to look at the different contexts in which literacy is practised and given meaning. This is especially important when relating literacy to how children and young people use digital technologies across contexts.

This implies that we must constantly ask the more general question of what it means to 'read' and 'write' in a culture, and thereby how we learn (Pahl & Rowsell 2005). In the *'Handbook of Literacy and Technology'*, with the subtitle *'Transformations in a Post-Typographic World'*, D. Reinking et al. (1998) present several perspectives on how the development of digital technologies changes conceptions of text, of readers and writers and ultimately of literacy itself. This implies that digital literacy relates to changes in traditional cultural techniques such as reading and writing, meanwhile opening up new dimensions regarding what it means to be a competent reader and writer in our culture.

The main question we need to ask is to what extent this really represents a new conception of literacy, or just an elaboration of former understandings. And is there something generic about literacy that transcends different modalities, like decoding, critical reflection, meta-cognition, and something more specific that is related to each technology? If literacy is understood as embedded in social practices and thereby as changing over time, we might say that digital literacy is just an elaboration and extension of former understandings through new cultural tools that give us new possibilities for relating to information and new ways to express our own meanings.

Four areas in which we see an impact of digital media on young people's media use and literacy practices are:

A participatory culture: This term from Henry Jenkins (2006) concerns the ways of participating and engaging in culture, and how these change over time, which is now becoming apparent in young people's use of social networking sites.

Information access: Since the introduction of World Wide Web, one of the most obvious advantages of digital media is access to information. The possibilities are endless and mark a significant difference from the book age in terms of the easy access to information provided by the Internet. In addition, the Web has created possibilities for everyone to provide and share information online. One example is Wikipedia, which is a Net-based lexicon to which everybody can contribute. This, of course, demands more of the user, who must evaluate the information provided and exercise responsibility in creating content.

Communication possibilities: The development of email, chat, sms and online communities has created new conditions for communication and communicative competence as a skill for the 21st Century.

Content production: An important change in literacy practices is that every individual can potentially be a producer of content that can be shared with a large number of other users on sites such as YouTube. Text production has greatly increased in our culture, and software tools make it easy to edit films, music and so forth.

The main questions then become: What are the key literacies and competencies for the 21st century, and how can we develop an education system that is adapted to face the challenges of competence development for the future? And what do young people really know about media, and what implications does this have for learning in educational settings? Technology serves both as a driver and lever for these transformations. In the next two parts of the article, I will relate these questions to some critical understanding of online practices among youth, and next, to how we can conceptualize dimensions of digital competencies related to school-based learning.

Participation, engagement and creative production – so what?

The new possibilities for user-generated content production represented by Web 2.0 make the personal voice more apparent. Information and communication technologies can be used for producing and consuming narratives in a whole new way by people around the world, as seen on Internet sites like 'MySpace' and 'YouTube'. In terms like my(space), you(tube) or face(book), we see combinations of personal expression and media used in an integrated way.

There are indeed critical points to be made concerning the autobiographical obsession inherent in the participation culture (Jenkins 2006) of these new sites. The large number of videos and texts is formidable, and this raises concerns about who will be heard or read. Many postings on these sites are not viewed by others at all.

At the same time, the age-specific use of digital media is shifting. On certain social networking sites, people in their 20s and 30s are even higher consumers than younger people are. However, there are certain aspects of the contextual embedding of such media for youth and that for adults that seem different. As shown in the articles in the book 'Digital Generations' (Buckingham & Willett 2006), there is a need to better understand the characteristics of different aspects of digital media, e.g., gaming, social media, sms. Similar examples of the different ways in which children and young people use different media and their implications can be seen in the many contributions found in collected works such as 'The International Handbook of Children, Media and Culture' (Drotner & Livingstone 2008) and 'Handbook of Research on New Literacies' (Coiro, Knobel, Lankshear & Leu 2008). Also the specific functions that digital media have in young people's lives have been explored in the large-scale 'Digital Youth' project lead by Japanese-American researcher M. Ito (//digitalyouth.ischool.berkeley. edu/). The increased writing activities of young people using digital media to produce and distribute texts have been revealed in the longitudinal study 'The Stanford Study of Writing' (2001-2006), lead by Andrea Lunsford (http://ssw. stanford.edu/). These studies show that there are some fundamental changes going on in the ways young people are communicating, producing texts and distributing content.

Two issues concerning the ways in which young people are using digital media are of importance here, because they deal with ways of engaging young people in learning activities across formal and informal contexts.

Productive practices

The development of digital tools has changed media production among young people in fundamental ways. The digitization of a wide range of media, computer capability and broadband access to the Internet imply that more students can work with photos, sound, text and moving images using standard software.

These new creative practices – often referred to as remixing culture given the ways in which different contents and modalities are put together – have been highlighted in the literature (Erstad 2008; Ito 2006). In the popular press, these practices are often celebrated as the literacies of the young generation. Although these cultural practices have become more common, and are new in the sense that digital media change both how and what people produce, far from all young people are involved in such practices. Potentially, most young people can take part in these production practices, but for different reasons they choose not to. These practices have primarily been studied as part of young people's everyday lives. However, such practices have increasingly found their way into more formal settings of school-based learning, for example with digital storytelling in different subject domains. In this sense, issues of digital competency become important in taking up such cultural practices and framing them as learning practices of importance to the development of skills and competencies needed in the 21st century.

Digital democracies in the making

Another example is the ways in which digital media might influence the civic engagement of youth (Selwyn 2002). In recent years, this has become an interesting area of research that documents how some groups of young people either become engaged in sites made for such purposes or create their own spaces to express their own opinions or make collective statements (Loader 2007; Rheingold 2008).

Both in research and in public debate there has been a fear that young people are losing a sense of the importance of community involvement owing to their involvement in the media culture (Buckingham 2000). And research shows that, for many youngsters, the Internet is not an important media for political engagement at all (Dahlgren & Olsson 2007; Livingstone, Couldry & Markham 2007). Even though political participation and conventional civic engagement, such as voting and knowledge of contemporary issues, have diminished, apolitical and community-related civic activities such as volunteer service continue to attract young people in significant numbers in many countries (Galston 2001). Some research shows that the Internet can serve as an information resource and community-building tool for civic engagement and political participation among young people (Rainie & Horrigan 2005). So perhaps the influence of the Internet on children and adolescents can play a positive role in their development, a role that other institutions in society are no longer filling.

One example of research that focuses on such issues is Justine Cassell's study of the Junior Summit online community, which consisted of 3,062 adolescents representing 139 countries, and a range of experience with computers. In studying this online community, Cassell and colleagues were interested in different aspects of how such communities engage young people, for example, with respect to leadership. Reporting on their research they write that:

> The importance of these findings about youth civic and community participation lies not only in the future of democracy, but also in what they tell us about the way in which young people create identities as individuals and as agents of community and organizational change in the era of the Internet. In this vein, it is important to examine one context in which new forms of leadership are prized, and one in which age may not prevent young people from participating on equal footing with their elders. This context is Internet communities, where leadership is often emergent rather than top-down, and where the lack of face-to-face cues in communication may allow young people to construct an identity more independent of the age, race, and gender cues available in face-to-face communication. Internet communities may be providing opportunities for young people to exercise leadership skills and become stakeholders in communities that they themselves have launched, in part, because they are able to construct their own identities as leaders online independent of public mores and expectations. (Cassell, Huffaker, Tversky & Ferriman 2006: 436-437)

This is an example of how skills in using digital media and navigating the Internet are the foundation for development of broader cultural competencies of importance to our evolving democratic processes. The Internet and media creation represent a new setting in which civic engagement and learning take place (Levine 2008; Raynes-Goldie & Walker 2008). In this sense, online forums for youth may become important tools for issues of collective identity (Erstad & Wertsch 2008). In the Nordic countries, we find examples of online communities for civic engagement among youth, from activist groups like 'Attack' to sites on environmental or other social issues (Østerud & Skogseth 2008). In the Nordic setting, this theme is directly related to education in the sense that civic education traditionally has been of great importance in teaching and learning. Kotilainen and Rantala (2007), for example, argue for the need to develop *civic media education* that takes into account all public media and considers young people as political as well as cultural actors. They have studied two cases of civic media education in Finland: Vaikuttamo.net, which is mainly operated in the schools, and Youth Voice Editorial Board, which is implemented as voluntary free-time activities in youth work.

One question that arises from reading about specific cases of how young people use and relate to digital media is: *Does this matter?* Does such engagement and general use of digital media have any impact on education and learning, and why does it matter in relation to digital literacies and competencies? Education has an important role to play both in increasing awareness and knowledge about the role of the Internet and digital media in our culture, and how it puts demands on the schools concerning how they define what constitutes civic education and teaching about democracy. Again digital literacies and competencies is the area in which such challenges are defined as key knowledge domains in the schools of today and of the future. In this way, the schools become important for participation in digital societies, and digital competencies become the mechanism for framing this in school curricula and practices.

Dimensions of digital competencies in schools

Some of the definitions and frameworks of media/digital literacy that have been developed conceive such literacy in a narrow sense as skills that can be broken down into specific operations. One example is the book 'Media literacy' (2001) by W.J. Potter, where specific skills and cognitive abilities in analysing content in the media are highlighted. However, other definitions and frameworks conceive of digital literacy more broadly. This is expressed in books by D. Buckingham (2003), where media literacy builds on a cultural studies tradition concerning how young people are engaged in using media in different ways. This also relates to the concept of 'Bildung' as part of media pedagogy and digital competence initiatives in the Nordic countries, as mentioned earlier in the article.

During the past decade, several initiatives have been taken for developing typologies and frameworks of digital literacies. The different definitions and conceptions of digital literacy have often been related to certain frameworks and the development of standards for educational practices. In January 2001, the Educational Testing Service (ETS), in the U.S., assembled a panel to develop a workable framework for ICT Literacy. The outcome was the report *Digital Transformation. A Framework for ICT Literacy* (ETS 2002).

The working group of the European Commission in their report 'Key Competencies for Lifelong Learning: a European Reference Framework' has identified digital competence as one of *"the confident and critical use of Information Society Technologies for work, leisure and communication. These competences are related to logical and critical thinking to high-level information management skills, and to well developed communication skills. At the most basic level, ICT skills comprise the use of multi-media technology to retrieve, assess, store, produce, present and exchange information, and to communicate and participate in networks via the Internet."* (European Commission 2006: 14). Digital competence in this framework encompasses knowledge, skills and attitudes related to such technologies.

Based on my own research on the educational use of digital technologies, I have suggested a few categories, elaborated from the ETS framework, to specify some aspects of digital competence in school practices (Erstad 2005). This is thought of as different aspects of how we understand young people's use of digital technologies in learning activities at school, and as a tool for assessing what they can and cannot do with digital media. These are:

Table 1. Different aspects and categories of digital competence

Basic skills	Be able to open software, sort out and save information on the computer, and other simple skills in using the computer and software.
Download	Be able to download different information types from the Internet.
Search	Know about and how to get access to information.
Navigate	Be able to orient oneself in digital networks, learning strategies in using the Internet.
Classify	Be able to organize information according to a certain classification scheme or genre.
Integrate	Be able to compare and put together different types of information related to multimodal texts.
Evaluate	Be able to check and evaluate the information one wishes to obtain by searching the Internet. Be able to judge the quality, relevance, objectivity and usefulness of the information one has found. Critical evaluation of sources.
Communicate	Be able to communicate information and express oneself through different mediational means (Wertsch 1998).
Cooperate	Be able to take part in Net-based interactions in learning, and to take advantage of digital technology to cooperate and participate in networks.
Create	Be able to produce and create different forms of information as multimodal texts, make web pages, and so forth. Be able to develop something new by using specific tools and software. Remixing different existing texts into something new.

This list is one step in the direction of breaking down what we mean by digital competence in school practices. The categories consist of general competencies that are not connected to specific subjects in school or specific technologies. They can be taught and are not only related to what is learned in school settings, but also to situations outside the school.

The critical point now is to bring the policy agenda and the more normative research arguing for the necessity of digital competence more in line with studying knowledge practices, and how digital media create conditions for change and transition within such practices. There are different frameworks to relate to in our understanding of digital literacy/competence. However, the key challenge is to go deeper into the implications of increased use of new technologies in educational practices.

Five dimensions can be elaborated, which highlight different aspects of how we understand digital competencies as part of school-based learning and how students might be empowered in the process of becoming educated.

Dimension 1: Basic skills

This has traditionally been expressed as certification of skills for teachers and students. It is a profile of how good you are at performing certain tasks in operating the computer, the Internet or software. The problem with this approach is that the technology changes all the time, and it is difficult to develop standardizations that will last over time. And, as expressed by the young people in the sections above, handling the technology is something you explore and learn when needed. Still, not all students have the same skills in operating the technology, and the teachers should have some tracking of their students' levels as a starting point for how technology will be used in learning activities.

Dimension 2: Media as objects of analysis

One aspect of digital competence in schools is the importance media and technology have as a knowledge domain per se. During the past 40 years, media culture has become more and more evident on all levels of society. In this sense, it has become a knowledge domain in its own right that is important for students to know about. This has traditionally been part of media education in school, but since the breakthrough of digital media, it has become an important part of many subjects in school. Based on what has been discussed above, the technology itself is something young people relate to, but do not have any understanding of. Thus, issues like media history, media genres and media and power would seem to be important.

Dimension 3: Knowledge building in subject domains

This relates to how new technologies change fundamental issues within established school subjects. We have seen this before, for instance when the calculator was introduced in mathematics, and the disputes this created about how mathematics as a subject changed because of this. The same can be said about different digital media and software packages that are introduced in different subjects. How do they change the knowledge structures within the subject itself, what is considered core knowledge elements, and also how students build knowledge and approach these knowledge structures? Knowledge is thereby seen as interconnected with the cultural tools we have available, and that knowledge changes over time.

Dimension 4: Learning strategies

This dimension cuts across different subject areas, and is more about the ways in which students approach information and knowledge. This has been important before regarding how students often have problems in developing good learning strategies and self-regulated learning. In relation to digital competence, this dimension has become even more important. Developments of information sources on the Internet place more demands on the competencies of students in terms of orienting themselves when searching for information, evaluating such sources and using information to build knowledge. Also how students need to develop good strategies for using information to learn more, and for learning how to learn.

Dimension 5: Digital Bildung/Cultural competence

This last dimension points towards broader issues of learning in our culture. Issues concerning what is called 'digital bildung', or cultural competence, are more concerned with the overall challenges of being part of a digital culture. This is a question of functioning optimally in a media culture and a knowledge society, and being able to make informed decisions of importance to oneself as a citizen and to society as a whole, for example when elections become digitalized and political debates take place on online sites. This is also a question of how learning is connected to identity and of what I have described above as students' learning lives across different contexts and our communicative competence in using the different cultural tools available to us. This approach to learning and literacy is more holistic and integrated with regard to educating the digital generation.

The future for digital competencies

Recent changes in the labour market indicate that many jobs that are in demand today did not even exist a decade ago. Not only is our labour market in transition, but also the competencies needed and the challenges faced by education. In order to proceed in exploring what digital competencies exist in our culture today, and the role of education, we need to go beyond simple political statements. There is a great need to establish strategies for research and educational practices using digital media to give direction to further developments.

There is one question, however, that is of key importance to the educational prospects of a digital generation: To what extent will we see new divisions in our societies, locally, nationally and globally, in terms of who will become included and excluded (Warschauer 2004)? The digital divide has mainly been discussed as an issue related to access, gender differences and so forth. More important today, however, is to see this as an issue of competence and literacy, or more generally as Bildung for a digital age. Bildung would imply knowing how to navigate in the information jungle on the Internet, to create, to communicate and so forth. This is where issues of digital competence and empowerment come in.

Which path one chooses to take in acquiring 21st century competencies is not insignificant. We could focus narrowly on skills in handling digital media, or we could see these as broader cultural competencies of great consequence for how we engage young people in the future development of our societies.

47

The main argument here is the necessity of critically embracing digital literacies/competencies as a new area of great importance to the digital lives of young people living in our complex media culture. Even though such literacies/competencies are increasingly defined as part of school curricula, like in Norway, the problem is still that these initiatives focus mainly on skills in handling the technology. In discussing the future of education, we need to understand the broader issues of digital competencies, as related to the five dimensions suggested in the present article. Two examples were mentioned showing the spectrum of these dimensions, one focusing on specific competencies related to working with multimodal texts, as in digital storytelling in the schools, and another showing broader issues of cultural competencies that concern civic engagement. The paths we decide to take with regard to digital competencies as an educational challenge will have consequences for educational policy, research and educational practices in the years to come. For the sake of our children, and their education, we need to start defining these paths and challenges today, as seen in the 'The Assessment and Teaching of 21st Century Skills Project'.

References

Barton, D. (1994) *Literacy. An Introduction to the Ecology of Written Language*. Oxford: Blackwell.

Bennett, W.L. (2008) Changing Citizenship in the Digital Age. In Bennett, W.L. (ed.) *Civic Life Online: Learning How Dgital Media Can Engage Youth*. Cambridge, MA: The MIT Press, pp 1-24.

Brandtzæg, P. & Heim, J. (2007a) *Patterns of Media User Communities in Countries Hosting CITIZEN MEDIA*. Oslo: SINTEF. (Citizen Media – Social Change)

Buckingham, D. (2000) *The Making of Citizens. Young People, News and Politics*. London: Routledge.

Buckingham, D. (2003) *Media Education – Literacy, Learning and Contemporary Culture*. London: Polity Press.

Buckingham, D. & Willett, R. (eds.) (2006) *Digital Generations. Children, Young People and New Media*. Mahwah, New Jersey: Lawrence Erlbaum.

Burn, A. & Durran, J. (2007) *Media Literacy in Schools – Practice, Production and Progression*. London: Paul Chapman Publishing.

Cassell, J., Huffaker, D., Tversky, D. & Ferriman, K. (2006) The Language of Online Leadership: Gender and Youth Engagement on the Internet. *Developmental Psychology*, vol. 42, no. 3, pp. 436-449.

Coiro, J., Knobel, M., Lankshear, C. & Leu, D.J. (2008) *Handbook of Research on New Literacies*. Lawrence Erlbaum: New York.

Cole, M. & Keyssar, H. (1985) The Concept of Literacy in Print and film. In Olson, D.R., Torrance, N. & Hildyard, A. (eds.) *Literacy, Language and Learning. The Nature and Consequences of Reading and Writing*, pp. 50-72. New York: Cambridge University Press.

Cope, B. & Kalantzis, M. (eds.) (2000) *Multiliteracies: Literacy Learning and the Design of Social Futures*. London: Routledge.

Cope, B. & Kalantzis, M. (2009) Multiliteracies: New Literacies, New Learning. *Pedagogy – An International Journal*, vol. 4, no. 3, pp. 164-195.

Dahlgren, P. & Olsson, T. (2007) Young Activists, Political Horizons and the Internet: Adapting the Net to one's Purposes. In Loader, B.D. (ed.) *Young Citizens in the Digital Age. Political Engagement, Young People and New Media*. London: Routledge, pp. 68-81.

Drotner, K. (1991) *At skabe sig-selv*. [To create your-self] Copenhagen: Gyldendal.

Drotner, K. (2001) *Medier for fremtiden: børn, unge og det nye medielandskab*. Copenhagen: Høst & Søn.

Drotner, K. & Livingstone, S. (eds.) (2008) *The International Handbook of Children, Media and Culture*. Los Angeles: SAGE

Erstad, O. (2008) Trajectories of Eemixing – Digital Literacies, Media Production and Schooling. In Lankshear, C. & Knobel, M. (eds.) *Digital Literacies. Concepts, Policies and Practices*. New York: Peter Lang. pp. 177-202.

Erstad, O. (2005) *Digital kompetanse i skolen* [Digital competence in the school.] Oslo: Universitetsforlaget (University Press).

Erstad, O., Gilje, Ø. & de Lange, T. (2007) Re-mixing multimodal Eesources: Multiliteracies and Digital Production in Norwegian Media Education. *Journal Learning, Media and Technology*. Special Issue: 'Media Education Goes Digital', Buckingham, D. & Bragg, S. (eds.) London: Taylor & Francis. Vol. 32, No. 2, pp. 183-199.

Erstad, O. & Wertsch, J. (2008) Tales of Mediation: Narrative and Digital Media as Cultural Tools. In K. Lundby (ed.) *Digital Storytelling, Mediatized Stories: Self-*representation in New Media. New York: Peter Lang Publishing. pp. 21-40.

ETS (2002) *Digital Transformation: a Framework for ICT Literacy*. Princeton NJ: Educational Testing Service.

European Commission (2006) *Key Competences for Lifelong Learning: a European Reference Framework*. Directorate-General for Education and Culture (Retrieved online at HYPERLINK " http://europa.eu/legislation_summaries/education_training_youth/lifelong_learning/c11090_en.htm" http://europa.eu/legislation_summaries/education_training_youth/lifelong_learning/c11090_en.htm on February 26th 2010)

Galston, W.A. (2001) Political Knowledge, Political Engagement, and Civic Education. *Annual Review of Political Science*, 4, pp. 217-234.

Heath, S.B. (1983) *Ways with Words. Language, Life, and Work in Communities and Classrooms*. New York: Cambridge University Press.

Ito, M. (2006) Japanese Media Mixes and Amateur Cultural Exchange. In Buckingham, D. & Willett, R. (eds.) (2006) *Digital Generations. Children, Young People, and New Media*. Mahwah, NJ: Lawrence Erlbaum. pp. 49-66.

Jenkins, H. (2006) *Convergence Culture. Where Old and New Media Collide*. New York: New York University Press.

Kellner, D. (2002) Technological Revolution, Multiple Literacies, and the Restructuring of Education. In Snyder, I. (ed.) *Silicon Literacies. Communication, Innovation and Education in the Electronic age*. London: Routledge. pp. 154-169.

Kotilainen, S. & Rantala, L. (2007) 'Media, Citizenships and Young People'. Paper presented in 8th Annual Conference of the European Sociological Association. Glasgow, 3rd-6th September.

Kress, G. (2003) *Literacy in the New Media Age*. London: Routledge.

Lankshear, C. & M. Knobel (2006) *New Literacies, Everyday Practices and Classroom Learning*. Berkshire, UK: Open University Press.

Lemke, J.L. (1998) Metamedia Literacy: Transforming Meanings and Media. In Reinking, D. McKenna, M., Laboo, L.D. & Kieffer, R.D. (ed) *Handbook of Literacy and Technology*. Transformations in a Post-Typographic World. Mahwah, NJ, Lawrence Erlbaum Ass.

Levine, P. (2008) A Public Voice for Youth: The Audience Problem in Digital Media and Civic Engagement. In W.L. Bennett (ed.) *Civic Life Online: Learning how Digital Media Can Engage Youth*. Cambridge, MA: The MIT Press, pp. 119-138.

Livingstone, S. (2009) *Children and the Internet*. Cambridge: Polity Press.

Livingstone, S., Couldry, N. & Markham, T. (2007) Youthful Steps towards Civic Participation: does the Internet Help? In Loader, B.D. (ed.) *Political Engagement, Young People and the Internet,* Routledge, London, pp. 21-34.

Loader, B.D. (2007) Introduction: Young Citizens in the Digital Age: Disaffected or Displaces? In Loader, B. (ed.) *Political Engagement, Young People and the Internet,* Routledge, London, pp. 1-18.

Ministry of Education, Research, and Church Affairs (1994) *Information Technology in Education*. Oslo.

Ministry of Education, Research, and Church Affairs. (2000) *ICT in Norwegian Education: Plan for 2000–2003*. Oslo.

Ministry of Education and Research (2004) *Program for Digital Literacy 2004-2008*. Oslo.

Pahl, K. & Rowsell, J. (2005) *Literacy and Education. Understanding the New Literacy Studies in the Classroom*. Thousand Oaks, Calif.: SAGE.

Potter, W.J. (2001) *Media Literacy*. London: Sage

Rainie, L. & Horrigan, J. (2005) *A Decade of Adoption: How the Internet has Woven itself into Americal Life*. Washington, DC: PEW Internet and Family Life.

Raynes-Goldie, K. & Walker, L. (2008) Our Space: Online Civic Engagement tools for Youth. In W.L. Bennett (ed.) *Civic Life Online: Learning how Digital Media Can Engage Youth*. Cambridge, MA: The MIT Press, pp. 161-188.

Reinking, D., McKenna, M.C., Labbo, L.D. & Kieffer, R.D. (eds.) (1998) *Handbook of Literacy and Technology. Transformations in a Post-typographic World*. Mahwah, New Jersey: Lawrence Erlbaum

Rheingold, H. (2008) Using Participatory Media and Public Voice to Encourage Civic Engagement. in W. Lance Bennet (ed.) *Civic Life Online: Learning How Digital Media Can Engage Youth*. Cambridge: The MIT Press, MA, pp. 97-118.

Scribner, S. & Cole, M. (1981) *The Psychology of Literacy*. Cambridge, Mass., Harvard University Press.

Selwyn, N. (2002) *Literature Eeview in Citizenship, Technology and Learning*. Bristol, Nesta Futurelab.

Snyder, I. (ed.) (2002) *Silicon Literacies. Communication, Innovation and Education in the Electronic Age*. London: Routledge.

Street, B. (1984) *Literacy in Theory and Practice*. Cambridge, UK: Cambridge University Press.

Thavenius, J. (1995) *Den motsägelsefulla bildningen*. Stockholm: Brutus Östlings Bokförlag Symposium.

Tufte, B. (1995) Skole og Medier: Byggesæt til de Levende billeders pædagogisk. Copenhagen: Akademisk Forlag. Doctoral thesis. .

Warschauer, M. (2003) Technology and Social Inclusion: Rethinking the Digital Divide. Cambridge, MA: MIT Press.

Wertsch, J. (1998) *Mind as Action*. New York: Oxford University Press.

Wertsch, J., del Rio, P. & Alvarez, A. (1995) Sociocultural Studies: History, Action, and Mediation. In J. Wertsch, P. del Rio & A. Alvarez (eds.) *Sociocultural Studies of Mind. pp. 1-34*. Cambridge, MA: Harvard University Press.

Østerud, S. & Skogseth, E. (2008) Å være på nett. [To be on the Net.] Oslo: Cappelen Damm.

2.0 – Children In and Outside School

Birgitte Holm Sørensen

Given the present prevalence of the Internet, mobile technology and Web 2.0 facilities, information technology must be seen as an environment requiring ICT-related competencies. Apart from basic skills in ICT operation, such competencies also include digital media production, critical search of information and interpretation of digital media's manifold representations. Another important competency is the individual person's ability to adjust to the constantly changing challenges and conditions of the digitalized world. With their informal learning strategies, children and young people are generally quick to adopt new technologies in their activities outside school. Their participation in Web 2.0 environments means that schools in the future must include both students' informal competencies and support them in developing ICT-related competencies.

Social development, digitalization and growing use of Web 2.0 constitute a challenge and a potential for change for teaching and learning. In a few years, schools will have wireless Internet and teachers and students will have their own mobilework station with built-in communication equipment such as web-cam, GPS and equipment for recording sound and pictures, while most software will be accessed online in the form of cloud computing. Furthermore, classrooms, project and conference rooms will have interactive whiteboards or multitouch tables.

To understand the conditions for the school's transformation from an industrial society school to a knowledge society school, we must acknowledge that different generations have different ICT experiences. These differences have a great impact on how students and teachers interact and perform in relation to ICT in school. The present article focuses on children's use of Web 2.0 outside school and on their ICT-related competence development; it also looks at how the schools must deal with the challenge of Web 2.0 in relation to developing students' ICT-related competencies.

Web 2.0

The concept of Web 2.0 deals with the second generation of the Internet. It focuses on new approaches to and use of the Internet in the digitally based business world, which has quickly spread to other areas of society (O'Reilly 2005). In Web 2.0, the Internet is seen as a platform on which all digital material is anchored. This change has resulted in a broad approach to the so-called services that, via the Net, allow users to share materials, construct materials jointly and take an active part in social communities that integrate a number of specific services offered on the Net, such as Facebook and Second Life. At the same time, Web 2.0 allows the individual to create ad hoc his/her own virtual room of possibilities and use it together with others by combining different services, such as Google Docs, Flickr, Wiki, Blogs, YouTube, MySpace, RSS-feeds and Mashups. The link with mobile and wireless Internet access, Web 2.0 and GPS are furthering the breakdown of the industrial society's physically well-defined space.

The employment of Web 2.0 has generated a number of new concepts. The concept *user-generated* content is tied directly to Web 2.0 and should be understood as the accumulation of users' own productions, which are either uploaded to the Net or produced directly in Web 2.0 services on the Net. Such productions can be processed further together with others in the same services. The concept covers several phenomena such as user-generated content on different websites, *peer-to-peer file sharing* and *social networking*. In addition, Web 2.0 features *social networking* and cooperation between users. With users' new status as active participants and producers, we might say that the concept *user-generated content* has appeared.

Digitalization and the Internet have caused radical changes in the schools. For years, the printed book has been the central learning artifact, but in the past decade, it has met with growing competition from digitalized teaching and learning artifacts and the facilities connected with Web 2.0. As a result, attention has focused on the importance of the learning artifact in relation to how it can be used in the classroom, and what effect this has on the teacher's teaching and the student's learning.

Children and IT

Computers and Internet have become so integrated into children's everyday life that most children have a mobile phone when they start school, and for every four 9- to 10-year-old children in Denmark, one has a profile on the Internet[1]. In recent years, many metaphors have emerged reflecting how children and young people are central users of digital media. Metaphors such as the game generation, Cyberkids, the Net generation, the digital generation, the globalization's front soldiers, digital nomads, New Learners, Power Users and Millennials are examples of concepts that point to children and young people as especially keen users of digital media (Haraway 1991; Tapscott 1998; Williams 1999; Papert 1999; Jessen and Sørensen 2003; Malyn-Smith 2004; Levinsen 2008). Each of these metaphors captures aspects of the difference between present-day children and young people familiar with ICT and adults. However, not all of them are equally well suited to describing or clarifying the differences and their implications.

Millennials and *the Internet Generation* are attempts to give the generation born after 1986 an original name relating to central events and cultural trends specific to the generation. However, the different forms of *digital divides* underline that far from all persons in this generation have gained special experience with ICT, even if the Internet and later the wireless and mobile solutions have existed during their entire lifetime. Similarly, the designations *New Learners* (Malyn-Smith 2004) and *Power Users* (ibid.:2004; Sørensen & Audon 2004; Ryberg 2007) refer to the generation that has had the opportunity to use ICT daily and indicate an extensive and advanced use of digital media on both a local and global level. This part of the generation is particularly interesting from an educational perspective, as it shows an inquiring and explorative approach to the media's potential (Malyn-Smith 2004; Sørensen & Audon 2004). However, research has not yet been able to determine to what degree Power Users' competencies stem from special ICT features and/or special characteristics of the persons who become Power Users. The special approach to ICT and learning reflected in Power Users is a challenge to the whole educational system, as their competencies are seen as particularly relevant in relation to a knowledge society (Sørensen & Audon 2004; Malyn-Smith 2004).

Attention has increasingly focused on children and young people as competent users of the media ever since Simon Papert argued in 1993 that the perception of children as competent media users was in contrast to the school's view. The school had apparently not yet noticed how competent children were as media users (Papert 1993). In recent years, many areas within the child and youth culture have been extended to include digital media, which must now be considered an integrated part of children's play, entertainment and information activities. The reason is partly that many private homes have acquired a computer and Internet access 'for the children's sake', as many parents see the computer not only as an entertainment media, but as a learning tool (Sørensen 2001). But because development has proceeded so rapidly, many children still grow up in homes with parents who do not and perhaps never will use a computer. Thus, children have had to teach themselves how to use a computer and the Internet. Children primarily learn how to use a computer by experimenting and getting help from other children (Livingstone & Bowill 2001; Drotner 2001; Sørensen 2002; SAFT 2003; Stald 2009). In other words, they use both an individual and a social learning approach.

The new digital media have resulted in new conditions for and changes in children's daily activities. The changes have occurred as children have embraced the new media and made them part of their lives and especially part of their social communities. This applies in particular to activities at home and in recreation centers, where children have integrated digital media into their games, creative activities, social relations, communication and information retrieval (Sørensen 2001).

The virtual room, interactivity, mobility and digital pervasion appear to have a crucial impact on the changes in children's daily activities (Drotner 2001; Sørensen 2002; Tingstad 2003; Dunkels 2009; Livingstone & Haddon 2009; Stald 2009). In the virtual rooms, children have found a qualitatively different room in which to express themselves. Interactivity complies to a great extent with children's need and desire to act, play, communicate and create social relations and situations by means of and through the new media. Children may bring their mobile phones wherever they go. It allows them to be in constant contact with others through calls, text messages and e-mails, just as it provides entertainment through games. Children's use of the mobile phone reflects concretely how digitalization changes in nature in the transformation from industrial society to knowledge society. From understanding digital media merely as well-defined tools with certain functions, digitalization and digital media have become pervasive; they prevail everywhere in the environment – in buildings, toys, articles for everyday use and clothes – in other words, they have become an integrated part of society's structure. In this way, digital media become both a condition for and a co-creative factor in children's actions and activities.

Today, children and young people's everyday life take place in both physical and virtual rooms. This means that children and young people's experience, play, learning, communication, social relations and identity are no longer tied only to physical rooms, but also to virtual rooms such as chat rooms, rooms for online games, social networks, news and discussion rooms, different websites, etc. In other words, children's everyday life has changed radically. Now, children play and communicate not only with children they know from the local physical room, but also with children from many other places both nationally and globally, which is a historically new situation.

Informal learning strategies

Growing up in a children's culture with computers and Internet, children have developed a number of different informal learning forms that function when children construct and share knowledge about, e.g., how they use different Web 2.0 resources. It is a question of learning hierarchies, learning communities and learning networks that function in different contexts (Sørensen 2003; Sørensen, Audon & Levinsen 2010). We might say that the learning forms are a set of learning strategies, i.e. approaches used by children to gain skills and obtain information about specific issues. Moreover, the learning forms describe the organizational forms that children construct or establish in their efforts to learn (ibid.).

When children from different age groups or with different skills are together, children's own organizational hierarchy starts to function as a learning hierarchy, where the youngest children learn from older children or the inexperienced children learn from those with experience (Sørensen 2003). Jean Lave and Etienne Wenger use the concept legitimate peripheral participation, referring to when participants are slowly trained into a community (Lave and Wenger 1991). The concept is related to the principle of apprenticeship, where learning is organized according to the apprenticeship hierarchy. Children's self-organization has a great deal in common with the legitimate peripheral participation. However, the difference is that the organization takes place in the children's own culture, where the children themselves decide whether or not they want to participate. If we look at how children organize themselves, e.g. in recreational centers or at home, where several children are present, we often see that the oldest or most competent child(ren) sits in front of the computer. In the next row, we find the second oldest or the second most competent children, and in the last row the youngest or the least competent children are standing. The rows in the hierarchy reflect a ranking where age, knowledge or ability are the parameters according to which children position themselves. Children establish and take part in the learning hierarchies, as they know they will benefit from an approach in which direct observation, copying, experimenting, discussions and conversations are part of the learning strategies (Sørensen 2003).

When children use a computer, it often takes place in a *community of learning* where they may play a game together. In such a situation, learning becomes an important element in the community, as it is *a means* that enables them to act and play in the game (Sørensen 2003). It may take place in the physical room as well as in the virtual room. Children's communities of learning share a number of features with Wenger's concept "communities of practice" (Wenger 1998). Children's online activities involve an ongoing negotiation of ideas, in which they develop a common understanding of the situation and process they are part of. It is a question of mutual commitment when children draw on, use and depend on each others' competencies, e.g. in an online game, where the object is to win a fight against another clan or group. It might often be a community of long standing, where the participants meet several times a week in the same game and the same clan, in which the community of learning is an integrated part.

When children use digital media, they establish *learning networks*, in which they develop strategies to retrieve information, share information with others and construct new knowledge. A network can be described as a combination of units in a general system. However, a children's network is not a solid, established network, but rather a loosely connected network. It is a question of informal networks, which actualizes Norbert Elias and his understanding of people as connected through chains of units he calls *interdependencies* (Elias 1998: 34-35). According to Elias, it is precisely the mutual dependency that provides a basis for creating networks (ibid.). In the different virtual rooms, children cooperate to create and develop ideas and communicate knowledge to each other. The same process takes place when children have to figure out, e.g., how to proceed in a computer game, a multimedia program, etc. The exchange of ideas and communication of knowledge take place via e-mails, the mobile phone, in computer game chat rooms, various discussion rooms on the Internet and in the time spent together around the computer. In networks established by children, they are in full control of who to contact in connection with problems that might occur when operating the digital media in different ways.

Global games, communication and networks

When children are able to communicate in English, their life in the global room begins. Children communicate and establish contacts and web-friendships with other children around the globe, and as such they take part in social and cultural globalization. On the Internet, children gain experience through games and social contacts, and they produce pictures, videos, home pages in English, etc., that are open to a global audience.

However, when we talk in general of children's use of digital media and the Internet, it is important to remember that while some children have an extensive and advanced use of digital media, others do not use the media very much at all. One group of children, the so-called Power Users[2], is a particularly active group of users. In their use of digital media, they have developed competencies that often are at a higher level than many adults' skills. These children develop new ways to use and combine digital media, and we might even say that they create new forms of cooperation and communication, which may be interesting to examine from a school and educational perspective.

It is characteristic of young Power Users that they are part of groups focusing on developing ICT-related competencies, and that such groups may be both local and global. In general, Power Users join or establish changing virtual groups as long as it serves a purpose or participation presents a challenge. The participants may gather and focus on momentary, common interests. The purpose may be to satisfy pleasure needs such as games, thematizing personal relationships or discussing and exchanging viewpoints on certain subjects. As long as it serves a specific purpose to participate, they will do so. When a subject is no longer interesting, an individual or part of the group will move to a new virtual community. As such, a large part of the Internet's virtual world is an ever-changing network (Jessen & Sørensen 2003).

Children and young people's different online activities, often based on interests in special areas, develop different forms of online communication, which enables them to differentiate between linguistic codes used in different online rooms. They take part in existing networks and adjust to the existing culture. If the networks are not adequate, they break out of them and establish new networks that meet their special needs. But an essential condition for participating is the ability to cooperate. In connection with online games where players often are divided into clans, cooperation is vital to win over a competing clan. Together, players work out the course of a game, plan sub-processes, develop alternative plans and make use of each others' competencies. In addition, they agree on the course of a game and who will fill the different positions. For better or for worse, the clan leader prepares the strategies for how to run the clan. Often, the clan leader must dismiss clan members and invite other players to participate. It is important to have skilled participants with different and valuable competencies. At the same time, leaders must handle negotiations and consult with their clan members. Some players know each other from the physical room, but often participants in a clan only meet online, and groups are established on the basis of online communication (ibid.).

A number of Power Users use English to communicate. Often they do not think about it, because it is a gradual process where English is used in more and more activities, and suddenly becomes the everyday online language. In other words, English becomes a functional language as a parallel to their native language used in the physical room (Sørensen 2001).

The oldest Power Users point to new ways of organizing, which is also reflected in some workplaces and in virtually based adult education. Through their activities on the Internet, these young people develop competencies in:

- online communication

- establishing and using online network

- cooperating online

- negotiating online

- online management

- using English as an online language

Such competencies are central in a knowledge society perspective, and they are first and foremost a result of young people's informal learning. We might say that, through virtually based leisure-time activities, children have achieved competencies that prepare them to participate in virtually based education and network-based jobs in a knowledge society. This is a 'spinoff' and was never the children's objective. They are interested in living a life where they engage in something that makes sense, allows them to gain experience and meet challenges, where they can do something together with others in "communities" and networks, and where they can communicate and interpret who they are. They look for situations in which they feel comfortable, and they challenge themselves and each other to gain new experiences and discover new types of social life.

Power Users are particularly interesting from an educational perspective, as they take an inquiring approach to the media's potential for activities and communication. The way in which they explore and apply the media calls for innovative thinking in relation to organization of teaching and learning processes, not only in the primary school, but also at other levels of education.

However, we must emphasize that only a small group of children possess the competencies described above. Some children do not spend a great deal of time on ICT outside school. In relation to these children, the school has a special responsibility. It would be desirable if all students had the above competencies when they leave school.

Web 2.0 and school

> Classroom teaching is like flying in a plane: "Sit down, look straight ahead, fasten your seatbelt and turn off any electronic equipment". If you are lucky the trip might be relevant, if not you can return to your life in 6-7 hours.

> The teacher had forgotten to book the computer room, which meant that we had nothing to do in the entire project week...it was a waste of time, the only thing we could do at school was to read something, talk together and wait to go home so we could start to work with our computer and Internet at home.

> I use the computer a lot at school – and the Internet, if I have to find something... I also use the video camera a lot and take photos with my mobile phone e.g. for projects. We have just been given interactive whiteboards, which we can also use during recess to listen to music.

These student quotations reflect very different school days in terms of access to and use of ICT. In an OECD report from 2004, the Nordic countries were placed high on the list in terms of number of computers in school. A Danish study shows that in 2007, 3.98 students were sharing a single computer[3]. But it is one thing to have a lot of computers, another to use them. A Nordic study from 2006 with figures from Danish schools shows that 29% of students in the 5th and 8th grades in a randomly chosen week in March 2006 had not used ICT in class, 42% had used ICT for 1-2 hours and 21% had used ICT for 3-5 hours. Only 7% had used ICT in 6 hours or more (E-learning Nordic 2006)[4]. These figures are completely at variance with children's use of media outside school. Several studies show that children and young people's use of media is far more advanced and differentiated outside school than in school (Drotner 2001; Livingstone & Bowill 2001; Sørensen, Jessen & Olesen 2002; SAFT 2003). Owing to the school system's traditional approach to teaching, it is difficult to break schools' passivity in introducing digital media into the classroom.

In recent years, a large number of digital teaching and learning tools based on different designs for learning and teaching have been developed. Parallel to this development, more and more Web 2.0 resources are made available. In this respect, affordance gains prominence as a central concept. Affordance comes originally from Gibson (1979), who uses the concept to refer to options available in terms of artifacts and actions in a given environment. The school's access to the Internet and Web 2.0 resources has expanded the options in artifacts and actions in the school's learning room. Many of the resources present new ways and forms of participation, sociality and cooperation, just as they present a new scope for students' production and publication activities. Such approaches to actions and forms are not new to the school, but digitalization, online technology and new forms of multimodality encourage the development of new designs for teaching and learning.

The digital media and the Internet confront the book as the primary learning tool in teaching and as such also the most used form of presenting an academic content for many years. There is a difference between presenting an academic content about astronomy in a textbook with static pictures and applying the multimodal resources available at the Internet in the form of animation, photos, videos and printed texts combined with different kinds of sound. The different types of expressions and media invite different formations of meaning.

> The form of representation has an impact on the content related aspects of what we may express about a phenomenon, which has epistemological consequences when e.g. we communicate in school......Thus, form and content can never be separated, which means that the selection of notation and media determines which content of information we may present (Rostwall & Selander 2008).

In order to use Web 2.0 in school, design for teaching and learning must be developed. In a Web 2.0 perspective and to comply with the aspects emphasized by students, it is relevant to draw on several approaches to design for teaching and learning. In a knowledge society school, design for teaching and learning is performed in a floating context, where technology presents a new scope for differentiating and designing in relation to individual students. Technological development is constantly challenging the school, which means that design for teaching and learning is also subject to constant development and change. Apart from theories of didactics, learning and different educational approaches, theories of multimodality, communication, play and games are gaining interest. Multimodality includes a number of clear options that consider both different approaches to learning and methods of expression. Communication in a teaching perspective does not only include face to face communication, but the media's diversity of approaches also depends on whether communication is taking place over Messenger, blogs, Twigger or Facebook. It means that the teaching repertoire is constantly expanding, allowing students in different ways to be active in their learning processes related to academic and interdisciplinary topics. For a number of years, play has been included in design for teaching and learning. In recent years, we have seen a new development in which playware, which focuses on digitally based play and learning objects, includes new options for school subjects such as sports, music and science. Similarly, games have been digitalized and developed in many forms, such as entertainment games that include learning potentials, e.g. Sim City, as well as learning games with a didactic view on different subjects.

Precisely because learning is not only tied to formal learning contexts, it is easier to see the learning potential of different objects and culture products. We begin to question different objects and culture products: Could they be used in students' learning processes? Learning and teaching resources that are seen as

59

relevant in a learning perspective are made available for students and teachers. Thus, they have an impact on development of designs for learning and also on students' learning processes and results. Children's use of and engagement in computer games is a good example of a culture product that has caught the interest of researchers, teachers and game developers. Subsequently, the product has been adopted by the school in a didactic adjusted form as a learning game[5] and as an "entertainment game" used didactically by teachers and students in relation to certain themes (Squire 2004).

Competencies that must be developed

As mentioned earlier, some children are for various reasons sorely lacking in digital competencies from a school and future perspective. The Internet has made an unsuspected quantity of information available, and while the quantity of information continues to grow, it appears in a complex mixture of expressions, with visual and auditive forms gaining in prominence. Wikipedia, e.g., features information consisting of texts, pictures, sound, video cuts, links, etc., all updated continuously.

In light of students' role as ICT users and the development of Web 2.0, information retrieval has become a central competence in teaching. Three other important competence areas include production and arrangement, analysis and communication, knowledge sharing and cooperation.

In classroom teaching, it is clear that most children lack skills in making a targeted search on the Net and relating critically to the information they find (Kryger 2004; Levinsen & Sørensen 2008). Often, this involves complex relationships that apply to digitally based information. When students use the Internet and digital technologies, they must learn how to find, interpret and summarize information in a systematic and critical manner. In other words, they must learn to identify their need for information, find the right means of information retrieval and use goal-oriented strategies for systematic retrieval. In addition, they must learn how to examine and evaluate information in a critical manner and understand how to screen, select and edit information for certain purposes as well as to correctly quote and reference different sources. In school, criticism of sources used to be a concept related to history in the highest grades. Today, it is a central concept applied at an early stage in school.

Digital technologies provide a long range of facilities for producing and communicating information, knowledge and experiences. In its logical conclusion, the entire world may be an audience to and user of knowledge produced by a student, if it is made available on the Internet. Central competencies include the ability to adjust the production and means to the message, recipients and publishing context and to take a critical view of which communication is relevant in the context and for the purpose at hand. In this connection, it is central for the student to reflect over choice of expression and media.

The multiplicity of texts is immense and increases demands on students' competencies in interpreting and analyzing texts to ensure that they can evaluate producers' interests and the digital media's presentation of the world. In addition, students must be able to understand how technological development and digital media production are related to cultural, social, political and financial issues.

Outside school, children are online via different platforms or increasingly advanced mobile equipment. Experience shows that such activities provide many new opportunities in a teaching context, but it requires other skills and social competencies than when communication between students and between students and teachers was based on a physical and simultaneous presence. Increasingly, communication, knowledge sharing and cooperation involve the use of, e.g., blogs, wikis, different social communities and teaching and learning platforms that can be used in many academic contexts. Students may sit by themselves at home, but still be working on a project assignment by cooperating and interacting online on Skype, MSN or Facebook with other project participants.

Conclusion

The school is faced with a real challenge in terms of developing students' ICT-related competencies. As mentioned, some students have ICT-related competencies at a high level, while others are in great need of developing their competencies. There are considerable differences in how well-prepared schools are to take on this competence development. How competence development should be handled differs from school to school and from teacher to teacher (Pedersen & Hornskov 2009). In fact, the issue is a real challenge in the training of teachers.

However, we should not only look at ICT-related competencies in relation to teaching and learning in school. ICT is woven into everything and therefore plays an active part in creating and converting the way in which we relate to each other, the world and our social structures (Castells 2000). We must also consider ICT-related competencies in a future perspective and tie them to the way in which an individual acquires his/her competencies. According to Castells, the way in which competencies are gained means a great deal to the individual person. Based on the need for labor in the future, he differentiates between self-programming and generic labor (Castells 2000: 12). The self-programming worker is able to meet new challenges in informal ways, train him-/herself in and adjust to new tasks, processes and types of information in line with the constant increase in technology's and society's rate of change. As distinct from this scenario, the generic worker is only able to change through formal training and as such may be either replaced or dismissed. In other words, generic workers constitute a vulnerable group. From an educational perspective, it is therefore important to create conditions in school that will allow students to develop self-programming competencies in addition to ICT-related skills. In fact, students must develop competencies that enable them through innovative approaches, self-studies, exploration and the use of social networks to adjust to and handle new types of assignments, processes and challenges in variable contexts.

Notes

1. http://andk.medieraadet.dk/Portal/Andk/Sikker_Internet_Dag/SID09/SID09_undersogelsen. aspx
2. The concept Power Users is used in an international project initiated by the Education Development Center, Boston.
3. http://cis.emu.dk/public_national_oversigt.do
4. http://www.elearningeuropa.info/files/media/media10112.pdf
5. E.g. http://www.dpu.dk/site.aspx?p=11097

References

Castells, M. (2000) Materials for an Exploratory Theory of the Network Society. *British Journal of Sociology,* 51, 1, 5-24.

Drotner, K. (2001) *Medier for fremtiden: børn, unge og det nye medielandskab.* København: Høst.

Dunkels, E. (2009) *Vad gör unga på nätet.* Malmö: Gleerup Utbildning AB.

Elearning Europa 2005: *A European Framework for Digital Literacy.* Retrieved January 15,2010, from http://www.elearningeuropa.info/directory/index.php?page=doc&doc_id=6007&doclng=6).

E-learning Nordic 2006: effekten af it i uddannelsessektoren. Retrieved January 22,2010, from http://www.elearningeuropa.info/files/media/media10112.pdf

Elias, N. (1998) *On Civilization, Power and Knowledge.* Chicago/London: The University of Chicago Press.

Gibson, J.J. (1979) *The Ecological Approach to Visual Perception.* Boston: Houghton Mifflin.

Haraway, D. (1991) *Simians, Cyborgs and Woman: The Reinvention of Nature.* London: Free Association Books.

Jessen, C. & Sørensen, B.H. (2003) Virtuel kommunikation og virtuelle fællesskaber – hvilke kompetencer? I: H. Mathiasen, *It og læringsperspektiver.* Vojens: Alinea

Kryger, N. (2004) *Skolen på nettet: læringens veje og vildveje.* København: Danmarks Lærerhøjskole.

Lave, J. og Wegner, E. (1991) *Situated Learning: Legitimate Peripheral Participation.* New York: Cambridge University Press.

Levinsen, K. (2008) Neomillenial Learning Styles og Mønsterbrydere. I: L.B. Andreasen, *Digitale Medier og læring.* København: Danmarks Pædagogiske Universitets Forlag

Levinsen, K. & Sørensen, B.H. (2008) *It, faglig læring og pædagogisk videnledelse: rapport vedr. Projekt It læring.* Gentofte Kommune /DPU, AU.

Livingstone, S. & Bowill, M. (eds.) (2001) *Children and their Changing Media Environment: A European Comparative Study.* New York: Erlbaum.

Livingstone, S. & Haddon, L. (2009) *Lids Online. Opportunities and Risk for Children.* Bristol: The Polity Press, Bristol University.

Malyn-Smith, J. (2004) *Power Users of Technology: Who are They? Where are They Going? Why does it Matter?* http://findarticles.com/p/articles/mi_m1309/is_2_41/ai_n6363954 (27.10.2007)

OECD (2001) *Meeting of the OECD education ministers,* Paris, 3-4 April 2001. Retrieved April 01, 2008 http://www.oecd.org/dataoecd/40/8/1924078.pdf.

O'Reilly (2005) What Is Web 2.0. Design Patterns and Business Models for the Next Generation of Software. Retrieved April 01, 2008 http://www.oreillynet.com/pub/a/oreilly/tim/news/2005/09/30/what-is-web-20.html

Papert, S. (1993) *The Children's Machine. Rethinking School in the Age of the Computer.* New York: Harvester Wheatheaf.

Pedersen, S.G. & Hornskov, M.B. (2009) It i skolen – erfaringer og perspektiver. Købenahvn: EVA

(English summary)

Rostwall, A.-L. & Selander, S. (2008) Design för lärande. Stockholm: Norstedts akademiska förlag.

Ryberg, T. (2007) *Patchworking as a Metaphor for Learning : Understanding youth, learning and technology.* Aalborg University: e-Learning Lab Publication Series; 10.

SAFT: Retrieved July 07, 2004, http://www.medieraadet.dk/html/saft

Squire, Kurt D (2004) *Replaying History.* Indiana:Indiana University.

Stald, Gitte (2009) *Globale medier – lokal unge.* Institut for Medier, erkendelse, formidling. København: Københavns Universitet.

Sørensen, B.H. (2001) Børns hverdagsliv med de nye medier. I: B.H. Sørensen, B.R. Olesen & L. Audon (ed.) *Det hele kører parallelt. De nye medier i børns hverdagsliv.* København: Gads Forlag.

Sørensen, B.H. (2003) Nye læringsformer med digitale medier. *Mediepedagogisk Tidsskrift,* Norge. Marts 2003.

Sørensen. B.H. & Audon, L. (2004) *Nye Læringsformer og rum – digitale medier i vidensamfundets skole.* Forskningsrapport. København: Danmarks Pædagogiske Universitet.

Sørensen, B.H., Audon, L. & Levinsen, K. (2010) *Skole 2.0.* Aarhus: Klim

Sørensen, B.H., Jessen, C., & Olesen, B.R. (ed.) (2002) *Børn på nettet. Kommunikation og læring.* København: Gads Forlag.

Tapscott, D. (1998) *Growing up Digital. The Rise of a Net Generation.* New York: Mcgraw-Hill.

Tingstad, V. (2003) *Children's Chat on the Net: A Study of Social Encounters in Two Norwegian Chat Rooms.* Trondheim: Norges teknisk-naturvitenskabelige universitet.

Wenger, E. (1998) *Communities of Practice. Learning, Meaning, and Identity.* Cambridge: Cambridge University Press.

Williams, P. (1999) The Net Generation: The Experiences, Attitudes and Behaviour of Children using the Internet for Their Own Purposes. *Aslib Proceedings,* 51 (9).

Global Digital Culture Requires Skills in Media Literacies

Sirkku Kotilainen

A 10-year-old boy is browsing YouTube, looking for different guitar versions of his favourite song, a part of which he has to learn for his next guitar lesson. Occasionally he checks his IM to see whether any of his friends are online. None of his mates appear, though, and the youngster moves on to an online game, puts on his headset and asks via the microphone whether any of his fellow players speak English.

The above situation is a fairly typical one in Finnish and Scandinavian homes. At a relatively young age, and through various Internet activities, children and young people engage in international interaction with fellow gamers and other online communicators. For example my own son, who is in primary school, often asks for translation help while he is playing games online. Yet this kind of informal learning young people are involved in is often disregarded – usually because discussions on media skills concentrate on the supposed risks these media may expose children to. However, in addition to assessing the risks involved, we should be considering the challenges presented to parents and teachers by the kinds of participatory, usually free-time activities young people are engaged in (e.g. Buckingham 2003). For instance, we need to ask what kind of media literacy skills children and young people should acquire so that they know how to deal with these global, mainly commercial media environments.

For young people, digital culture is not a separate technology or a virtual world; on the contrary, it is inseparably linked to their other activities and interests, for instance, making independent films or participating in societal activities. I am suggesting that their upbringing should not merely prepare them for adulthood, but also for responsible activity taking place in the present. This kind of responsibility includes multiple skills in media literacies.

Activities online are a part of current youth cultures

Community services, such as Youtube and MySpace, along with Wikipedia and blogs, allow users to get engaged in public and social knowledge creation, mostly in international, digital media cultures. These kinds of online *public media* interest young people because they provide opportunities for interaction and creation of their own media work. Youth researchers talk about "mediated youth cultures," in which the uses of different media (e.g., the Internet, mobile phones, television) – as well as the modes of cultural expression, i.e. music, text and images added to their multimodalities – are integrated into the everyday lives of the young through participatory cultures online (e.g. Hodkinson 2007; Jenkins et al. 2009).

How is one to be visible and how is one to be heard in information societies if not through media? This question is linked to mediated youth cultures and to discussions of citizenship, especially in contemporary Western societies. For young people in the West, acting on media publicity, for example in online communities, can be a part of everyday practices. However, researchers have found 'digital divides' among the young concerning the quality of online activities. Low-speed broadband access or less up-to-date software mean unequal access to opportunities for online self-expression. Other discriminatory factors among users include poor media literacy skills or even media illiteracy (Livingstone & Helsper 2007; Jenkins et al. 2009).

Sonia Livingstone, Magdalena Bober and Ellen Helsper (2004) were among the first researchers in Europe to study how especially young people interact online in the United Kingdom. They distinguish three types of participatory users of the Internet: the interactors, the civic-minded and the disengaged. The civic-minded are mainly concerned with political participation, while the interactors use the Internet for more cultural and creative purposes. The disengaged are not interested in the ICT and Internet, or do not have access to them. Empirical data collected in Finland (e.g., Kotilainen & Rantala 2009) elaborate on this classification somewhat. For instance, those who are disengaged on the Internet can take part in civic activities through more traditional media (see Table 1). This typology is based on two public action-orientated case studies that examined Finnish young people aged 13-18 years using several methods (Kotilainen & Rantala 2009).

Table 1. Four types of civic identities of young people in relation to media

	Weak civic self-image	Strong civic self-image
Weak mediated civic connectedness	Seekers	Communalists
Strong mediated civic connectedness	Communicators	Activists

Source: Kotilainen & Rantala 2009.

The seekers are young people who are still looking for civic issues to become engaged in, communities to connect to and spaces in which to act. They could also be considered as potential civic agents in their own right when the issues, communities and spaces are discovered. The communalists refer to a more traditional type of citizen who often thinks he/she can influence what goes on in his/her own life sphere, but does not feel it is important to act more publicly. Alternatively, she/she does not see media as a valid channel of influence, but rather acts in peer and hobby communities. The communicators are young people who are connected through media to multiple communities, but often do not see this interaction in political terms. Finally, activists have common issues they want to make public, and they also find the public space to carry out their actions. In other words, these youngsters have the knowledge, means, willingness and courage to take public action. Moreover, they can be seen actively practising their media literacy skills (Kotilainen & Rantala 2009).

Active youngsters who practise their media literacies and their learning paths, also in digital media, are also found in the collaborative Scandinavian research project "Making a Filmmaker", which focuses on how young filmmakers learn their craft (Gilje, Frølunde, Lindstrand & Öhman-Gullberg 2010). All of the young people – who practise active filmmaking, for example, in their free time – appear to use different learning contexts for filmmaking, whether formal, non-formal, or informal contexts, and they also position themselves differently. The findings indicate four different types of filmmakers, with varying priorities as to finding their own, individual 'learning paths'. There are differences where gender is concerned: the findings indicate that young female filmmakers appreciate the institutionalized aspects of contexts, for example, learning in school courses; young male filmmakers, on the other hand, tend to actively look for new knowledge and practise on their own, and for example, to browse supportive material online.

Children, young people and media have been studied since the 1920s, mainly in the more prosperous parts of the world; the focus, however, has mostly been on the effects of media, ways of using the media or interpreting media performances. Research on the viewpoints of young people, especially their everyday practices of media literacies, is only beginning (e.g. Jenkins et al. 2009). However, the European Commission and UNESCO are developing their strategies of media literacy education. Media and information literacy is considered a human right, alongside the more traditional type of literacy. Moreover, media literacy is considered a key skill of citizenship in the global world (cf. UN 2009).

The ongoing comparative study "Global Research on Youth Media Participation" (2009-2011), which is coordinated in Finland, approaches media literacies defined not only as individual abilities, but as social practices embedded in certain cultural and political contexts (see, e.g., Lankshear & Knobel 2006). 'Writing', i.e. doing and creating media, is regarded as just as central as 'reading' and interpreting media. This kind of understanding stems from new literacy studies (NLS), which "encourages us to be reflective about the everyday practices that we are all part of, to ask questions, rather than to assume that already know what literacy is" (Hamilton 2000). This notion of the social nature of literacy replaces the singular 'literacy' with 'literacies' – skilled and purposeful engagements with the meanings people produce. Moreover, the notion challenges us to reflect on the multimodalities that require competencies in many codes (Burn 2009; Cushman 2009; Buckingham 2003).

Cognitive and cultural approaches to media literacies

From the educational point of view, analysing the roots of media literacy from the view point of civic agency takes into account the histories of national awakening, utilitarianism, and the rise of labour movements in Western societies since the late 18th century, in conjunction with the rise of modern media. In Scandinavia in general, and in Finland in particular, the roots go deep into the long-standing tradition of folk education. Basic literacy had an important impact on workers' efficiency, but it also developed their awareness of their rights and gave them an overall sense of empowerment in society. The multiple new literacies, such as media literacy, refer to the various competences, coping strategies, and survival skills needed in current times (Kotilainen & Suoranta 2007).

The skills related to media literacies can be summarize in four areas of ability: access, analysis, evaluation and creative production or, alternatively, in three areas: to use, to understand and to create. All of these abilities promote aspects of personal, cognitive development: consciousness, critical thinking and problem-solving abilities (cf., e.g., Buckingham 2003; Varis 2009). Henry Jenkins et al. (2009; cf. Knobel & Lankshear 2007) list cultural competencies young people should acquire in order to be full participants in the emerging participatory culture online, where the key elements are *sharing and taking part*. For example, play and simulation are current media literacy skills "that enable participation in new communities emerging in networked society." Furthermore, other important competencies include judgement (the ability to evaluate the reliability and credibility of different information sources) and negotiation (the ability to travel across diverse communities, discerning and respecting multiple perspectives). But what about having the courage and motivation to take part in public discussions, on the one hand, and having the risk awareness necessary to protect one's privacy, on the other? These two aspects – social participation through media and risk awareness – are both regarded as important elements of contemporary media cultures, at least in Western societies (cf. Kotilainen 2009b).

The comparative study "Global Research on Youth Media Participation" is being conducted mainly in Finland, Argentina, Egypt and India among youngsters between 11-17 years. We are exploring, among other things, the kinds of media literacies that are activated in relations and engagements in literacy events with media or access points for media literacy, for example, while playing video games, watching TV, reading newspapers and in diverse activities online (cf. Street 2003; Hamilton 2000; Cushman 2009). Special attention is paid to media participation, i.e. youth engagement with public media, especially while creating media work (cf. Lewis 2006; Tyner 2003). In order to get closer to the cultural practices of media literacies, we will examine challenging situations in which young people are motivated to develop a specialized expertise (cf. Barton & Hamilton 1998; Hamilton 2000).

Thus, in the project, the concept of children, young people and audiences rests on theories that regard people – even children and young people – as active subjects both in their own lives and in society in general (Arendt 1958; active audiences see, e.g., Ross & Nightingale 2003; Livingstone 2005). Finnish media researcher Seija Ridell (2006, 247-249) argues that, when talking about audiences, audience research focuses too intensely on the question of *being an audience*. Instead she suggests, in contemporary times, the questions should relate more to *acting as audience*– for instance, how do different young people in different cultures act as audiences? Ridell suggests that future research should focus more on the actor positions of the audiences.

Initially, media participation is broadly defined as a young person's active interaction with media, such as creating one's own opinion while watching a reality television programme, while some kind of action is involved, for example, discussions with friends about the programme, or perhaps use of the available ways of communicating with the programme (mobile voting, for instance). Public media participation includes positions of negotiator, visible expresser and creative actor. In all of these positions, young people can act in media publicity, for example by taking part in online discussions or creating content for communal radio (cf. Ridell 2006). In addition to media participation, we assume that non-participation exists, too. One side of non-participation is related to the media themselves, which position young audiences as objects – or do not address children and young people as audiences at all. For example, Ulla Carlsson and Cecilia von Feilitzen (2006, 10) have found, especially concerning young people globally, that there exist 'huge divides as regards access to media and information'. According to them, the current process of media globalization favours the interests of more affluent countries, while countries with fewer resources – such as those in Africa, Asia, Latin America and Eastern Europe – often testify to having been taken by surprise or unawares by this swelling media flood.

In our comparative study, the preliminary interviews were conducted among young people in 2009. Regarding Finland and Egypt, for instance, the interviews reveal an intensive relationship between youngsters and media. Most of the interviewed young people seem to have access to the Internet and mobile phones, although in Egypt this seems to apply more to the area around Cairo as compared to rural areas, and to youngsters from wealthy families. In Finland, the socioeconomic differences are more linked to the cultural ways of using the Internet and mobile technologies; this aspect has also been reported among youngsters in the United Kingdom (cf. Livingstone & Helsper 2007). In both countries, one of the main differences in participation and uses online seems to be gender based; this aspect has been noted in previous Western studies (e.g., Livingstone et al. 2004): gaming mainly attracts boys, whereas girls tend to interact with peers. In Finland, the interviewed young immigrants used the net actively for networking with relatives abroad and with their culture of origin (Hirsjärvi & Tayie 2010).

The importance of special interests among the young is also evident in a Finnish boys group. For example, the 10-year-old boy, T – who was mentioned at the beginning of the paper – provided an interesting contrast to the interviews with the two youngest, 9-year-old boys, O and U, who were very similar to each other. Overall, these three interviews revealed that meaning-making processes start to become evident during the pre-teen years: the interview with T highlighted this phenomenon. T's technological competence was remarkable, at a level that could only be glimpsed in the discussions of the 9-year-olds. While O and U concentrated on comparing their skills and talking about the solutions to certain games, T was capable of more analytical discussions pertaining to the meaning of gaming while he was playing. For him, the most important thing was to be good at the particular game, and to have fun – fame was not so important. T also talked about the limitations of media use due to technological solutions, age limits and money (Hirsjärvi & Taiye 2010).

The first interviews were mainly carried out at home or in other places where youngsters could talk and, at the same time, show how they usually engage with the media, mostly online (for more information on the focused interview method, see Merton, Fiske, Kendall 1990/1956). The other methods of this comparative study include questionnaires and data collection through a special "One day media" diary during spring 2010. These diaries are also being collected in several other countries on different continents, 80-100 in each country thus, in this case, the number of participating countries is greater. In addition to practices of media literacies, researchers look at the cultural practices of participation and engagement with media. The expected results of the entire research project include descriptions of the global variations and commonalities in youth media participation and youth media literacies, in different media environments, and in several cultural contexts: global perspectives on youth media participation, audience agency and media literacies.

Towards responsible participation in global media cultures

Schools in particular should prepare pupils for dealing with different phenomena of media culture, and they should approach this issue methodically, providing support for as many children and young people as possible. In Finland, as in other Scandinavian countries, schools do offer an increasing amount of media literacy guidance; however, from the national point of view, the situation is uneven. When it comes to groups that need special support, this increasingly important, informal part of students' life can be ignored altogether. These kinds of groups exist in every school: children and young people who are enthusiastic gamers, for instance, but who do not get any support for their media use at home. The importance of informal media culture in the lives of young people has not been sufficiently understood, either in schools or in teacher training (e.g., Kupiainen et al. 2008; Kotilainen 2009c).

Global media cultures challenge teachers and parents to pay attention to the importance of supporting especially intercultural interaction and versatile media literacies among children and young people. Also of importance are the social and cultural aspects of media literacies, such as sensitivity to cultural and communicational differences and skills for intercultural social activities online. Moreover, one should pay attention to the practice of ethical communication and the structures of global commercial media. For example, educators should engage young people in discussions on the rights associated with publishing material from different sources and what it means to get global publicity for one's work, i.e. the possibility of reaching global audiences. These kinds of media literacies, which include working with multiple aspects of intercultural communication, could be called *global media competence*.

A global view of media cultures would also take immigrants into account, for instance here in Scandinavia. In what ways, for example, could audiovisual communication and media education help immigrants in their adjustment to a new culture? The media environment seen fit for children and young people in the country of origin may differ considerably from our Western media culture (cf. Carlsson et al. 2008). The media cultures of children and young people are made up of global, partly converging media streams, as well as of local, cultural specificities (cf. Kotilainen 2009c).

The challenges pertaining to the media cultures of children and young people are now being solved, for instance in Finland, with the aid of several parties. Media literacy education enthusiasts come from several sectors: school, youth work organizations, libraries, cultural organizations – such as media and film centres – and administrators from local and national governance. In 2005, re-searchers and other experts of media literacy education established a national association for generating cooperation among experts from different fields, and increasing media literacy in Finland. For example, the Finnish Society of Media Education is developing online services for national actors in the field, mainly with the funding of the Ministry of Education (www. mediaeducation.fi). Moreover, the association is conducting some small-scale studies. For example, in 2010, it is working to develop a method for regular national monitoring of the media uses of small children (max. age eight years): a kind of media barometer. Lately, in regards to the development of educational practices in media literacy, media pedagogy has been developing faster in other sectors of society than in the cumbersome structures of the formal school system (Kupiainen et al. 2008; Kotilainen 2009a).

Global enhancement of media literacy in children and young people is a timely issue. For example, the International Clearinghouse on Children, Youth and Media at NORDICOM and the UN Alliance of Civilizations' Media Literacy Education Clearinghouse have this goal in mind, including research and dialogue among actors in this area. In addition to these, other strategies have been suggested in different parts of the world: training teachers in media skills and national planning for media literacy skills (e.g., Carlsson et al. 2008; UN 2009).

Questions of media literacy in general, and the media cultures of children and young people in particular, should be handled methodically all over the world, and be regarded as the contents of global education and intercultural communication. Establishing the groundwork for this requires frequently updated, intercultural research on the media cultures of children and young people – cultures that are both global and local, and tied to the contemporary media, cultural policies and special issues pertaining to the field.

References

Arendt, H. (1958) *The Human Condition*. University of Chicago Press.

Buckingham, D. (2003) *Media Education: Literacy, Learning and Contemporary Culture*. Cambridge: Polity press.

Barton, D. & Hamilton, M. (1998) *Local Literacies: Reading and Writing in One Community*. London: Routledge.

Burn, A. (2009) Process and Outcomes. What to Evaluate and How? In Verniers, P. (ed.) *Euromeduc: Media Literacy in Europe. Controversies, Challenges and Perspectives*. Brussels: Euromeduc Project, pp. 61-71.

Carlsson, U. & von Feilitzen, C. (2006) 'Foreword', In Carlsson, U. & von Feilitzen, C. (eds.) *Yearbook 2005/2006: In the Service of Young People? Studies and Reflections on Media in the Digital Age*. Nordicom, The International Clearinghouse on Children, Youth and Media, University of Gothenburg, pp. 9-12.

Carlsson, U., Tayie, S. Jacquinot-Delaunay, J. and Perez Tornero, J.M. (2008) (eds.) *Empowerment through Media Education. An Intercultural Dialogue*. Nordicom, The International Clearinghouse on Children, Gothenburg University.

Cushman, M. (2009) *Decoding Literacy: Literacy, Literacy, all is Literacy*. Paper for the Euromeduc Conference, 21-24 October 2009, Bellaria, Italy.

Gilje, Ø., Frølunde, L., Lindstrand, F. & Öhman-Gullberg, L. (2010, forthcoming) 'Mapping Filmmaking across Contexts; Portraits of Four Young Filmmakers in Scandinavia' In Kotilainen, S. & Arnolds-Granlund, S-B. (eds.) *Media Literacy Education: Nordic Perspectives*. Göteborg: Nordicom & Finnish Society on Media Education.

Hamilton, M. (2000) *Sustainable Literacies and the Ecology of Lifelong Learning*. Paper for Supporting learning Global Colloquium, July 5-7, 2000, University of East London.

Hirsjärvi, I. & Tayie, S. (2010, forthcoming) *Youth Media Participation. Notions of the Methodological Approach of the Interviews in an International Comparative Project*.

Hodkinson, P. (2007) Youth Cultures: A Critical Outline of Key Debates. In P. Hodkinson & W. Deicke (eds.) *Youth Culture. Scenes, Subcultures and Tribes*. London: Routledge.

Jenkins, H. et. al. (2009) *Confronting the Challenges of Participatory Culture: Media Education for the 21st Century*. MacArthur Foundation. An Occasional paper on digital media and learning. www.digitallearning.macfound.org.

Knobel, M. & Lankshear, C. (eds.) (2007) *A New Literacies Sampler*. New York: Peter Lang.

Kotilainen, S. & Suoranta, J. (2007) Mot en dialogisk mediepedagogikk i Finland. In Vettenranta, S. (ed.) *Mediedanning og mediepedagogikk: Fra digital begeistring til kritisk dommakraft*. Oslo: Gyldendahl Akademisk, pp. 104-123.

Kotilainen, S. & Rantala, L. (2009) 'From Seekers to Activists: Characteristics of Youth Civic Identities in Relation to Media', *Information, Communication & Society* 12(5), 658-677

Kotilainen, S. (2009a) Promoting Youth Civic Participation with Media Production: The Case of Youth Voice Editorial Board. In *Mapping Media Education Policies in the World: Visions, Program-*

mes and Challenges, New York: United Nations, Alliance of Civilizations, UNESCO, European Commission, pp. 243-259.

Kotilainen, S. (2009b) Media Literacy: Appropriation and Empowerment. In Verniers, P. (ed.) *Euromeduc: Media Literacy in Europe. Controversies, Challenges and Perspectives.* Brussels: Euromeduc Project, pp. 143-150.

Kotilainen, S. (2009c) Lasten ja nuorten mediakulttuurit kasvatuksen haasteena. [Media Cultures of Children and Young People as a Challenge for Education] In Lampinen, J. & Melen-Paaso, M. (eds.) *Tulevaisuus meissä. Kasvaminen maailmanlaajuiseen vastuuseen. [The Future is Us. Growing to a Global Responsibility]*, Publications of the Finnish Ministry of Education, 40, pp. 96-100.

Kupiainen, R., Sintonen, S. and Suoranta, J. (2008). *Decades of Finnish Media Education.* Helsinki: Finnish Society on Media Education & Tampere University Centre for Media Education (TUCME). Available online: www.mediaeducation.fi/publications (17.03.2010)

Lankshear, C. & Knobel, M. (2006) *New Literacies: Everyday Practices and Classroom Learning.* 2 ed. London: Open University Press.

Lewis, C. (2007) New Literacies. In Knobel, M. & Lankshear, C. (eds.) *A New Literacies Sampler.* New York: Peter Lang, pp. 229-237.

Livingstone, S. & Helsper, E. (2007) 'Gradations in Digital Inclusion: Children, Young People and the Digital Divide', *New Media & Society* 9:4, pp. 671-696.

Livingstone, S. (ed.) (2005) *Audiences and Publics: When Cultural Engagement Matters for the Public Sphere.* Bristol: Intellect.

Livingstone, S., Bober, M. & Helsper, E. (2004) *Active Participation or Just More Information? Young People's Take up of Opportunities to Act and Interact on the Internet.* A research report from the UK Children go Online Project. http://www.children-go-online.net

Merton, R.K., Fiske, M. & Kendall, P.L. (1990/1956) *The Focused Interview. A manual of Problems and Procedures.* Glencoe, IL: Free Press.

Ridell, S. (2006) 'Yleisö. Elämää mediayhteiskunnan normaalina jäsenenä' [Audiences. Living in a mediated Society]. In *Mediaa käsittämässä [Understanding Media]* Ridell, S., Väliaho, P., Sih-vonen, T. (eds.) Tampere: Vastapaino, pp. 233-257.

Ross, K. & Nightingale, V. (2003) *Media and Audiences. New Perspectives*, Open University Press, Maidenhead.

Street, B. (2003) What's "new" in New Literacy Studies? Critical Approaches to Literacy in Theory and Practice. *Current Issues in Comparative Education* 5(2), 77-91.

Tyner, K. (2003) Beyond Boxes and Wires: Literacy in Transition, *Television & New Media* 4(4), 371-388.

UN (2009) *Mapping Media Education Policies in the world: Visions, Programmes and Challenges*, New York: United Nations, Alliance of Civilizations, UNESCO, European Commission.http://www.unaoc.org/images//mapping_media_education_book_final_version.pdf (17.03.2010)

Varis, T. (2009) *Communication and New Literacies in the Multicultural World.* Presentation in UNESCO Chair Forum 15.-20. September 2009 in Nanjing, China.

Understanding Media Literacy

Tapio Varis

It is widely understood that the most important skills of the future would be communication skills. Today everyone is able to access vast amounts of data without a mediator. Critical thinking skills are needed as a productive and positive activity. Critical thinkers see the future as open and malleable, not as closed and fixed. They are aware of the diversity of values, behaviours, social structures, and artistic forms in the world. Critical thinking is a process, not an outcome, and it is emotive as well as rational.

In my understanding we face three kinds of problems. First we have to try to understand what is the learning process of becoming literate and what does communication competence and media skills mean in the information society. Second, we have to analyse the increasing neo-illiteracy. Third, we should discuss of what kind of skills should we give to the citizens now as compared to the earlier skills of writing and reading.

In an intercultural world communication necessarily mediates different values and cultural behaviours. Great civilizations and cultures have very different patterns of communication and use different senses in a different way. In consequence, if a truly global information society is to be created, more attention should be given to the diversity of cultures and the co-existence of different civilizations and cultures.

Media literacy has been defined as the ability to access, analyze, evaluate, and communicate messages in a wide variety of forms. Media literacy is a concept whose broad definition and range of applications lead to diverse approaches, creating some intriguing conflicts and tensions. Educators and scholars with disciplinary backgrounds in media studies, the fine and performing arts, history, psychology and sociology, education, and literary analysis each may vigorously defend one's own understanding of what it means to access, analyze, evaluate, or create media texts without a full awareness of the extent of complexity, depth or integrity of various other approaches (Hobbs 1998).

The concept of digital literacy in a broad sense is a way of thinking but it can also be understood as complementary to the concept of media education and even synonymous with media literacy. Digital literacy as media literacy aims to develop both critical understanding of and active participation in the media. In the discussions in UNESCO Communication and Information Sector, for example, digital literacy is understood to enable people to interpret and make informed judgements as users of information supports and sources and it also enables them to become producers of media in their own right. Digital and media literacy is about developing people's critical and creative abilities.

According to José Manuel Pérez Tornero digital literacy is not just a simple operative and technical consciousness that is made up of nothing more than technical knowledge. Digital literacy is the complex acquisition process of an individual of humanity combined with their abilities and intellectual competencies (perceptive, cognitive, emotive) and practical competencies (physiological and motor). In Pérez's view these correspond to the technological transformation of the last decades in the twentieth century – the technological change of the Information Society.

To reduce digital literacy exclusively to the skills of using a computer is a crude simplification and a loss in meaning. Using a computer requires diverse and complex previous knowledge. It also introduces the individual and humanity to new contexts, which demands mental, intellectual, profound and complex changes. In essence, digital literacy is a complicated process that consists of acquiring a new tekne. This Greek term means the ability of art or craft by an individual or humanity. According to Pérez we are facing the transformation of the most profound tekne that humanity has ever experienced (Pérez Tornero 2004).

The challenges to peace and open, multicultural communication can be characterized by the transition from an industrial society to an information society with the need of digital competences. The dynamics of globalization, mobility and pluralism result in a multicultural world. A higher degree of individual flexibility in combination with the need for tolerance and responsibility are connected to the demand for sustainable development. The promotion of higher quality and equal educational opportunities become central issues of educational institutions.

The study of complexity has brought science closer than ever to art, Knowledge has gone through a cycle from non-specialism to specialism, and now back to interdisciplinarity, even transdisciplinarity. Art deals with the sensual world (media as the extension of senses) and the holistic concept of human being. Traditional knowledge has been disciplinary based although increasingly interdisciplinary. In the vocational field knowledge is also contextual and needs to be created in application – learning by doing. This also reflects local and regional realities. The Western philosophy is characterized by analytical, scientific, objective, rational and critical thinking while the Eastern approach is characterized by synthesis, literature and art with a subjective and emotional thinking. Both cannot and should not dominate other, but should have close dialogues between them. In a sense, many of the basic issues where already discussed in ancient Greece by

Socrates, Plato and Aristotle. Aristotle's "Poetics" is of particular importance to understand the balance between different senses of the human being and the combination of sound, drama, and text like in modern multimedia. Also Aristotle's definition of rhetoric as the faculty of discovering in any given case the available means of persuasion is a relevant approach to analyse the influence of modern media.

In order to learn new technologies and become digitally literate new forms of learning paths have to be developed utilizing all forms of learning, especially at work and non-formal environments. At the same time special attention should be given to teacher education in information and communication skills and competences. The period of transition that we are now living differs from the periods of change of older dominant media. Traditional print and electronic media were introduced within a period of reasonable length and when we moved to the active use of a new form of communication, we could also have a rough estimation of the economic and social impacts of it, and train new professionals for the media and support people for the institutions. Now different forms of communication and technologies integrate and converge with a speed that hardly anyone has the time or ability to assess all of the consequences, real possibilities, or problems. In a positive sense, people may be able to speak more directly to each other without former restrictions.

The cultural dimension in the communication and technology applications bring also the dimension of emotions and affection and the spirit of sharing and caring to the process. The social dimension require inclusive policies. Internet does not automatically promote social understanding and integration. In an intercultural world communication necessarily mediates different values and cultural behaviours. Great civilizations and cultures have very different patterns of communication and use different senses in a different way. In consequence, if a truly global information society is to be created, more attention should be given to the diversity of cultures and the co-existence of different civilizations and cultures.

The European Union Digital Literacy Expert Group proposed in 2007 concrete measures to evaluate and promote digital literacy. The Group concluded in 2008 that connectedness in the digital world is increasingly becoming integrated with other forms of social and societal interaction. Questions of digital and media literacy and e-inclusion can no longer be artificially separated from wider questions of social inclusion or engaged citizenship. As 'quality of use' becomes a dominant theme, it will be necessary to develop appropriate criteria, evaluation methodologies and benchmarks that can be used effectively to target resources to areas of need and to measure impact and value for money.

The Group recommended to develop and use appropriate evaluation and impact assessment frameworks including more socioeconomic background variables and more indicators related to motivation, critical thinking and quality of use. It also supported research leading to the development of more sophisticated evaluation and benchmarking tools for digital and media literacy programmes, and critical academic research.

Our study "Current trends and approaches to media literacy in Europe" in 2008 pointed out that the new digital technologies present unprecedented opportunities for far wider participation in the continuing development of Europe's cultural heritage and civil traditions in a global context. At the same time however, these technologies offer profitable opportunities for misinformation, unwanted surveillance, abuse of the vulnerable and infantilization of public discourse. The rapid development of digital technologies has thus made more urgent an issue that has been pressing for some time: the need for European citizens to fully understand the means by which information, ideas and opinions are now created, circulated and shared in modern societies: in other words, for a media literate population.

Promoting media literacy among European citizens has become a **strategic and integrationist objective** for the whole of Europe. A fundamental requirement for the promotion of this new capacity is to have a suitable model for media literacy, and to know all its dimensions, its strategic value and the specific benefits that it can bring to the development of information society in Europe. The question facing the European Commission, therefore, is what can be offered at Commission level that will add value and encouragement to National efforts, diverse as these are. Using this model, we will describe the existing and possible approaches to media literacy and their implications for a policy of promotion and support.

The skills related to media literacy can be summarised in four areas of ability: *access, analysis, evaluation and creative production*. All of these skills boost aspects of personal development: *consciousness, critical thinking* and *problem-solving abilities*.

When considering other elements that help to define the field of media literacy conceptually and thematically, one must remember that it is the result of a process of learning (and teaching) in any given context, but particularly in formal, informal, social, family and media settings. This multi-contextual process leads to the acquisition of specific abilities and competences, in addition to attitudes and values. This process is known as *media education*.

Media literacy should not be treated as an isolated or independent skill. On the contrary, it is a skill that involves and encompasses other skills and forms of literacy: *reading and writing literacy, audiovisual literacy* (often referred to as image or visual literacy) and *digital or information literacy*.

Furthermore, media literacy is a necessary part of *active citizenship* and is key to the full development of *freedom of expression* and the *right to information*. It is therefore an essential part of *participative democracy* 29 and *intercultural dialogue*.

It is convenient to develop with greater precision the different components of the media literacy and digital literacy abilities. We have distinguished between operative, cognitive, and social abilities:

Operative or technical abilities – that is, the ones related to the technical devices – include capacities related to the comprehension and use of these instruments, as well as others that are developed in order to adapt these tools to the specific users and their needs.

However, due to their very nature, technical abilities include some aspects related to certain decoding capacities (especially interfaces) and of personal appropriation – for specific ends – of the functionalities – and of the interfaces, that media tools have. From this point of view, they could to some extent be integrated in the cognitive field. However, given their relative simplicity, we prefer to see these as belonging to the operative field.

Cognitive abilities, include capacities related to the production of meaning that affect media texts (messages) and their signification. In general, they are the abilities of capturing, assimilating and producing information; they include also the use of this information for generating outlines and models of comprehension that allow to obtain an appropriate diagnosis of the external environment and to use the information obtained for strategies oriented by individuals' actions: problem-solving, strategies of creation and production of meaning, etc.

Finally, **communicative and social abilities** are the result of applying technical and cognitive abilities in the development of communication and social relations. These abilities allow possibilities that range from a simple contact to the creation of complex cooperation and collaboration strategies that use media tools as their base.

Another relevant summary has been given by Henry Jenkings and his colleagues for the Macarthur Foundation (2007). They found that according to a recent study from the Pew Internet & American Life project (Lenhardt & Madden, 2005), more than one-half of all teens have created media content, and roughly one third of teens who use the Internet have shared content they produced. In many cases, these teens are actively involved in what we are calling *participatory cultures*. According to them a participatory culture is a culture with relatively low barriers to artistic expression and civic engagement, strong support for creating and sharing one's creations, and some type of informal mentorship whereby what is known by the most experienced is passed along to novices. A participatory culture is also one in which members believe their contributions matter, and feel some degree of social connection with one another (at the least they care what other people think about what they have created).

Jenkings identifies the following forms of participatory culture: **affiliations** (memberships in online communities), **expressions** (producing new creative forms), **collaborative problem-solving** (working together in teams), **circulations** (shaping the flow of media, the participation gap (the unequal access to the opportunities), **the transparency problem** (the challenges young people face in learning to see clearly the ways that media shape perceptions of the world), and **the ethics challenge**.

The study emphasizes that schools and afterschool programs must devote more attention to fostering what we call the new media literacies: a set of cultural competencies and social skills that young people need in the new media landscape. Participatory culture shifts the focus of literacy from one of individual expression to community involvement. The new literacies almost all involve social skills developed through collaboration and networking. These skills build on the foundation of traditional literacy, research skills, technical skills, and critical analysis skills taught in the classroom.

The new skills that Jenkins present could well be the base for assessing digital literacy. These skills include include:

Play – the capacity to experiment with one's surroundings as a form of problem-solving

Performance – the ability to adopt alternative identities for the purpose of improvisation and discovery

Simulation – the ability to interpret and construct dynamic models of real-world processes

Appropriation – the ability to meaningfully sample and remix media content

Multitasking – the ability to scan one's environment and shift focus as needed to salient details.

Distributed Cognition – the ability to interact meaningfully with tools that expand mental capacities

Collective Intelligence – the ability to pool knowledge and compare notes with others toward a common goal

Judgment – the ability to evaluate the reliability and credibility of different information sources

Transmedia Navigation – the ability to follow the flow of stories and information across multiple modalities

Networking – the ability to search for, synthesize, and disseminate information

Negotiation – the ability to travel across diverse communities, discerning and respecting multiple perspectives, and grasping and following alternative norms.

Many concepts are related to media literacy, including: Access, Understanding and Create, 3Cs Culture, Critical and Creative, 5Cs adding Comprehension and Citizenship, Read and Write the media, 3Ps Protection, Promotion and Participation, etc.

Therefore it may be productive to convert media and digital literacy criteria into social indicators to provide a multi-layered instrument and involve different indicators that can be pulled together to form an overall picture of a people's media literacy competence across different media, different age groups of people and including the dimension of critical understanding. According to the European understanding media literacy is the **competence** (skill, ability) to cope, autonomously and critically, with a communicative and media environment established by the information and knowledge society.

Finland and global education

Today, knowledge and skills for international and intercultural interaction are needed in nearly all fields. This is why multicultural studies should be made an integral part not only of general education but also of adult and vocational education and training. It is essential to consolidate global education in the curricula, teaching and operational cultures of schools and vocational institutes. Instruction must offer tools for finding out the causes and effects of different phenomena and for drawing conclusions, which at its best leads to growth into active, critical and mediacritical world citizens.

For global education to be realised, it must be planned, analytical and systematic. Good planning will facilitate and clarify the currently somewhat diffused global education in schools. Multiculturalism and global education constitute an increasingly important part of teachers' professional competence. Global education must be made part of the school everyday and operational culture, lest it remain merely rhetoric and a topic of theme days. Safeguarding high-quality global education requires feasible plans, effective methods, clear objectives and systematic evaluation. Global education must permeate education at all levels, it must be equitably available to all, and it must be comprehensive and rich in content.

Internationalism may either be the object of teaching/learning or a means of teaching/learning. The substance of different teaching subjects highlight the shared features and the differences of cultures and international pupil/student exchanges add experiential knowledge and understanding. Methods and procedures themselves can sustain the principles of peace education, inclusion and tolerance. Joint projects, problem-solving, a discussive and attentive atmosphere and democratic decision-making, on their part, train for respect of human value and human rights and for cooperation. Global education is motivating; at its best it gives room for pupils' and students' own ideas. Similarly motivating are opportunities offered by visits and exchange programmes to get to know different cultures.

The process from literacy to media literacy includes abilities:

- to communicate by means of different media, be they verbal, visual, oral, auditive, digital, iconographic or any combination of these

- media literacy relates to socio-cultural frames of reference and to the competence required in the midst of cultural change

- "media civilized" citizens

Media education is an important part of the Finnish teaching and education system. It is carried out in day-care centres, elementary schools and upper secondary education. Media education is not a subject but a point of emphasis in teaching and education. The training of people in the education and teaching field is constantly being developed because of the evolution of media and the need for new media skills.

Media education research is a recent endeavour in Finland. By nature, the research is multidisciplinary: related research is being done for instance in the departments of humanities, social and educational sciences and information research. In Finland, universities emphasize the different points of view of various sciences and media education centres, which offer studies as a minor subject or as separate courses, have originated within universities. The challenge of developing media education study modules is the fact that they are often project-financed.

Teacher training in Finland is of high quality and teaching studies aim at a master's degree. Although the amount of media education in teacher training has been increased over the years, it is still possible to graduate without completing a course in media education. Usually the media education content can be studied as a minor subject or a stand-alone course. Many media education courses, most of which deal with technology teaching, are available in post-graduate studies programmes. A study published in 2007 stated that also in teacher training the emphasis is clearly on the use of media equipment in teaching and educational work whereas the content-related themes are given less attention

Media education in early childhood education has advanced considerably in the 21st century. It is focused on developing a child's capacity to live within the media culture and the understanding of the child's own relationship with the media, taking into account the age and developmental stage of the child. Additionally, it furthers well-being and the child's participation in the information society. Media education is based on events, experiences and learning as a form of playing. The results that are generated by the activity are made available, studied and discussed. Media education is integrated into other early childhood education, enriching and deepening its function. It can be implemented in a goal-oriented fashion in separate activity sessions or as a part of daily care, teaching and education. The Ministry of Education's Media Muffin-project, which was carried out in 2006-2007 in co-operation with The National Institute for Health and Welfare produced a national guideline for media education. The guideline was published as a guide booklet that was mailed to all day-care centres in Finland. In 2009, a guide describing the media education themes for pre-primary and pre-school education was also published.

Finland is regarded as one of the model countries when it comes to education. The school system which guarantees all children and young people an equal opportunity for free of charge basic education near one's home has been listed as a key factor behind the success. Also, the high educational standard of teachers, the high authority of the individual schools and teachers in the implementing of teaching and the significant role of the co-operation between home and school are all considered important factors that benefit the learning of students.

National and regional development projects have been initiated and continuing education has been increased to activate the use of technologies in schools. In 2008, the Ministry of Transport and Communications, the Ministry of Education and the Finnish National Board of Education started a project to utilise information and communications technology in teaching and studies. The vision of the "Information and communications technology in everyday school work"-project is that in the year 2011, schools in Finland will be equipped with innovative and creative operating models and practices that can be used in teaching information and communications technology and the utilisation of digital media.

In the compulsory or upper secondary school curriculum ratified in 2004, media education has been integrated into one cross-curricular theme. Cross-curricular themes are points of emphasis in teaching and education that include content which is connected to many different subjects. They are unifying themes in teaching and education. The themes are also used to meet the contemporary educational challenges. When drafting school and municipality-specific curricula, these themes are to be included in common and elective subjects and they are to be visible in the operating culture of the school.

In basic education the cross-curricular subject media education is called communications and media skills. The other cross-curricular themes in basic education are called growing as a human being, cultural identity and internationality, committed citizenship and entrepreneurship, responsibility for the environment, well-being and a sustainable future, security and traffic and man and technology.

The media education content of the upper secondary school curriculum is part of a cross-curricular theme called communication and media competence. In addition to that theme, the cross-curricular themes common to all upper secondary schools are active citizenship and entrepreneurship, well-being and security, sustainable growth, cultural identity and cultural knowledge

The challenge now in the 21st century is to bring together scientists, public authorities, businesses, academics, civil society organizations and other interested groups and stakeholders to understand challenges for sustainable education and cultural literacy in the global context; identify the potential of ICT to advance and improve education; share knowledge and best practices about successful policies in global education; create venues of collaboration; and consolidate responsible communities for multi-literacies. (Varis & Alagtash 2008).

In the UNESCO Report on Knowledge Societies (2005), there is a general agreement on the appropriateness of the expression "knowledge societies"; the same cannot be said of the content. Special efforts have been made to develop the new renaissance education and build global cultural bridges together with artists. It is widely understood that the most important skills of the future will be communication skills. Critical thinking skills are needed as a productive and positive activity. Critical thinkers see the future as open and malleable, not as closed and fixed.

References

Confronting the Challenges of Participatory Culture: Media Education for the 21st Century, Henry Jenkins, Director of the Comparative Media Studies Program at the Massachusetts Institute of Technology, MacArthur Foundation 2007, An occasional paper on digital media and learning

Current trends and approaches to media literacy in Europe, http://ec.europa.eu/avpolicy/media_literacy/studies/index_en.htm

Finnish Media Education Policies – Approaches in Culture and Education. Finnish Society on Media Education 2007: http://mediakasvatus.fi/files/u4/mediaeducationpolicies.pdf

Global Education 2010. Series of Publications; Publications of the Ministry of Education, Finland 2007: 12

Hobbs, R. (1998) The Seven Great Debates in the Media Literacy Movement. *Journal of Communication*, Winter 1998, Vol. 48, No 1, 16-32.

Merilampi, Ritva-Sini (2002) Facts behind Young Finns' Success in Literacy Comparisons. Unpublished paper, Ministry of Education, Helsinki, Finland, May 2002

Pérez Tornero, J.M. (2004) Promoting Digital Literacy. European Commission 4th Workshop "Media Literacy, Digital Literacy, e-Learning", 27 February, Brussels.

UNESCO (2005) Towards Knowledge Societies, UNESCO World Report 2005. Paris

Varis, Tapio: European and Global Approaches to Digital Literacy. *Digital Kompetanse*, Vol. 3, No 1, 2008.

Varis, Tapio & Salem Alagtash (eds) Ubiquitous Ict for Sustainable Education and Cultural Literacy, 2008, http://www.minedu.fi/OPM/Kansainvaeliset_asiat/kansainvaeliset_jaerjestoet/unesco/suomen_unesco-toimikunta/sutjulkaisuja?lang=fi

Part II.
Young People and the Nordic Digital Media Culture

From TV Viewing to Participatory Cultures
Reflections on Childhood in Transition

Ingegerd Rydin & Ulrika Sjöberg

Today, media have become more or less unconsciously intertwined in our everyday routines, not only integrated into the furniture of our homes, but also companions wherever we go. As the media environment is continuously in a phase of transformation, as exemplified by the current processes of media convergence and globalization, it becomes relevant to gain knowledge about the consequences of people's uses and practices, in this case children's and young people's. However, when addressing young people, discourses on morals and protections also have to be taken into account, as these groups have always been surrounded by restrictions established by the adult community. Therefore, when reflecting on the various changes in young people's media use and practices that have taken place over the years, it is important to contextualize the discussion and address issues of the views and discourses on children and childhood and of growing up in Western societies today.

The present discussion will be confined to television and the Internet, as they are the most prominent media among children and young people (*Nordicom-Sveriges Mediebarometer 2008*). In particular, the focus will be on our own research in a Swedish context, which extends about forty years back in time. What are the main changes? For example, have young people's media practices and meaning-making processes changed as a consequence of emerging new media? Or is it a question of continuity regardless of the dramatic changes in the media landscape?

In this chapter, we present, in brief, "a research journey" that starts out from our own research. We provide a historical review that points out landmarks in the study of children and media and then proceed to a discussion of our most recent research topics and projects, which will be described in somewhat more detail. Along this journey, methodological and theoretical reflections will be made.

A historical look at children and TV
– milestones and discourses

Television, as a very pervasive medium, was gradually introduced in the United States and Western Europe after the Second World War, although the medium as such was developed prior to the war. By the end of the 1950s, most countries in the Western hemisphere had access to one or more television channels, and in the 1970s, the majority of the households were equipped with at least one television set. At the end of the 1990s, television was still the most pervasive medium in European households: about 90 percent of children had access to a television in their home. The dissemination of television was also rapid in the Third World, and by the end of the twentieth century, most people, at least in urban electrified areas, had a set (Rydin 2004).

Television gradually replaced radio as the medium most used by children; primarily attracting children in the younger ages (up to the teenage years). The amount of television viewing is dependent on the output of children's programmes as well as the output of entertainment programmes. Thus, children have increased their viewing time as a consequence of more national channels as well as the deregulation of the television market, which led to increased access to commercial mainstream entertainment. Time spent with television varies across countries, depending on differences in cultural patterns as well as differences in production. By the 2000s, the average child viewer in the United States watched about 3 to 4 hours of television a day, whereas the European viewer watched about 3 hours, with some national variations (Rydin 2004). In Sweden, for example, preschool children watched somewhat more than 60 minutes of television a day, whereas school children watched about 1 hour and 30 minutes around the year 2000. Since then, viewing time has increased slightly, but more important is the fact that television in Europe and the United States has changed its function from the early days, when it was a medium that gathered the family in the living room, to a more privatized and individual activity, as there is an increasing tendency for the children of today to have their own television set in the bedroom (Livingstone and Bovill 2001).

"Impacts and effects"

Children's fascination with television has concerned researchers, parents, educators and other groups dealing with children's well-being ever since the medium was introduced. Much of the public debate has been focused on the effects of media violence; this debate has resulted in a great deal of scrutiny by psychologists and sociologists and has given rise to a massive body of research. But the debates and research have also dealt with whether television viewing in itself is a passive activity, and sometimes television has been compared to a drug, which has a tranquilizing or seducing effect on the viewer. Television has also been blamed for causing negative effects on reading skills and some claim that too much television use negatively affects children's intelligence. Other worries have concerned children's physical condition, such as their getting too little exercise or that radiation from the screen may affect their brain or eyes. Television viewing has also been linked to obesity in children (Rydin 2004). Children's television viewing has, in other words, mainly been described in terms of displacement and substitution.

In the history of media effects, a "direct effects era" was predominant for a long period of time. The reception of television was viewed in a linear and one-dimensional manner. Later, researchers realized that children did not react uniformly to the same programme, but that there were intervening variables such as age, gender, predispositions, perceptions, social environment, past experience and parental influence. However, even though years of research has stressed that there are a number of so-called intervening variables, the "direct effects model" has been very influential in the public debate on children and television (Wartella and Reeves 1985).

When research was done in more realistic settings, rather than in the laboratory, the effects of exposure to television were attenuated and long-term effects were weak or even non-existent. Long-term research conducted both in the United States and in Europe has come to the conclusion that television violence is but one of a number of factors responsible for violent aggressive behaviour among young people. Aggressive behaviour is mainly related to factors other than exposure to television violence, such as personality or sociocultural variables, for example, family conditions, school, and peers. However, researchers also point to the fact that the frequent occurrence of screen violence reinforces the idea of violence as a solution to problems (von Feilitzen 1993). The globalization of the television market has contributed to an increased production of violent programming and to the worldwide dissemination of such programmes (for example animated cartoons and action adventures) (Rydin 2000b).

Learning and the social benefits of television

At the end of the 1960s and the beginning of 1970s, there was a belief among researchers, politicians and educators that television could be used for promoting learning and social behaviour. The medium was deliberately used for preschool learning and compensatory education in the United States, in Europe, and in some developing countries, for example, in the Latin American countries of Mexico and Brazil. Producers, educators, and researchers started investigating the possibility of using television to reach out to underprivileged groups in society. In the United States, the educational programme Sesame Street was developed and became a success also in other countries, where the programme was sometimes adjusted to the domestic child audience. For example, Brazil, Germany, Israel, and Spain developed their own versions of Sesame Street. In Scandinavia, the domestic public service companies expressed a certain resistance against Sesame Street, owing to its commercial format. The young audience was not used to commercial programmes and advertisements and should not be exposed to that kind of format, according to the programming policies; this idea has survived in countries like Sweden within channels governed by public service missions. However, in Sweden a wave of programme series inspired by Sesame Street were produced, teaching elementary skills in reading, concept formation as well as promoting pro-social behaviour, such as solving conflicts without violence or strengthening children's self-confidence (Rydin 2000a). And in Norway, a version of Sesame Street called "Sesam stasjon" was released in 1991 (Seip Tönnessen 2000). In Sweden, public television produced its own long-running programme series "Fem myror är fler än fyra elefanter" (Five ants are more than four elephants), which has reached more or less cult status and is still re-broadcasted from time to time. The outlook on children and childhood that was predominant during the seventies was that children's knowledge of the world should be broadened and that the young audience, at an early age, should be prepared to meet the demands of life outside the nursery. Children should not be overprotected, yet there was a contradiction here in that children were also perceived as vulnerable and it was thought that they should not consume too much media violence or other types of content that could lead to negative effects (Rydin 2000a).

The active viewer – uses and gratification

Another line of research, which can be seen as a reaction to the stimulus-response model that guided effects research, stressed the idea of "the active viewer", which had its origin in the uses-and-gratification approach that asked questions such as "What do viewers do with the media?", rather than asking "What does the media do to the audience?" This implies that the audience actively chooses programmes that fit its needs and interests. Television provides the audience with certain gratifications (Katz, Blumler and Gurevitch 1974). Pioneers such as Hilde Himmelweit and Wilbur Schramm presented such a view, thus recognizing children's active choices and selectivity (Dorr 1986). The original theory, however, has been problematized and media ethnographers such as James Lull (1995) claimed much later that the notions of "needs" and "motives" were diffuse and that the model was mechanistic. Other approaches stressing the active viewer came from cognitive psychology (e.g. Noble 1975; Dorr 1986) as well as from cultural studies and semiotics, i.e. contributions from humanistic sciences (e.g. Hodge and Tripp 1986), and paved the way for the so-called cultural turn, which became a landmark in much of the European media research. Not only was meaning-making a process of negotiation between the individual and the media content. It was also apparent that media uses and practices were situated in social contexts and that meaning-making was often a collective project in peer groups or in the family. The need to examine the interplay between various micro-settings and as macro-structures was emphasized. This so-called cultural turn ran parallel with changes in the media landscape of deregulation and more media-intense environments (increasingly mobile) at large, which required a methodology that could handle people's more complex relations with the media.

Deregulation and postmodern childhood

The television market has been more regulated in most European countries than it has in the United States. As a rule, the European broadcasting landscapes are organized as "dual systems" with public service broadcasters not just being a supplement to commercial stations, but a central pillar of the broadcasting system (Livingstone and Bovill 2001). In Northern Europe, children's programmes have a particular position and status. Programmes for children are offered on a regular basis. For example, by the 2000s in Sweden, about ten percent of the output on public service television was aimed at children and young people. About half of this output consisted of domestic productions, with programmes in a variety of genres: fictional dramas, sports, news, documentaries, magazine programmes (Rydin 2000b). However, deregulation has been both a challenge and a threat to public service television. The general tendency in Europe that public service television has weakened, entailing fewer investments in domestic children's programmes in favour of cheap imports. Public broadcasters face competition from global (American) commercial children's channels like Cartoon Network, The Disney Channel, Nickelodeon, and Fox Kids Network (Rydin 2000b).

In line with transformations in the media landscape, one can also observe changes in childhood and views of children, e.g. the idea of "post-modern child-hood" (Brembeck and Johansson 1996), which is a metaphor for the transition from modernity to a more individualistic and consuming type of childhood established by the end of the twentieth century. In Sweden, for example, it was a landmark when public service television, with its monopoly on children's programmes, was challenged by commercial television and the video-movie in-dustry. And later when people had access to the Internet on an everyday basis, discussions about the blurring boundaries between the private and the public domains of life became an issue for debate and research. This issue became even more relevant after Web 2.0 was introduced and with the rise of so-called "social media". The terms "push" and "pull" point out the interactive possibili-ties offered by digital and social media and the main difference between these and the traditional media. Young people's relation to media and its implications for childhood were expressed using terms like "growing up digital". Different voices were raised concerning changes in childhood and the role of media in children's lives – either as a tool for young people's empowerment, providing them with new liberating competences that are needed in a global and digital media environment (Tapscott 1998), or as something mainly harmful to the young and from which they have to be protected (Postman 1982). In other words, the same worries appear as for television. These contrasting positions have been criticized for their essentialist perception of childhood and youth (conceived as either innocent/vulnerable or media literate) and for their deterministic view on the relation between the audience and the media (e.g. Buckingham 2000). But on the whole, we can safely say that computers have been more welcomed than television was, because authorities from the education field foresaw the teaching potential of computers and the Internet.

What will happen to television in the future?

At the end of the 1990s, television was still the predominant medium in Swedish children's and adolescents' lives. It was a medium that most young people had access to and spent the most time with, compared to other media. Surveys conducted today show that, in the age range 15-24 years, more time is spent on the Internet compared to television (120 minutes and 90 minutes, respectively). For the younger ages, the 9-14 years, television is still the most used medium (76 minutes and 54 minutes, respectively) (Mediebarometern 2008). But nonetheless, major changes are taking place in the type of media we use to gain access to certain content or functions. TV producers know this and are increasingly directing their efforts towards the Net as a platform for audiencehood. New criteria are to be applied in production, distribution and marketing, because television viewing is changing in nature as are the specific meanings attached to TV content on the Net. See further 'Presenting oneself and building networks' below.

The traditional television was the main medium used by children and young people at the end of 1990s, even if the Internet had started to make its entrance. When compared to other media, a number of advantages of television were mentioned. One of the reasons for its popularity among young people was the social context of exposure: meeting friends and simultaneously watching television. Another aspect was that the medium provided company, and was a way to avoid the silence when home alone. It was also appreciated for its entertaining content, which was preferred when the young person wanted to relax, had no energy for other things, or was just tired. It would be interesting to know whether the same thoughts come up today when the Internet and mobile phones are part of everyday media use. In the 1990s, television was labelled a family medium; it was well integrated into family life and gathered the family in front of the screen (Sjöberg 2002). It was also during this period that more and more households acquired multiple TV sets and we came to see the emergence of increased individualization of media use. Terms like bedroom culture began to emerge and reflected children's increased access to different media in their own bedroom, which in turn is assumed to have implications for parental regulation, type of media use, leisure opportunities, and family communication (Bovill & Livingstone 2001).

Today, interactivity has become a buzz word, and the need to be constantly online or available via one's mobile phone 24 hours a day is a natural part of daily life. Our pattern of media use has become increasingly simultaneous, as opposed to use of separate media at different times. Already in the 1990s, the Internet was appreciated by the young as a means to search information, to chat with one's friends, but still the "passivity" offered by traditional television was not to be forgotten. The word passivity is seldom used in today's digital age or in media research. Just sitting in front of the TV screen, not having to concentrate at all, was sometimes appreciated in contrast to the interactive computer or mobile phone. When young people in the 1990s were asked about what will happen to television in the future, their immediate answer was "It will still be here!" At that time, watching television on the Internet was not common and few programmes were offered, as compared to today when most TV channels have their own websites with the possibility to download programmes or watch them in stream format, etc. In our digital age, producers are also trying to find new ways of building relations with their viewers (or should we say visitors), and the emergence of social and personal media has changed the conditions of such a relation. In the 1990s, traditional television served other purposes than the Internet, but today an increased convergence of the two is seen. Thus, the two media have a higher degree of interchangeability and are able to meet the same needs.

In today's digital media environment, traditional television has developed and adapted its character, especially after Web 2.0; this allows the viewer increasing access to various types of content on the Net, to more individual freedom of choice, to chat with other viewers or with, for example, celebrities, journalists, etc. Another change is that anybody who wishes to can produce their own programme, which in a second can be distributed to a worldwide audience. With this said, it is apparent that new media cultures are developing. But we must also remember that even the "old media" have changed their functions and modes of use. Viewing patterns do not look the same as before. We think about the TV set's various shapes and sizes, such as flat-TV, plasma screen, etc., which allow for new types of viewing patterns, e.g "home cinema". And the monitor does not necessarily look like a TV set. It may be quite small and used in the car or in bed and handled by most children from toddler age. Children can use the monitor as a toy in their room and select movies from their own albums of DVD:s. Web-TV offers opportunities to postponed viewing. Overall, media use is individualized in home settings, but the simultaneous use of multiple media is increasing, such as surfing on the Net while watching TV on the flat screen, and becoming difficult for audience researchers to track and study.

And despite these changes, preferred genres among the young tend to be quite stable over time, where both Swedish and international series and soaps (including reality shows) top the list. Realism (Barker and Andre 1996) can be one of the explanations for the popularity of various soaps over the years. Being able to identify oneself with the contents, its events, experiences and characters, and getting a glimpse into the adult world have always been of interest to the young, even in today's digital media landscape. The importance of identification is also seen in young people's talk about and use of Internet sites (see below).

Internet – a moving target

How do we actually study a moving target like the Internet? How changeable and transformative is use of the Internet among young people? Can any continuity in their net use and the meanings attached to its various contents and functions be discerned? The Internet started to enter Swedish households in the late 1990s, and at that time it was families of high socio-economic status that were most likely to have access to the Internet. Today these differences are levelled out in Sweden. In the 1990s, the Internet had just begun the process of finding its position, spatially and temporally, in the homes and in comparison to television, which was watched almost every day and for several hours a week, whereas the Internet was logged on to about once a week. At that time, the most popular usage of the Internet was to surf, search information, download software, chat and send e-mails (Sjöberg 2002). On-line games were barely mentioned and sites like *Facebook* or *Youtube* did not exist – not to mention the increased amount of various types of blogs on the Net, written by politicians, artists, employees, etc., but also by the young people themselves. In addition, over the years visual means have become more widely used in young people's communication on the Net as compared to the 1990s (see further below). Much more research is needed on mediated visual communication in relation to meaning-making among the young. Thus, what are the implications of our increasingly visual media culture for self-perception, social relations, modes of learning, the blurring of private and public, etc. (e.g., how rather private images are placed on the Internet, the use of diaries on the net)? All of the above-mentioned uses are common even today, when fifteen years have passed. However, new types of usages among the young are also seen, and the Internet has an even more prominent position in daily life, along with the mobile phone. In the 1990s, Swedish households had access to Internet through a phone modem; lower costs after 6 p.m. and parents' restrictions on the extent of Internet use also had implications for how and when the Internet was used at the time. Children growing up today have access to broadband and mobile Internet, which seems to trigger the need to be constantly online. Technology is thus helping to shape new social habits.

Presenting oneself and building networks

That the Internet offers a platform for young people to socialize and experiment with self-presentation, thereby becoming part of the identity formation process, has made it a popular medium. Childhood and adolescence are periods in life when the young person develops differently and simultaneously along several interrelated dimensions – biologically, culturally, psychologically, cognitively and socially – and the Net has become a kind of playground in this transition in life. It is a platform with less involvement and influence on the part of the adult world compared to the traditional school yard, or traditional media for that matter. This increased "freedom" has led to a risk discourse in society, especially among adults, but children themselves also talk about the possibility to lie and be anonymous, which in turn has implications for their net use. As a comparison, in the TV era, the risks were called "effects" or "impact", often referring to effects of violence such as aggressive behaviour, as we touched upon in the beginning of this chapter. Concerning the Internet, the risk discourse has dealt with violent computer games, on the one hand, and with issues related to sex and pornography, on the other. There is increased awareness of these issues now as compared to the 1990s, probably due to for example news coverage on paedophiles using the Net as an arena to reach children. In parallel to this risk discourse, young people today increasingly turn their attention to communities and meet people they already know, or a friend's friend, rather than chatting with strangers (cf. Sjöberg 2002; boyd 2008; Stern 2008). A European consortium of researchers has recently presented a series of comparative research reports on this topic with the purpose of promoting safer use of the Internet within the European member states (www.lse.ac.uk/collections/EUKidsOnline/). Survey polls indicate that children sometimes do get sexual invitations through the Net. However, this has turned out to be rather unusual. Also, it has been shown that, in Sweden, young adolescent girls who do make appointments with strangers already belong to exposed groups and that they tend to have profound personal and emotional problems of their own (Rydin 2010). Such findings demonstrate the complexity of this issue and the fact that regulations of the Internet may not reach groups already on the margins of society.

In a four-year project, which started last year, we are collaborating with Swedish Television (SVT) Interactive in an attempt to explore young people's thoughts and uses of television sites, and how traditional television companies (public service) can use the Internet in new innovative ways suited to the needs of a young audience[1]. In these studies so far, communication and interaction are essential, but also the graphical design and not the least making a site personal and, as above, using the Net as a platform for self-representation. Another important factor in the popularity of a site is the possibility to identify oneself with a character or person that is portrayed on the site, thus the importance of identification (like with soaps and series, see above) is central. The old ways of thinking of a so-called mass audience no longer exist among the young; personalized and social media are on the agenda. Just sitting and reading content on a site is not appreciated at all; instead young people wish to participate through chat forums, playing games, or producing their own content and thereby gaining control over the site.

The role of transnational movements and globalization – New types of audiencehood

Along with the introduction of the Internet on a more general scale, many societies have also changed their demographic profile. Changes in the global political and economic order, the opening of borders in Europe, the outbreak of wars, have created a new wave of migration processes. These demographic changes have also affected the media market and the distribution of media. By providing an equal flow of information and promoting communication among people, media are seen as facilitators of a living democracy. However, in today's media-saturated society, with increased access to different media (e.g., minority, transnational, national and local media), claims are being raised that democracy is under threat and that multicultural civil society tends to be fragmented, encouraging exclusion rather than inclusion between cultural groups. After the Second World War, Sweden faced increased migration, which has made the country a multicultural community in terms of ethnicity, culture, religion, language. This change has taken place rather rapidly. In 2008, almost 14 percent of the Swedish population had an immigrant background, which can be compared to about 3 percent in 1950 (Hultén 2009).

Naturally, changes in the demographic structure of the population had implications for the media situation in a media environment such as the Swedish one, with its strong focus on national issues. New types of audiences and new types of media practices were assumed. Research was initially geared towards studying representations of migrants and ethnic minorities, and was thus based on textual analyses. The empirical data in these studies have been a specific media text such as a TV programme, radio programme or newspaper and have focused on concepts such as racism and anti-racism (see, e.g., Löwander 1998; Brune 2008), whereas issues concerning media use and practices were not looked at. And research with children and young people was non-existent. The work by Rydin and Sjöberg (2007; 2008) on media usage among families with immigrant backgrounds in Sweden was therefore an important contribution to this research field. The project 'Media practices in the new country' was conducted during the period 2004-2006 and was aimed at highlighting the role and utilization of the media in families (mainly with children in the age range 12-16 years) with an immigrant background. We chose to emphasize the concepts of generation and family for studying relations to the media, in order to better understand transition processes, where parents and children are in different stages of life. For example, generational tensions in family life may be evoked when entering a new cultural sphere. The concept of generation also has a temporal dimension, which stretches from tradition to modernity and thus is a matter of cultural change. Children and adults may cope with the process of cultural change differently, which may lead to family disputes and conflicts (Rydin and Sjöberg 2007). The question is: What is the role of the media in this coping process? The media themselves are also structured along age dimensions, thereby inviting different generational practices.

Among the young people, Sweden was considered home, but a home geared towards participation in Swedish society, as far as their rational selves were concerned. Emotionally, however, young people could have their hearts in their parents' homeland, especially regarding bonds of friendship and kinship. For these youngsters, the Net came to have additional meanings in relation to their "Swedish peers" (Rydin and Sjöberg 2010). While it was not common for the young people to search for information about their parents' or their own homeland on the Net, other ways of bonding could be seen. Children could use e-mail and MSN Messenger to keep in touch with friends and relatives in the country of origin or to become members of Swedish chat rooms as a way to get to know peers whose parents come from the same country. As for the latter type of use, it was not so much about exchanging thoughts about the homeland as about local matters and the importance of identifying oneself with peers who looked alike (physical appearance) and who all used the mother tongue as an identity marker, thereby distinguishing oneself from the majority in Swedish society.

Compared to the Internet, transnational television became a much more important means for the parents to preserve their mother tongue and cultural heritage, including norms, traditions, values, religious beliefs. The children, on the other hand, mainly preferred English, US American and Swedish entertainment programmes. This difference depended partly on the limits set by language proficiency and partly on preferences. Even if it was not so common among the children, viewing television from the parents' homeland might evoke the feeling of being in the country (Rydin and Sjöberg 2007). This type of bonding could also be seen while watching music videos from the native country; both parents and children recognized places and houses in the video. No informants in the study stated that they merely preferred international or national programmes. One example of a hybrid between the two is seen in programmes where the formats and genres have been adjusted to the local viewers, like the Swedish *Fame Factory*. The fact that a programme in the child's or the parents' own mother tongue is preferred may indicate the use of this type of programme as an identity marker, that is, as a means to distinguish oneself from the mainstream programme in Sweden, but also to find similarities between the two and thereby connecting different cultures. In addition, compared to their Swedish peers, these children and young adolescents often had to translate the news for their parents, who lacked sufficient skills in Swedish. But the children did not only have this specific role while watching television; they were also a key in helping their parents with practical matters and in contacts with various authorities. For these families, traditional power relations between child and parent were turned upside down (Rydin and Sjöberg 2007). The children's media use also seemed to be influenced to some extent by their parents' need for help with translation in order to keep informed about Swedish society. For example, these youngsters seemed to watch more news programmes than their Swedish peers do. To conclude, the young participants' childhood was at least in these respects different from that of young people in the majority culture.

Popular culture goes to school: learning and participation

The issue of children and the media (particularly television) has also been a target for the United Nations since the Convention on the Rights of the Child became valid in 1989. One issue of concern has been to increase children's participation in terms of media education. In the United States and Europe, media education has been added to the school curriculum to varying extents. The implementation of media education has been a slow process, often met with resistance by defenders of established school ideals.

In Sweden, for example, educational television was accepted in preschool as a tool for learning for a time, particularly in the seventies. But quite soon it was rejected, and the television set was literally moved out. In elementary schools, on the other hand, educational television has had a somewhat different status and gained recognition, at least by some teachers. However, media education with a focus on television literacy skills has not been implemented on a regular basis, despite assistance through the programming of the public service educational channel (Utbildningsradion).

However, the discourse around the Internet as a source for learning and social benefits has been pursued in a more positive spirit. Children have been taken for the digitally competent ones, with advanced skills compared to adults. And the computer and the Internet in particular have been received with open arms by educational authorities and teachers. Still too much focus has been placed on physical access and the technical aspects, rather than on issues related to media literacy, which include a set of skills: "[...] involves not only ways of understanding, interpreting, and critiquing media, but also the means for creative and social expression, online search and navigation, and a host of new technical skills" (Ito et al. 2008: viii). Thus, media literacy embraces a wide range of skills. And sometimes we use expressions such as digital literacy, visual literacy, multimodal literacy, print literacy and games literacy. It is a field of research that is expanding right now, and here media scholars with their particular knowledge of media theory can provide with substantial contributions. We are both involved in different projects looking at media literacy in the schools, including young people's media production, but also at young people's media usage during leisure time. It has been claimed that there is a generation gap in relation to new technology and that young people possess a rich repertoire of media skills that are not taken seriously by the educational system (Drotner 2008). But in this discussion, it is as if young people's media competences are taken for granted, without any reflection on the individual variations that exist. Based on our research, for example, we see that when pupils are asked how they would like to use media in a teaching context, few new ideas or suggestions are heard; the wall between popular culture and school is not easy to break down, which stresses the need to rethink our use of media already in preschool, so as to develop children's media skills, but also support them in developing the skills needed to navigate in our society.

Concluding remarks –methodological challenges

In this chapter, experiences from research with young people (including small children) and their media use over the past 40 years have been presented and discussed. Research, of course, does not occur in a vacuum, but is rather in a constant interplay with surrounding discourses in society on media and childhood as well as with the changing media landscape. Our recent studies in various social contexts – such as following the everyday life of migrant families or in-depth studies of media practices in classroom settings – have convinced us that there is a need for new methodological skills and theoretical approaches to studying our increasingly symbolic and mobile mediated environment. In order to understand the new media situation, researchers must have a toolbox of various methods that can deal with people's more complex relations with the media.

In attempting to grasp today's complexity with regard to globalization, media convergence, intertextuality, etc., media ethnography has gained a great deal of interest among scholars, including ourselves. Not only is the contextual nature of media use stressed, but also the child as a reflective individual, living and acting in a complex web of integrated environments. We, as media scholars, have to conduct empirical studies that take their point of departure from the children and adolescents themselves and the various contexts they navigate within and between. In other words, the challenge is to capture the relational nature of meaning-making in young people's encounters with media. In addition, we can see how the process of meaning-making is much more tied to communication than ever before. It is about creating relationships and building social networks, where visual elements have just as strong a position as the written word. These contexts can be both physical and mediated. Applying a contextual perspective also makes the researcher attentive to various power relations, including both structure and agency. A young person's media usage is not always a matter of free choice. What might seem as an act of empowerellt and participation might occur under the restrictions of commercial interests. And when studying media literacy in the schools, power relations within that system may inflict upon and affect processes of learning. In other words, we need methods that can capture how relations, networks and alliances, etc. are constituted. Finally, research also needs to look at variations among subgroups as well as at gender, ethnicity, lifestyle and class.

Note

1. The project is called 'Organized producers of young net cultures: Actors, practices, ambitions' and is funded by The Knowledge Foundation (KK-stiftelsen) during the period 2009-2013.

References

Barker, C. and Andre, J. (1996) Did You See? Soaps, Teenage Talks and Gendered Identity. *Young: Nordic Journal of Youth Research*, 4 (4), 21-38.

boyd, D. (2008) Why Youth ♥ Social Network Sites: The Role of Networked Publics in Teenage Social Life. In: D. Buckingahm (ed.) *Youth, Identity, and Digital Media* (pp. 119-142). London: The MIT Press.

Brembeck, H. and Johansson, B. (1996) *Postmodern barndom*. Göteborgs universitet: Etnologiska föreningen.

Brune, Y. (2008) Bilden av invandrare i svenska nyhetsmedier. In: M. Darvishpour and C. Westin (eds.) *Migration och etnicitet: Perspektiv på ett mångkulturellt Sverige* (pp. 335-361). Lund: Studentlitteratur.

Buckingham, D. (2000) *After the Death of Childhood: Growing Up in the Age of Electronic Media*. London: Polity Press.

Dorr, A. (1986) *Television and Children: A Special Medium for a Special Audience*. Beverly Hills, CA: Sage Publications Inc.

von Feilitzen, C. (1993) Våld – sett på olika sätt. Perspektiv på medievåldets påverkan och betydelse. In: C. von Feilitzen, M. Forsman & K. Roe (eds.) *Våld från alla håll: Forskningsperspektiv på våld i rörliga bilder*. (pp. 25-49) Stockholm: Symposion,

Drotner, K. (2008) Leisure is Hard Work: Digital Practices and Future Competencies. In: D. Buckingham (ed.) *Youth, Identity, and Digital Media* (pp. 167-184). Cambridge: The MIT Press.

EUKidsOnline: http://www.lse.ac.uk/collections/EUKidsOnline

Hodge, R. and Tripp, D. (1986) *Children and Television: A Semiotic Approach*. Cambridge: Polity Press.

Hultén, G. (2009) *Journalistik och mångfald*. Lund: Studentlitteratur.

Ito, M. et al. (2008) Foreword. In: D. Buckingham (ed.) *Youth, Identity, and Digital Media* (pp. vii-ix). Cambridge: The MIT Press.

Katz, E., Blumler, J.G. & Gurevitch, M. (1974) Utilization of Mass Communication by the individual. In: J.G. Blumler, & E. Katz (eds.) *The Uses of Mass Communications – Current Perspectives on Gratifications Research* (pp. 19-32). Beverly Hills, CA: Sage Publications Inc.

Livingstone, S. and Bovill, M. (eds.) (2001) *Children and Their Changing Media Environment: A European Comparative Study*. London: Lawrence Erlbaum.

Livingstone, S. and Haddon, L. (eds.) (2009) *Young People in the European Digital Media Landscape*. Gothenburg: Nordicom.

Löwander, B. (1998) *Rasism och antirasism på dagordningen. Studier av televisionens nyhetsrapportering I början av 1990-talet*. Umeå: Umeå University, (diss.).

Noble, G. (1975) *Children in Front of the Small Screen*. London: Constable.

Nordicom-Sveriges Mediebarometer 2008 (2009) University of Gothenburg: Nordicom.

Postman, N. (1982) *The Disappearance of Childhood*. New York: Delacorte Press.

Rydin, I. (1996) *Making Sense of TV-narratives. Children's Readings of a Fairy Tale*. Linköping: Linköping University, (diss.).

Rydin, I. (2000a) *Barnens röster: Program för barn i Sveriges radio och television 1925-1999*. Stockholm: Stiftelsen Etermedierna i Sverige/Prisma.

Rydin, I. (2000b) Children's TV Programs on the Global Market. *News from the UNESCO International Clearinghouse on Children and Violence on the Screen*. 1:17- 20.

Rydin, I. (2004) Television. In: P. Fass (ed.) *Encyclopedia of Children and Childhood. In History and Society*. (pp. 813-815) New York: Macmillan Reference USA.

Rydin, I. (2010) Försvinner barndomen med Internet? Reflektioner kring forskning och debatt om möjligheter och risker. In: U. Carlsson (ed.) *Barn och unga i den digitala kulturen* (pp. 19-37) Gothenburg: Nordicom, The International Clearinghouse on Children, Youth and Media.

Rydin, I. and Sjöberg, U. (2007) Identität, kulturelle Veränderungen und das Generationsverhältnis. In: H. Bonfadelli and H. Moser (eds.) *Medien und Migration: Europa als multikultureller Raum* (pp. 273-302). Vorgesehener Verlag: VS Verlag fur Sozialwissenschaften.

Rydin, I. and Sjöberg, U. (2008) Internet as a Communicative Space for Identity Construction among Diaspora Families in Sweden. In: I. Rydin and U. Sjöberg (eds.) *Mediated Crossroads: Identity, Youth Culture and Ethnicity. Theoretical and Methodological Challenges*. (pp. 193- 214) Gothenburg: Nordicom.

Rydin, I. and Sjöberg, U. (2010) Everyday Life and the Internet in Diaspora Families. Girls Tell their Stories. In: T. Olsson and P. Dahlgren (eds.) *Young People ICT:s and Democracy* (pp. 147-169). Gothenburg: Nordicom.

Seip Tönnessen, E. (2000) *Barns møte med TV – teks og tolkning i en ny medietid*. Oslo: Universitetsforlaget.

Sjöberg, U. (2002) *Screen Rites: A Study of Swedish Young People's Use and Meaning-making of Screen-based Media in Everyday Life* (published Ph.d. thesis). Lund Studies in Media and Communication 5. Lund University.

Stern, S. (2008) Producing Sites, Exploring Identities: Youth Online Authorship. In: D. Buckingham (ed.) *Youth, Identity, and Digital Media* (pp. 95-117). London: The MIT Press.

Tapscott. D. (1998) *Growing up Digital: The Rise of the Net Generation.* New York: McGraw-Hill Companies Inc.

Wartella, E. and Reeves, B. (1985) Historical Trends in Research on Children and the Media: 1900-1960. *Journal of Communication,* 35, no. 2: 118-133.

Winn, M. (1977) *The Plug-in-Drug.* New York: The Viking Press.

The Extensions of Youth
A Long Term Perspective

Thorbjörn Broddason, Kjartan Ólafsson
& Sólveig Margrét Karlsdóttir

> To behold, use or perceive any extension of ourselves
> in technological form is necessarily to embrace it.
> To listen to radio or to read the printed page
> is to accept these extensions of ourselves
> into our personal system and to undergo
> the "closure" or displacement of perception
> that follows automatically.
>
> Marshall Mcluhan (1964)

Researchers are familiar with the idea that children are the vanguard of technological progress (Rushkoff 1996). Children are supposed to be naturally inclined to embrace new means of communication and test their potential (Lee 2005). Results from the long-term research project *Children and Television in Iceland* provide an opportunity to look into this question. Its origins can be traced to the year 1968, when a written questionnaire was given to a sample of school children. The original purpose was to collect data on the introduction of television in Icelandic society and make the most of the circumstances, where only some geographical areas had access to the services of the recently established national television service (Broddason 1970). As the years went by, however, it became evident that the 1968 survey was a unique source of knowledge about a phenomenon that was attracting the steadily increasing interest of social scientists. This was the background of the second survey that was launched in 1979. Although the new survey was not an exact copy of the previous one, its basic purpose was to provide the researchers with comparative material to the 1968 results. And now the ball was rolling: what had started as an isolated spot-check was transformed into a long-term project, which presently consists of seven individual surveys, the latest one having been carried out in 2009.

The following pages contain a discussion of the development of a few key factors in the media behaviour of young people as it can be extracted from some of the evidence provided by repeated questionnaire surveys over a period of 41 years. The issues highlighted here do not give an exhaustive idea of the information available from the database built up within the project *Children and Television* in Iceland; rather the purpose is to throw light on the interplay between the new media, in particular the Internet and mobile phones, and more traditional media and on how this interplay has affected trends that have remained relatively stable for a number of years. From the communication technology perspective, it is quite appropriate to call the latter half of the 20th century the Golden Age of Television. Now we have several indications to the effect that a fundamental change has occurred with the spread of high-speed Internet services during the first years of the 21st century.

Data from all seven survey occasions will be utilized. On all occasions, the survey questions have been given to samples of children in the upper grades of the compulsory school system in three communities, namely Reykjavík, the capital of Iceland, Akureyri, the largest township in the North of the country (without television in 1968), and Vestmannaeyjar, an island community off the South coast. Table 1 shows the total sample sizes and response figures. In the first six surveys, random samples of children were drawn from selected schools in the three communities, whereas in the seventh survey the whole population of the selected schools was asked to participate. Hence the much larger numbers of respondents in the seventh survey round.

Table 1.   Children and Television in Iceland: Sample sizes and response rates. Age group 10 to 15 years

Survey Year	Sample Size	Number of Respondents	Response Rate
1968*	733	601	82%
1979	864	795	92%
1985	896	824	92%
1991	961	817	85%
1997	984	857	87%
2003	1008	786	78%
2009	3202**	2876	90%

*Age group 10 to 14 in 1968.
**This is the total population of 10-15 year olds in the selected schools in 2009.

In 1968, the survey was conducted by the first author single-handedly, while in later rounds he was joined by fellow researchers and students. On no occasion was the data collection left to persons unconnected to the project. The upper age limit of the sampling population was dictated by the school leaving age (14 in 1968; 15 from 1979 onwards), while for the lower age limit the line was drawn where the researchers were confident that the overwhelming majority of respondents had acquired sufficient reading and writing skills to successfully complete the questionnaire (Broddason 1970; 1996).

Various tools of communication

The aim of the first study in 1968 was to collect data on the introduction of television in Icelandic society. As it turned out, television ownership was already widespread in the spring of 1968 in the areas within the reach of television signals. Some 92 percent of respondents living in the two communities where television signals could be picked up had a TV set at home just 18 months after the Icelandic state broadcasting service had started its television services. Already in the first survey, we see a pattern that is to emerge in later surveys, with boys living in homes where TV sets have been present for a longer time than is the case in homes where girls are living (Ólafsson 2000). Thus, the mere presence of a boy in the household seems to contribute to the household acquiring a TV set.

At that time, the idea of more than one television receiver in an ordinary Icelandic home was rather far-fetched, not only due to the cost involved but also because at that time the vast majority of people only had access to a single television channel, and video recorders were not yet commercially available. All this changed during the 1980s, when the state monopoly on broadcasting was cancelled and with the introduction of the privately owned Channel two (Stöð 2) in 1986. Thus in the 1991 survey, we introduced a question about the number of TVs in the respondents' homes. Table 2 shows a steep growth in the number of TVs per household during the last decade of the past century and the first decade of the present century.

Table 2. Number of TVs in Respondents' Homes 1968-2009 (per cent)

	1968*	1979	1985	1991	1997	2003	2009
One TV	92	na	na	47	28	11	13
Two TVs	na	na	na	36	40	33	25
Three or more TVs	na	na	na	17	32	56	61
Mean number of TVs	na	na	na	1.7	2.2	2.9	3.0

*Excluding respondents in Akureyri where no television service was available at the time.

In the 1979 survey, a question was added regarding the respondent's personal ownership or possession of certain communication tools, i.e. a radio, a record player and a cassette player. By 2009, the list had grown to 18 items. The wording of the question was: "Do you own or is there in your room any of the following?" In Table 3 the progress of four key items towards varying levels of saturation is shown from 1991 onwards.

Table 3. "Do you own or is there in your room any of the following?" Per cent giving an affirmative answer in the past four surveys

	1991	1997	2003	2009
Television	29	46	66	65
Mobile phone	na	3	79	91
Personal (table top) computer	na	na	36	29
Laptop	na	na	7	38
Internet connection	na	na	30	51

The pattern that we see in Table 3 as well as when television was introduced in Iceland is in line with the general idea that the diffusion of innovations follows an S-shaped curve (Rogers 1995; Livingstone 2002). Thus we see that already in 1968 when television was relatively new in Iceland almost all respondents had access to a TV set at home. Similarly, between 1997 and 2003 mobile phones go from being almost non-existent to being owned by nearly all respondents.

However, the steepness of the diffusion curve is different across different media, with television (first set) and mobile phones having a much steeper curve than computers and additional TV sets. Also there is a point of saturation that is not necessarily 100%. This is, for example, the case for television sets in the respondent's own room, which does not rise between 2003 and 2009.

The general pattern for all new introductions to the media market seems to be that there is a time when that particular medium changes from being new and exotic to being an everyday phenomenon. For television in homes, this time was at the introduction of Icelandic television services in the late 1960s. For television sets in the bedrooms of adolescents, it was the mid-1990s. For mobile phones, it was the beginning of the millennium. For computers it was the first decade of the new millennium, and these computers were increasingly being connected to the Internet (in 2009, some 9% of our respondents possessed both kinds of computers, hence the net percentage for ownership of either or both kinds of computers was 58%).

We notice that personal ownership of television among our respondents, which increased by leaps and bounds between 1991 and 2003, seems to have levelled off entirely by 2009, but (and this is of importance) at different saturation levels for boys and girls. In Table 4 the well-known truth that boys acquire gadgets faster than girls do is handsomely demonstrated.

Table 4. The frequency of personal ownership of a TV 1991-2009. According to gender (percentages)

	1991	1997	2003	2009
Boys	38	53	73	71
Girls	18	39	58	58
Total	29	46	66	65

In spite of these suggestive figures, it would be unwise to jump to the conclusion that what we are witnessing here is a stagnation in adolescent interest in moving images; rather we should look at these figures in the context of changes in computer ownership, in particular the dramatic growth in laptop ownership between 2003 and 2009 (Table 3). Apparently the personal computer, in particular the laptop, is to some extent replacing ordinary television receivers in the communications arsenal of Icelandic youths. In response to two questions, "How do you use the computer" and "How do you use the Internet", some 50 per cent claim to watch movies, series or video clips at least once a week with the help of these tools. This overall figure conceals considerable gender differences in favour of boys as well as age differences.

The most conspicuous change revealed in Table 3 is related to the ownership of mobile phones. Practically a non-existent phenomenon among adolescents in 1997, only six years later it had become nearly pervasive among the older respondents, and in 2009 the situation was even closer to saturation. Clear gender differences, which were apparent already in 2003, persist in 2009. A mobile phone constitutes the exception to the above-mentioned rule that boys acquire new gadgets ahead of the girls. Not unexpectedly, mobile ownership increases with age, even though the extremely high ownership percentage within all age groups is perhaps more noteworthy (Table 5).

Table 5. "Do you own...a mobile phone?" (per cent)

Age	10 yrs	11 yrs	12 yrs	13 yrs	14 yrs	15 yrs	All age groups
Boys	83	85	88	89	90	92	89
Girls	89	91	94	95	98	99	95

Although Marshall McLuhan's characterization of the media as the "extensions of man" was coined several decades before cell phones were nearly omnipresent, as they are today, it aptly reflects the uses of the mobile phone, as reported by our respondents. Not only is mobile phone ownership more widespread among girls than the boys, it is also of considerably more importance to them (Tables 5, 6 and 7). It is not an exaggeration to claim that in mid-adolescence, the mobile phone has become a social lifeline for a large proportion of girls, but less so among boys. It is also noteworthy that the traditional use of the phone as a speech medium is important both to keep contact with parents and friends, whereas the texting function is primarily reserved for contacts with friends.

Table 6. 2009 Survey: Speak at least once daily via mobile phone (per cent)

Age	With parents		With friends	
	Boys	Girls	Boys	Girls
10 years	23	30	11	18
11 years	32	37	21	21
12 years	26	39	25	37
13 years	28	47	38	45
14 years	26	47	37	56
15 years	31	44	46	62

Table 7. 2009 Survey: Send an text message at least once daily via mobile phone (per cent)

Age	To parents		To friends	
	Boys	Girls	Boys	Girls
10 years	6	9	3	9
11 years	10	10	9	12
12 years	5	14	10	27
13 years	6	13	21	37
14 years	7	18	20	50
15 years	6	14	26	57

As we have now examined the introduction of new media during the last decades of the 20th century and at the beginning of the new millennium, it is time to see how older media have fared at the same time.

Book reading:
An alarming decline followed by a perplexing rise

From the very outset of the research project Children and Television in Iceland, we have included questions on leisure reading. Consequently, we are able to speak with some confidence about changes in reading habits. The following question has been put to our respondents in each survey:

If you think carefully, how many books, apart from school books, do you think you have read during the past 30 days? (1968 and 1979).

Have you read any books during the past 30 days? (Here we do not mean books that you may have read in relation to your school work) (1985, 1991, 1997, 2003, 2009).

The participants wrote down what they considered the appropriate figure. As the survey material has accumulated over the years, the responses to this question have brought into light a picture of clear differentiation in terms of age and gender. With every fresh survey, these findings have been further confirmed.

What has changed, however, over the years is the number of books consumed by our respondents, both in terms of averages and with regard to the number of youths reading no books at all "during the past 30 days" as well as those who claim to read a great deal (Table 8).

Table 8.   Book reading "during the past 30 days" 1968-2009

	1968	1979	1985	1991	1997	2003	2009
None	11%	11%	15%	18%	27%	33%	28%
One to nine	79%	63%	72%	76%	65%	64%	68%
Ten or more	10%	26%	13%	6%	8%	3%	4%
	100%	100%	100%	100%	100%	100%	100%
Mean, boys	3.5	6.0	3.8	2.4	2.2	1.5	2.0
Mean, girls	4.4	6.7	4.5	3.2	3.3	2.2	2.5
Overall Mean	3.9	6.4	4.2	2.8	2.7	1.8	2.2

The overall trend between 1968 and 2003 is unmistakable, especially with regard to the "non-readers" whose ranks are constantly swelling. The diminishing numbers of the very heavy readers are also apparent, with the most dramatic downturn occurring between 1997 and 2003. Admittedly, the figures for 1979 stand out as something of an anomaly in this context; this is in all likelihood best explained by the new *comic book* genre, which had been recently introduced on the Icelandic market in 1979 and enjoyed considerable popularity at the time of the second survey. These publications take much less time and effort than ordinary books, and they can even be enjoyed without being "read" in the proper sense of the word. Since the 1985 survey, comic books have been covered by a separate question (for a more comprehensive discussion of this problem, see Broddason 1996: 120-123).

Researchers have traced this consistent trend to the growing importance and prominence of television during the latter half of the 20th century, and more recently the other new media as well, in particular the Internet (Knulst and Kraaykamp 1997; Koolstra and van der Voort 1996; Neuman 1988; Livingstone, Bovill og Gaskell 1999; Broddason 2006). Those concerned with the future of reading have seen a worrying sign in the declining averages, but the growing numbers of "non-readers" may appear even more alarming. The figures from the 2009 survey, however, tell a different story (Table 8): The number of "non-readers" has fallen back to the 1997 level, and the overall book reading mean is higher than it was in 2003. After all these years of decline in book reading, we have indeed anticipated that the bottom might be reached one day; yet it is intriguing that we should observe it while at the same time the new media continue their undeterred expansion. Computer ownership has increased since 2003, Internet connections have become even more common and the number of TVs per household has continued to increase. The only development that seems to be levelling off is the number of TVs in the respondent's personal possession, but the explanation for this might very well be that the youths prefer to watch television programmes on their computer screens rather than bothering to switch between the TV with its single function and the computer, where other communication activity goes on. We are thus left with the perplexing question of why the decline in book consumption has not only halted, but actually turned around at a time of continued expansion of the new media. The explanation, or a part of it, may be found in a campaign that has been run in the Icelandic schools for a while, called "The Bookworm". This is a computerized version of an old custom that enables school classes and whole schools to compare their progress in reading with other classes or schools. It is evident from the campaign's website that it generates considerable activity. The campaign obtained the European School Net Award in 2007. Another recent effort is "The Great Public Reading Competition", a country-wide event held in the 7th class. The declared purpose of the competition is to increase the general level of reading skills, heighten pupils' respect for others as well as their self-respect and especially to encourage individuals with reading difficulties to fight on (Karlsdótttir 2009).

Newspaper reading: an alarming decline continues

Right from the beginning, we have included a question about the daily reading of newspapers. Although the wording of the question has varied slightly across surveys, comparability has been preserved (Table 9).

Table 9. Per cent claiming to read a newspaper every day or almost every day

1968	89
1979	90
1985	72
1991	68
1997	61
2003	40
2009	29

The similarities with the trend in book reading are obvious throughout, that is to say until the 2009 survey. Whereas the spell on book reading was broken by the time of the 7th survey, the spell on newspaper reading remains as strong as ever. We can offer two explanations for this parting of ways. The first has to do with what we regard to be the inherently weak position of traditional printed newspapers in their competition with the increasingly sophisticated electronic news media (including of course the newspapers' own websites). In terms of immediacy, depth, background and flexibility, the comparison is increasingly to the newspapers' disadvantage. The end of the old-fashioned newspaper seems to be in sight. Ordinary printed books, e.g. fiction, perhaps several hundred pages in length, on the other hand, have not met with equally serious electronic competition thus far. Consuming tens or hundreds of pages of leisure reading on the screen simply has not caught on. Most likely, however, this is only the lull before the storm. At the time of writing, there are already on the market electronic alternatives to the printed book, whatever its length or content, that appear to have such huge advantages and may have such wide ranging consequences for the reading public that not only the newspaper part of the next questionnaire, but also the book reading questions will have to be completely rewritten.

Concluding remarks

Researchers agree that a fundamental change has occurred in the communication environment and the communication behaviour of young people in the industrialized world during recent years and decades. The material gathered in the research project Children and Television in Iceland throws some of these changes into sharp relief. From one point of view, the Golden Age of television is approaching its end more rapidly than many of us would have anticipated, but at the same time television is becoming an integral part of the new electronic media environment and will survive in a recognizable shape, if not in name. Nothing, it seems, will stop the rapid decline of printed newspapers, whereas books in the traditional sense of the word, although handsomely defending their position for the time being, will probably undergo a monumental transformation in the near future.

References

Broddason, Thorbjörn (1970) *Children and Television in Iceland*. Unpublished MA-thesis: Lund University.

Broddason Thorbjörn (1996) *Television in Time: Research Images and Empirical Findings*. Lund: Lund University Press.

Broddason, Thorbjörn (2006) Youth and New Media in the New Millennium. *Nordicom Review, 27*(2), 105-118.

Karlsdóttir, Sólveig Margrét (2009) *Yndislestur ungmenna í upplýsingasamfélagi*. [Leisure Reading in the Information Society]. Unpublished BA-thesis: University of Iceland.

Knulst, W. & Kraaykamp, G. (1997) The Decline of Reading: Leisure Reading Trends in the Netherlands (1955-1995) *Netherlands Journal of Social Science, 33*(2), 130-150.

Koolstra, C.M. & van der Voort, T. (1996) Longitudinal Effects of Television on Children's Leisure-time Reading: A Test of Three Explanatory Models. *Human Communication Research, 23*(1), 4-35.

Lee, L. (2005) 'Young People and the Internet: From Theory to Practice'. *Young, 13*(4), 315-26.

Livingstone, S. (2002) *Young People and New Media*. London: Sage.

Livingstone, S., Bovill, M. & Gaskell, G. (1999) European TV Kids in a Transformed Media World: Findings of the UK study. In P. Löhr og M. Meyer (eds.) *Children, Television and the New Media. A Reader of Research and Documentation in Germany* (pp. 8-24). Luton: Luton University Press.

McLuhan, Marshall (1964) *Understanding Media: The Extensions of Man*. New York: McGraw-Hill Book Company.

Neuman, S.B. (1988) The Displacement Effect: Assessing the Relation between Television Viewing and Reading Performance. *Reading Research Quarterly, 23*(4), 414-440.

Ólafsson, Kjartan (2000) Tómstundastörf og fjölmiðlanotkun íslenskra ungmenna 1968-1997. [Leisure activities and media use of Icelandic youth 1968-1997] Unpublished MA thesis. University of Iceland.

Rogers, E.M. (1995) *Diffusion of Innovations* (4th ed.). New York: The Free Press.

Rushkoff, D. (1996) *Media Virus! Hidden Agendas in Popular Culture*. New York, NY: Ballantine Books.

Growing up in a Commercial World
Reflections on Media, Marketing and Young Consumers[1]

Ingunn Hagen

Commercial childhood is not primarily about children's stacks of cuddly animals, or useless products, but the fact that most experiences and products have a price tag attached to them, not least the intense marketing to have such products sold (Nordisk ministerråd, 2005: 13; my translation).[2]

Children today are exposed to a growing number and range of commercial messages. These extend far beyond traditional media advertising, and involve activities such as online marketing, sponsorship and peer-to-peer marketing. Commercial forces also increasingly impact on children's experiences in areas such as broadcasting, education and play (Buckingham 2009: 4).

The driving force behind this exploding media culture is the exponential rise in children's spending power during the past several decades, prompted in part by the very changes in family structure that are confounding the role of parents. Never before have children and youth played such a powerful role in the marketplace (Montgomery 2007: 7).

"Everything costs money." This is the impression one gets about children's lives and leisure time. Lately there has been public concern about the increasing commercialization of childhood. Commercial actors have discovered that children have purchasing power, both directly and indirectly through their role in the family. The present article will address the role of media in children and young people's consumption. Media and especially TV increasingly address children using advertising. During the past 15-20 years, the Internet has also been increasingly used in marketing aimed at children and youngsters, alone or in combination with other media. Media institutions are agents in this commercialization, and different brands use media in order to reach new and more individuals in the niche market of children and youth.

Thus, the development in the media field is central to understanding the pressure to consume that is put on children and youngsters, and how children have become an interesting target or niche for marketing.[3] In Norway, where TV advertising aimed at children is not allowed, only Norwegian channels that broadcast from abroad (like TV3 that broadcasts from England) and international channels (such as Cartoon Network and Nickelodeon) provide advertising on Norwegian TV screens. The latter, however, provide commercials for everything, from toys and food to media products. There is also indirect purchasing pressure, through spinoff products related to popular programs, even on the Norwegian Public Service Broadcaster NRK.

When children use media, they become available as a target audience. Due to their direct and indirect purchasing power, children have become interesting as a segmented group, which is divided into niches according to gender and age (Tingstad 2006). A number of global media products have long been available for Norwegian children, and such products are now in increasing numbers, as they are in many countries. In the present article, I intend to discuss a few contemporary examples. Satellite TV has opened up for global competition, and consequently the Norwegian national public service broadcaster NRK is competing with an increasing number of commercial channels, especially the Disney channels. The TV channels also have websites, which they use to communicate with and attract children to their channels. While this article takes Norway as its focal point, there are similar developments going on elsewhere.

Commercialization and children as consumers

The phenomenon of children as consumers is closely linked to the development of welfare in the Western part of the world. In Norway, one of the wealthiest countries in the world, this has led to increasing commercialization of the lifeworld generally, in the sense that money and profitability are the dominant measures in society (cf. Tingstad 2006; Bjørnebekk 1992). This wealth has also "trickled down" to the children. Norwegian parents (and grandparents) are wealthier than even before, and many wait longer before they have children. Moreover, most parents want their children to have what they perceive to be the best. Thus, children are sometimes talked about as "small emperors" or "trophy children".[4] Children's consumption is from the beginning a symbol of the status of their family.

Studies show that children themselves, when they grow older, have more money and thus more purchasing power than they did earlier. Furthermore, more and more activities in children's leisure time require payment for participation (Brusdal 2001). As indicated, children also have an indirect influence on family decisions about consumption – everything from what type of cereal they eat to what media technologies the family buys. Children can be very intense when there are products they want. In English this is labeled rather negatively as children's "pester power" or the "nag factor" (see Strasburger, Wilson and Jordan 2009). When children say that "everybody has this", parents often go out of their way to provide their children with the same object. Children have also become an attractive niche in the market because they represent a potential for long-lasting brand loyalty, and thus secure future profit (cf. Nakken 2007; and also Harris 1999).

The commercialization of childhood is the point of departure of the research project "Consuming Children: Commercialization and the Changing Construction of Childhood", which this author is part of. [5] This project is an interdisciplinary endeavor involving teamwork; it includes studies of both production, texts and products, and consumption. The empirical focus is on two age groups: preschool children and so-called tweens ("in-betweens" – the age between children and teenagers, about 8- to 12-year-olds). The latter category has received increased attention as a target of marketing in recent years. Such age-segmented think-ing has also been actualized in connection with the new children's channels in Norway, a topic we will return to later in the article.

The commercialization of childhood raises questions that are difficult to answer, but still very important to ask. For example, what are the media political conse-quences of commercialization? Equally important is the question of how children can learn to become competent and critical consumers. At the same time, it is worth questioning the assumption that children's consumption is problematic, while adult consumption is not questioned to the same extent. It is also typical that children (and women) are almost automatically considered to be more vul-nerable than men are when it comes to influence (cf. Hagen 2004/1998).

Marketing and advertising via TV

With its central position in culture, the TV medium is an important arena for marketing products to children. For example, American children are on average exposed to 40,000 TV commercials during a year (Arnett and Tanner 2005; see also www.newdream.org/kids/facts.php). In the multi-media society, TV has received competition from digital media, but there is also a tendency toward integrative marketing, where use of several media reinforces marketing. For example, children's channels have websites that offer spin-off products. The mobile phone has also become central in the interaction between broadcasting institutions and their viewers. Tingstad (2006) gives the example of voting related to the TV program *Idol*, which was a great source of income for the Norwegian channel TV2. In the following, we will focus on how TV contributes to both direct and indirect commercial pressure.

Daily TV viewing and exposure to programs and commercials may create strong desires among children (cf. Brusdal 1999). Children are often emotionally attached to or identify with TV characters (see Hake 2003; Rydin 2003), and they often find great pleasure in imitating these characters. Thus, children may wish to have clothes or gear that characters in children's TV have. Similarly, advertising is often shaped to create desire among children, and children are not always able to separate the advertising clearly from the programs. With exposure every half hour, commercials can cause children to develop brand recognition and also desires for some of the products. The line between marketing and programs can also be blurred; since the 1980s, TV channels and toy producers have sometimes cooperated on programs, which have often been produced for the purpose of promoting children's toys (Strasburger, Wilson & Jordan 2009).

As mentioned earlier, Norway has strict rules regarding children and TV commercials compared to other countries. The Norwegian broadcasting regulations state that "there cannot be commercials in connection to children's programs or advertising directly addressing children".[6] This means that Norwegian commercial channels (like TV2 and TVNorge) need to adhere to these regulations, and cannot send commercials addressed to children. However, the regulations only include channels broadcasting from Norway. Thus, Norwegian channels broadcasting from another country can have commercials, such as the previously mentioned TV3, which is broadcast from England. The Children's Ombudsman sued TV3 for broadcasting illegal commercials to Norwegian children, but it did not get anywhere in the EFTA courts; it is the laws of the broadcasting country that apply, not the laws of the receiver country.[7] As indicated earlier, despite the regulations, international channels – among others Cartoon Network and earlier Jetix – broadcast rather aggressive commercials. Examples of products are toys, like dolls or action heroes, candy, and fast food (like McDonald's).

Cartoon Network is worth examining closer, as one of the global, commercial channels that has very intensive advertising directed at children, including Norwegian children. Cartoon Network is originally an American cable-TV network, now broadcasting all over the world. The channel mainly broadcasts cartoons. The commercials are primarily for toys, but also for cereals, snacks, and fast food. An analysis in the spring of 2007 suggested that almost one fifth of Cartoon Network's broadcast time was commercials, and that the commercials came in 5-minute slots every half hour.[8] The commercials were introduced by advertising intros and a story teller who informed viewers that there would be commercials. The commercial itself lasted 20 seconds and was often filled with action and pictures, music, text, and a Norwegian story teller. About two thirds of the commercials were gender specific, clearly directed toward either girls or boys, while one third were more gender neutral. Examples of advertising directed at girls were Cinderella Barbie, Bratz dolls and My Little Pony, while commercials directed at boys were about Spectrobes and Transformers figures (robots for play). More gender-neutral commercials included products like Kinder Surprise, Moon sand and the Donald Magazine.

We see that Cartoon Network follows the principle that the commercial should be clearly separated from the TV program itself. However, for certain products, this distinction may be difficult for children to perceive (cf. Tingstad 2006). Part of the concern about advertising to children relates to whether small children can distinguish between commercials and other content. According to Harris

(1999), the worries are also regarding whether smaller children understand that commercials are supposed to persuade them, or how commercials are interconnected with the economy of commercial TV. Even though very small children can identify commercials, they do not have sufficient understanding of the purpose of commercials. Children may also have problems understanding details in commercials, for example so-called disclaimers – which may partly contradict that main message and which are often written in small print or expressed very rapidly (cf. Strasburger et al. 2009).

From direct to indirect advertising

The most popular channels among 2- to 11-year old children in Norway are the NRK and Disney channels (see Hagen and Wold 2009). Cartoon Network had for example only 5 % market share. In this way the Norwegian children's market is surprisingly free of commercials – Disney has less advertising in the traditional sense, but they do promote other products. TV2 has many commercials addressing a family audience with products that also are consumed by children. However, this channel does not have advertising spots that interrupt the programs. Thus, compared to other countries the advertising on Norwegian children's television is not particularly aggressive.

But marketing can also occur more indirectly, as indicated earlier. On many TV channels, including NRK and TV2, the program is almost like a commercial for characters from the series. This means that the program content is used to sell other products, such as toys or clothing. It may be the character itself or toy products, such as Postman Pat, Lego Star Wars, Dora the Explorer, Sponge Bob Square Pants, Winnie the Pooh, or clothes with a logo or characters printed on them. The channels sell the rights to produce these products for different companies, so-called merchandizing (Bjørnebekk 1992). If the program becomes popular, a whole industry of spin-off products may develop. Through copy rights and licensing there is great income potential for TV companies. One Norwegian example is when TV3 introduced action characters like Ninja Turtles and the Transformers in the 1990s. This lead to a great spin-off wave related to toys on the TV market.

Income from merchandizing is becoming increasingly important for commercial companies. Their goal is often to have new characters or concepts – He-man, Bob the Builder, Spiderman, Beyblades – all of which have the ability to attract children on a broad basis. Here they use all the expressions from popular culture: excitement, romance, and humor – and produce these over and over again. Thus, the commercial channels largely build on serials that are run every day and that run for infinity, and they broadcast reruns constantly. If we enter the websites of these channels, for example Cartoon Network or Nickelodeon, we can see how such characters are in focus. "Heroes" they are called, and they are presented visibly, like in a banner. Thus, children are supposed to immediately find "their own" character. It is also important to play on multiple media expressions; the same characters are available on film, in games, on CDs, in books etc. Multimodality is the keyword here, something I will return to. The relationship can also be the reverse, that popular characters from other media become TV serials. This was the case with Pokémon, which first started as a Nintendo game. Later the characters and concept were sold to TV (Tobin 2004).

When one has hit one's target and created a popular character, the "road" continues to games, bed linens, curtains, clothes, bread, furniture, etc. Then the marketing strategies become broader; one has to develop the character into a brand. As with all brands, one then needs a logo – such as Batman's spooky wing profile or Hannah Montana's star sparkling name. Donald Duck, for example, has had the same heading in his magazine since the 1950s, more or less unchanged. A slogan is also useful – Pokémon's "Gotta catch 'em all!" is just as catchy as Nike's "Just do it!" Through the use of different campaigns, one seeks not only to get children hooked, but also their parents, siblings, grandparents, etc. However, directing commercials at children is not without its problems. There may be legal regulations and restrictions. However, equally important is the resistance from parents and society generally regarding aggressive marketing toward children. The alternative is to develop strong brands, which generate sufficient revenues. The Disney corporation, for example, has such a strong brand and such a diversified business that they manage to run their channels with fewer external sponsors.

NRK – now also with spin-off products

In the past, the monopoly situation of the public broadcaster NRK allowed this institution to go happily protected from competition with commercial channels for a long time. However, when a more competitive situation arose, it also had consequences for how the content of these public service channels developed. When there is competition for viewers, all actors focus on appealing to the target group and on making them loyal (to the channel). In this way, a commercial logic as well as children's TV esthetics have developed, also in NRK (cf. Hagen 2004/1998). Still, NRK's aim is to be an alternative to the commercial channels for children, something their vision also indicates: "We are to create a world in which children develop and are important" (see Bøe 2009; my translation).

The NRK produced series *Sesam Stasjon* (based on the concept of the American series Sesame Street), which began in 1991 and is generally considered to be the beginning of the commercialization of children's TV in Norway (Tønnessen 2000). The series developed a commercial esthetics in the sense that the story line was constantly interrupted (where commercials were supposed to have been). In this way, the TV expression became more fragmented, in contrast to the more coherent and calm story telling tradition of NRK. Moreover, the *Sesam Stasjon* series was accompanied by a number of spin-off products that were connected to the TV series. This practice had not been very common in Norway prior to this series.

Since then, NRK has continued the commercial exploitation of popular series. Examples include the NRK-produced Christmas series (like *Amalies Jul*, 1995; *Jul i Blåfjell*, 1999 with many annual reruns; *Jul på Månetoppen*, another version of the latter series 2002; and *Barnas Superjul* 2004). NRK has created their own company, NRK Aktivum[9], which is supposed to manage the licensing of spin-off products. In Norway, the characteristic blue hats/caps of the Santas in *Jul i Blåfjell* became a "craze" among children for years when this series and versions of it were broadcast. The very popular *Jul i Blåfjell* series was accompanied by 40 spin-off products (http://www.orapp.no/vil_stoppe/, retrieved 15.12.2008). This was done both to earn money and to strengthen the brand of NRK. Later on, the follow-up series *Jul på Månetoppen* was accompanied by 50 different spin-off products (Blindheim 2004).

The surplus money from NRK Aktivum goes to those NRK departments that have produced the programs that the spin-off products are based upon, which can supplement NRK's licensee fee money. However, this is not without problems for NRK, as the channel was originally financed through state support and the licensee fee and is not supposed to "do business". Not everyone appreciates the fact that the "solid NRK" has thrown itself onto this "commercial wave". The debate has been about the fact that such activities may reduce editorial freedom as well as tarnish the reputation or image of NRK as a public service broadcaster. For example, one media researcher (Nyborg 2007) expressed that NRK has "a raw commercial pressure toward children which includes licensing and product placement."[10] He characterized the series broadcast by NRK as quality productions, but thought that "the programs in practice function as long commercials" (my translation).

Web Commercials directed at Children

In recent years, TV channels have experienced hard competition from the Internet and the marketing going on there. The Internet as a marketing medium has been rapidly increasing, and since the millennium shift, more and more money is being used on advertising and net marketing. Net advertising can be even more difficult to recognize than for TV commercials, especially for (small) children. Thus, Nordic consumer ombudsmen have developed common guidelines for marketing aimed at children and youth via the Net. It is emphasized that children should understand that this is advertising. Combining games and marketing has been criticized and reacted against (such as the WebPages of Dinolife and Kinderegg).

In a study by Borch (1998; see also Borch 2003), she identified commercial websites as the most common way to market products to children and youth. She analyzed the commercial websites of tine.no (the main Norwegian dairy producer), lego.com/no and Donald.no. These pages mix information, advertising and games in ways that can be difficult to realize, even for adults. Here children are getting free advertising material, can become club members and play in return for consumer information, such as their name, interests etc. This non-recognizable form of marketing makes it more difficult for children to be as critical and on guard as they would have been if the marketing had been easier to identify. By solving tasks and games, they provide information that again can be used to target the marketing toward them. Such commercial websites can be regarded as "branded environments", where children may interact with characters, logos, jingles, games, and small films. This interaction in web-based play and activity rooms is expected to increase the brand loyalty of children.

Indeed, the Internet is increasingly a central element in the build-up of different media brands. All the large actors in the children's culture market have their own websites, where they offer large amounts of extra material related to their fictional world. The greater the actor, the greater possibilities they have for developing attractive websites. For example, the official Disney pages Disney.no (which is different from Donald.no) have a rich offer of games, easy access to excerpts from the series, and – not least – links to all the "heroes" mini-pages. This is a form of indirect marketing, where the website is supposed to contribute to building up brand loyalty, as discussed above. In addition, the website provides for direct marketing of Disney products, with suggestions to buy films, CDs, etc. NRK as well have their website NRK Super Nett, which is actively used to cross-promote the TV programs of NRK Super (see Bøe 2009). However, unlike other websites, like those of Lego and Cartoon network, the NRK Super website does not actively promoting the spin-off products. Lego.com, for example, actively promotes sales by informing about new Lego products. Lego.com also promotes brand loyalty through their Lego Club, games, and by allowing children to have their own Lego network (Lego social networking site). On Cartoonnetwork.com, children can find games, small videos, fan talk and shopping possibilities.

The problem of identifying what constitutes marketing is the main focus of a study of Ingrid Kjørstad (2000), published in the report *Barn og Internettreklame* (Children and Internet Advertizing). In this report, Kjørstad claims that, increasingly, new forms of commercial messages are appearing, and she asks children whether they are able to recognize commercial messages in different kinds of Internet advertising. One main finding is that children appear to have more positive attitudes toward advertising on the Internet than via other channels. This could be a reflection of the fact that the Net is perceived as a "cool" and modern medium. Most of the children expressed that it was easy for them to recognize advertising on the Internet. However, three kinds of marketing were difficult for the children to recognize: sponsoring, newsletters, and chat commercials. For example, it was not obvious to the children that the dairy producer Tine earns their customers' "goodwill" when they sponsor voluntary organizations (like "soccer school" for children). Thus, Kjørstad suggests that the regulations should be made stricter with regard to these kinds of marketing.

We will now have a closer look at Disney, a company or brand that has had great influence on the children's culture in Norway; like in many countries.

Disney – from Donald to Hannah Montana

Disney's media products have been popular in Norway since the second world war, especially through the weekly magazine Donald Duck & Co, but also through NRK's Christmas Disney broadcast. Thus, Disney has been one of the first examples of modern popular culture with a broad appeal in Norway. For years, getting the Donald magazine was one of the highlights during the week for many children (see Hagen 2001). Now-a-days, it seems as if "use and throw away" toys made of plastic are supposed to assist the traditional Donald magazine in competing with the myriad of magazines targeted at children and youth.

Disney started with what was important popular media at the time: cartoon movies (shown at the cinema) and cartoons. Cartoon stripes and the movies came first, and for a long time, the most popular character was Mickey Mouse. Later Donald came into focus, and this character became the driving force behind the cartoon magazines. Eventually Disney developed into a giant entertainment corporation with associated companies in many countries and a number of media products, like TV channels, websites, computer games, DVDs, books, etc., all of which are widely available in Norway (see Hagen 2001). The Disney corporation also has its own Disneyland and Disneyworld in the US, and later in France.

Lately, Disney has become available for Norwegian children via new media, such as websites, DVDs, computer games and the new TV channels. In 2003, Canal Digital (distributor) obtained the rights to broadcast the three Disney channels called Disney channel, Toon Disney and Playhouse Disney to satellite, cable TV and broadband customers in the Nordic countries. Also Viasat customers can watch the Disney Channel and Toon Disney. The latest addition among Disney's channels is the boy's channel Disney XD. This channel, which was launched on September 12[11], 2009, aims at providing boys age 6-14 years a broad selection of series, films and sport.[11] The channel is a merging of the two earlier channels, Jetix and Toon Disney.

There is often less advertising on the Disney channels. However, merchandizing is an important part of Disney's success (cf. Buckingham 2001; Wasko 2001). Disney media products – especially the popular cartoon movies that become box office successes – have been followed by DVDs and numerous spin-off products (cf. Hagen 2001; Drotner 2003). Disney is making the most out of this on their channels. They advertise intensely for their spinoff products.[12] In this way, the channels function like a grand advertising poster for Disney's own media and spin-off products.

However, both Disney's media products and spin-off products experience competition from other brands. Thus, it is not surprising that the traditional Donald magazine's sales figures are on their way down. As a means of facing the increased competition, the magazine is accompanied by small toys and advertising. A toy attached to the front of Donald seduces children into buying the magazine, and inside there is advertising for the latest Disney films and spin-off toys. But despite the decrease in sales, the Donald magazine is still popular.[13] The development in Norway mirrors the fact that Disney has become a leader in the global children's culture, with many legs and massive marketing efforts. The Disney characters have become icons that children all over the world recognize and identify strongly with. Throughout their childhood, children are surrounded by channels, films, websites, magazines, toys, clothes, bed linens, and clubs with a Disney identity. In addition, Disney has a film menu that caters to the whole family: The Aristocats, 101 Dalmatinians, Beauty and the Beast, The Little Mermaid, Lion King, Narnia, Pirates in the Caribbean, Alice in Wonderland and others. By buying up other characters, such as Winnie the Pooh, the Disney Corporation has been able to reach new target groups, including small babies.

The latest addition to the Disney tribe is called Hannah Montana, a series that started on the Disney channels in 2006. Together with High School Musical, these are the flagships among the series targeting the so-called tweens group. In these series, Disney is not using cartoons, like we are used to with Disney, but real characters and a soap opera serial format. With Hannah Montana, Disney has created a figure that plays on a number of elements: music, humor, romance and the dream of being a star. There is enough slap stick humor in the series that the youngest get their share, while the dialogue is quite advanced, including irony that mainly older children understand. The core of the plot is that Hannah Montana has a double life: During the day time she is an ordinary girl by the name of Miley Stewart. In the evening, however, she is transformed into the superstar Hannah Montana. Of course nobody knows about this, except her and her family.

In this way, the character is a girl with whom (female) viewers can identify – in her ordinary life as a school girl – while she at the same time has all the glamour and pop star qualities. Because the series is a situation comedy, it also has a twist that may appeal to boys. For example, they can identify with her cool big brother or father, or laugh at her hysterical teacher. The music is also an important element; it is catchy, but with enough rock edge to give the series a cool image. With this music and the casting, Disney has hit the target so well that the main character Miley Cyrus has become a pop star in real life.[14] And there are of course numerous Hannah Montana spin-off products: clothes, necklaces, guitars, mouse mats, cups, wallets, purses, books, and dolls – the list is endless.

One of Disney's success factors is the fact that they approach all age groups: preschool children, school children, teenagers, parents and grandparents. Their products also appeal to both girls and boys. No wonder that the expression 'a Disney classic' is suitable. A number of children read the Donald magazine into their teenage years – even as adults. At the same time, Disney have been able to renew themselves, by using new characters and new forms of expression, as shown by the Hannah Montana series. Thus, the cartoon magazines, the TV series and the movies are all genuine popular culture expressions that appeal to the whole family.

Concluding remarks

Commercial media expressions for children, fashion trends and crazes are nothing new in Norway, like elsewhere. With the development in the media field over the past decades, this commercialization has accelerated. There has been commercial television, a more commercial TV esthetics and increased commercial pressure with advertising and marketing through mobile phones and the Internet. Schor noticed the potential social consequences of commercialization for children's lives: "Children's social worlds are increasingly constructed around consuming, as brands and products have come to determine who is 'in' or 'out', who is hot or not, who deserves to have friends or social status" (2004: 11). In other words, commercialization emphasizes materialism and what is "cool", that is, the norms for popularity and inclusion/exclusion. The debate about children, youth and consumption resembles the views expressed in the field of children, youth and media: Are children competent consumers, able to evaluate advertising and other commercial pressure, or are they vulnerable individuals who have problems protecting themselves against marketing strategies? Moreover, how can regulation and prohibition be combined with information and consciousness raising?

Norwegian authorities have in recent years been working toward what they perceive to be a massive commercial pressure on children and youth. One of the former ministers of the Ministry for Children and Equality wrote a newspaper article entitled "Children need to be made conscious about commercial pressure" (my translation).[15] The article came in connection with the Ministry's relaunching of the website www.foreldrepraten.no (website for "Parental talk"). This website offers parents a resource for discussing issues related to children's consumption and media use. In order to make children more conscious, the Ministry for Children and Equality has also launched a work book on advertising entitled "Are you influenced?" (my translation). In colored, bright paper and with commercial esthetics, the booklet is supposed to be used as a teaching tool in secondary and high school.

It is necessary for schools to assist children in developing the critical competence needed to evaluate advertising and marketing, especially via the Internet. With both the Internet and TV as popular channels, marketers have broad access to children and young people. For an actor, it may be a coup if he can create brand loyalty and shape consumer habits while children are small and easiest to shape. If a brand has succeeded here, the foundation has been laid for long-lasting consumption.[16] When children have been persuaded by successful marketing, this can lay the foundation for influencing other children, so-called "peer pressure" (Lindstrom and Seybold 2003). Moreover, the children will continue this loyalty when they grow up, and transfer it to their own children.

However, teaching and consciousness raising are not enough, according to the Norwegian Consumer Ombudsman. His agency suggests strengthening the law on advertising to children. Among other things, they think that there must be a demand for special care when marketing to children; such advertising should not be scary, contain sex, violence, drugs or play on children's bad consciousness or lack of self-confidence. Moreover, they want to prohibit marketing of unhealthy foods and direct advertising. Still, the question is what such legal acts lead to in practice. For example, it is already forbidden to use bonus gifts and prices in marketing aimed at children. However, such strategies are often used, for example in McDonald's Happy Meal concept and in the plastic toys that accompany children's cartoon magazines. It also happens that commercial actors themselves make small steps toward taking social responsibility. For example, the tele-companies Netcom and Telenor – after advice from the Consumer ombudsman – cooperated in making rules regulating mobile phone advertising to children. Also Disney has been involved in some campaigns in recent years, for example related to raising environmental consciousness and to teaching children how to act smart and safe on the Internet.

The largest problem is that many TV channels broadcast from other countries, and thus cannot be regulated. Moreover, Internet and web marketing are even more difficult to regulate. Still, there is a great need for updated regulation. However, one should not tamper with children's rights to be informed and to gain experience with marketing. In the words of Buckingham: "Although there is a continuing need for regulation, we also need to ensure that children are informed and empowered consumers" (DCSF News 14.12.2009). Such empowerment requires that media and consumer competence become a must for children. The efforts to develop such competence should focus on the strategies used by marketers to create desires and brand loyalty, and should also address such topics as the ethics of overconsumption in a global perspective, sustainable consumption, and the social implications of overly materialistic values.

Notes

1. The present article is a revised version of Chapter 8, called "Mediebruk og kommersialisering" (Media Use and Commercialization) in the book *Mediegenerasjonen. Barn og unge i det nye medielandskapet* (The Media Generation. Children and Young People in the New Media Landscape, by Hagen and Wold, 2009). A number of people have contributed their ideas to this article or the Norwegian point of departure: my son Odin Andrè Hagen Jacobsen, Dan Y. Jacobsen, Thomas Wold, Kari Brudevoll and my colleagues in the "Consuming Children" project: David Buckingham, Vebjørg Tingstad, Tora Korsvold, Gry Mette Haugen and others.
2. From the report *Kommersielt press not barn og unge i Norden. Foreldre og barn i en kommersiell oppvekst* (Commercial pressure toward children and youth in the Nordic countries. Parents and children in a commercial childhood), published by Nordisk Ministerråd (Nordic Council of Ministers).
3. Purchasing or commercial pressure could be defined as someone being pressured to buy certain goods, almost against their will (op. cit. p. 14). If one assumes that children have less resistance and fewer critical abilities with regard to commercial influence, such concepts are especially relevant to discuss related to them.

4. This was a concept used by consumer researcher Ragnhild Brusdal when she was one of the keynote speakers at the International Conference on 'Child and Teen Consumption 2008'.

5. See the website for the project on http://www.svt.ntnu.no/noseb/Consuming/ or Buckingham and Tingstad's (2007) article in the journal *Barn*.

6. In Norwegian: "det kan ikke sendes reklameinnslag i tilknytning til barneprogram eller reklameinnslag som er særlig rettet mot barn". Source: The Broadcasting law, see for example http://www.lovdata.no/all/tl-19921204-127-003.html#3-2.

7. Source: the article "TV3 sends commercials to children" by Harald Espeland (http: //wwe.bt.no/bergenspuls/tv/article589512.ece?service=print).

8. This analysis was a student project (PSY 1007), carried out by Martine Romstad and Nina Nogulic spring 2007. The two of them analyzed 24 hours broadcast by Cartoon Network.

9. NRK Aktivum AS was, according to their webpage, "established in 1997 as a fully owned daughter company of the Norwegian Broadcasting Corporation in order to take care of the commercial aspects of NRKs business".

10. This is from the article "NRK must be cleansed from commerce" (my translation) in the Net Magazine Vox Publica (http://voxpublica.no/2007/08/nrk-ma-renses-for-kommersen). Nyborg was also the leader of the Committee that wrote: NOU: 2001:6, *Oppvekst med prislapp? Om kommersialisering og kjøpepress mot barn og unge* (Growing up with a price tag? About commercialization and purchasing pressure toward children and youth).

11. See the article "Ny guttekanal fra Disney" (New Boy's Channel from Disney, see http://www.barnevakten.no/sider/tekst.asp?side=26455).

12. Typically, the same spots appear again and again, and they can even be followed by a countdown watch on the screen, which shows the days, minutes and seconds left before the next Cheetah Girls CD will be in the store.

13. A journalist in the Norwegian Central Bureau of statistics wrote: "Donald Duck has been and is still is, without comparison, the most popular cartoon magazine. One out of three people read the cartoon when they read cartoon magazines. Regardless of gender, age and region this is the most popular cartoon magazine." (Pedersen, 2004; my translation, see: http://www.ssb.no/vis/magasinet/slik_lever_vi/art-2004-04-27-02.html). The numbers are obvious: In 2007, the number distributed of Donald Duck & Co published was 111,367 and in 2006 this number was 117,926. In comparison, during its best years, in 1979 and 1986, the magazine sold on average 250,000 issues (cf. Hagen, 2001).

14. Hannah Montana/Miley Cyrus has had several major concert tours that have attracted a huge audience. In Norway, the concert film played in several cities, in Disney 3D.

15. Adresseavisen 28.1.2008, s. 33.

16. The goal of many brand builders is to create emotional brand loyalty. This goal is based on the assumption that customers can establish a psychological or emotional "attachment", a feeling of duty and faithfulness toward the brand"(Bjørn Ulvær, see http: www.markup.no/att/sCFt45t7.pdf, my translation).

References

Arnett, Jeffrey J. and Jennifer L. Tanner (eds.) (2005) *Emerging Adults in America: Coming of Age in the 21ˢᵗ Century*. Washington: The American Psychological Association.

Bjørnebekk, Ragnhild (1992) Barn og kommersielt fjernsyn [Children and commercial television]. I: Sand,Therese og Wenche Walle-Hansen (red.) *Sosialisering i dag* [Socialization Today]. Ad Notam Gyldendal. 164-199.

Blindheim, Trond (2004) Forbruk som lyst og nytelse [Consumption as desire and pleasure". In: Blindheim, T.; T.Ø. Jensen; F. Nyeng; & K.F. Tangen, *Forbruk. Lyst, Makt, Iscenesettelse eller Mening?* [Consumption, Desire, Power, Staging or Meaning?] Oslo: Cappelen forlag as., p. 139.

Borch, Anita (2003) Reklamens makt i en digital hverdag [The Power of Advertizing in a Digital Everyday Life]. In: Engelstad, Fredrik and Guro Ødegård (Red.): *Ungdom, makt og mening* [Youth, Power, and Meaning]. Oslo: Gyldendal Akademisk.

Borch, Anita (1998) *Reklame rettet mot barn på Internett: en forstudie* [Advertizing towards children on the Internet. A pilot study]. Arbeidsrapport nr. 2, Statens institutt for forbruksforskning (SIFO).

Brusdal, Ragnhild (2001) *Hva bruker barn og unge penger på? En beskrivelse av ulike forbruksmønstre blant barn og unge i alderen 8-24 år* [What are children and youth using money for? A description of different consumption patterns among children and youth age 8-24 years]. Arbeidsnotat, Statens Institutt for forbruksforskning.

Brusdahl, Ragnhild (1999) *Kommersielt trykk og markedsføring mot barn og unge.* [Commercial Pressure and Marketing towards Children and Youth]. Arbeidsrapport nr. 5, Statens Institutt for forbruksforskning (SIFO).

Buckingham, David (2009) *The Impact of the Commercial World On Children's Wellbeing: Report of an Independent Assessment.* For the Department for Children, Schools and Families and the Department for Culture, Media and Sport. (http://publications.dcsf.gov.uk/default.aspx?Page Function=productdetails&PageMode=publications&ProductId=DCSF-00669-2009)

Buckingham, David (2001) United Kingdom: Disney Dialectics: Debating the Politics of Children's Media Culture. In: Wasko, Janet; Mark Phillips and Eileen Mehan (eds.) *Dazzled by Disney? The Global Disney Audience Project.* London and New York: Leichester University Press.

Bøe, Ida Lovise (2009) *Vi skal skape en verden hvor barn vokser og er viktige. NRKs posisjonering overfor barn* [We are to create a world where children develop and are important. NRK's positioning towards children]. Master thesis, NTNU.

Drotner, Kirsten (2003) Medier og dannelse i en global verden [Media and cultivation in a global world]. In: Selmer-Olsen and Sando: *Mediebarndommen* [Media Childhood]. Trondheim: DMMHs publikasjonsserie. Nr. 2/2003.

Hagen, Ingunn and Thomas Wold (2009) *Mediegenerasjonen. Barn og unge i det nye medielandskapet* [The Media Generation. Children and Youth in the New Media Landscape]. Oslo: Det Norske Samlaget.

Hagen, Ingunn (2004/1998) *Medias publikum. Frå mottakar til brukar?* [Media's audience. From receiver to user]. Oslo: Ad Notam Gyldendal

Hagen, Ingunn (2001) Norway: Norwegian Memories of the Disney Universe. In: Wasko, Janet; Mark Phillips and Eileen Mehan (eds.) *Dazzled by Disney? The Global Disney Audience Project.* London and New York: Leichester University Press. P. 222-257.

Hake, Karin (2003) Five-Year-Olds' Fascination for Television. A Comparative Study. In: Rydin, Ingegerd (eds.) *Media Fascinations. Perspectives on Young People's Meaning Making.* Göteborg: Nordicom. s. 31-51.

Harris, Richard J. (1999) *A Cognitive Psychology of Mass Communication.* London: Lawrence Erlbaum Associates.

Kjørstad, Ingrid (2000) *Barn og Internett-reklame. En studie av 12-åringers forståelse og kunnskaper om reklame på Internett* [[Children and Internet Advertising. A study of 12 year olds' understanding and knowledge about advertising on the Internet]. Rapport nr. 7-2000. Oslo: Statens Institutt for forbruksforskning (SIFO).

Lindstrom, M. and Seybold, P.B. (2003) *Brand Child. Remarkable Insight into the Minds of Today's Global Kids and their Relationship with Brands.* UK: Kogan Page Ltd

Montgomery, Kathryn C. (2007) *Generation Digital. Politics, Commerce, and Childhood in the Age of the Internet. Cambridge,* MA & London: The MIT Press.

Nakken, Øyvind (2007) *Captain Sabertooth – Adventurous Brand Loyalty.* MA Thesis, Department of Psychology, Norwegian University of Science and Technology.

Rydin, Ingegerd (2003) *Media Fascinations. Perspectives on Young People's Meaning Making.* Göteborg: Nordicom.

Schor, Juliet B. (2004) *Born to Buy: The Commercialized Child and the New Consumer Culture.* New York: Schribner.

Strasburger, V., Wilson, B. and Jordan, A. (2009) *Children, Adolescents and the Media.* Second Edition. Sage Publications, Thousand Oaks, California.

Tønnessen, Elise Seip (2000) *Barns møte med TV. Tekst og tolkning i en ny medietid* [Children's meeting with TV. Text and interpretation in a new media age]. Oslo: Universitetsforlaget.

Tingstad, V. (2006) *Barndom under lupen. Å vokse opp i en foranderlig mediekultur* [Examing Childhood. Growing up in a Changing Media Culture]. Oslo: Cappelen Akademisk Forlag.

Tobin, Joseph (2004) *Pikachu's Global Adventure. The Rise and Fall of Pokèmon.* Durham and London: Duke University Press

Wasko, Janet; Mark Phillips and Eileen Mehan (eds.) *Dazzled by Disney? The Global Disney Audience Project.* London and New York: Leichester University Press.

Advertising Directed at Children
Harmless Trifle or Gold Mine?

Gunilla Jarlbro

Advertising directed at children is prohibited in Sweden, as it is in Norway. The salient points of the Swedish ban are that advertising must not be designed to capture the attention of children under 12, nor be broadcast in direct connection to children's programming, whether before, after or during commercial breaks in the programme. The regulations apply only to channels that broadcast from Sweden, while channels that broadcast from other countries are subject to regulations in the broadcast country. The Swedish ban has triggered keen interest abroad. Various commercial actors on the European level are devoting a good deal of time and energy to the issue, probably because they see the ban as a threat. Nowadays, however, focus should not be limited to television commercials; we should also be looking at advertising that shows up on the Internet. The latter form of advertising is also considerably more sophisticated than the former.

Why do advertisers spend so much money to design and direct advertising to children as a target group? Does advertising influence our children, or is advertising a harmless trifle, not worth the bother of any special attention? Even as enormous sums are spent on advertising, many commercial actors claim that advertising has very little impact. Research findings can be conflicting, and those debating the issue can always find arguments to support their position, whether they are for or against advertising to children. For every political or financial interest, it seems at least one research report can always be found to suit the ulterior motive. The question naturally arises: how can some research on advertising directed at children support its proponents, while other research supports its detractors? The most central research questions in this context are most likely the following: First, at what age are children able to differentiate between advertising and other media content? Second, at what age do children develop the ability to understand the intent of advertising? These two questions are important because it is only when children can differentiate between advertising and other content and understand the intent of advertising that we no longer need regard them as helpless victims of the consumer society.

The explanation for why research findings can support both advocates and opponents of children's advertising can be found in the fact that the majority of studies pertaining to children and advertising have been controlled by extra-scientific interest groups – interest groups whose opinions on whether advertising directed at children should be banned or regulated diverge. This has allowed conflicting perspectives to control the research or study process, which has in turn led to conflicting results. European research on children and advertising since the mid-1990s seems to have been concentrated primarily to England and Germany and, to a certain extent, Denmark. However, when it comes to spreading information about the issue of children and advertising in general and television advertising in particular, the focal point shifts to Belgium.

That it should be easy to identify advertising as advertising is an important principle of democracy. After all, a critical stance is predicated on understanding that one is being exposed to advertising. If we refer only to the intra-scientific studies performed in this area, we find that, although certain studies maintain that children age 3-6 have developed sophisticated "advertising savvy", there is no empirical evidence that this "savvy" is a natural element of the cognitive repertoires of very young children. Furthermore, it seems that most children do not develop the ability to explain and understand the underlying purposes of advertising until they are 10-12 years old. From this perspective, advertising directed at children is not a harmless trifle, because children under the age of 10-12 do not even understand that they are being exposed to commercial influences. I mentioned that online advertising is incredibly sophisticated, and the question thus becomes whether having reached the ripe old age of 12 is sufficient to understand that one is the target of commercial influence. Online advertising is definitely not a harmless trifle, at least not when counted in money. In a November 2008 forecast, the Swedish Institute for Advertising and Media Statistics predicted that 2009 would be the third-best year ever for online advertising, and estimated that online advertising revenues would outstrip revenues from television advertising that same year.

A report on Nordic marketing channels aimed at children and adolescents[1] outlines various types of marketing channels and clearly shows a strong increase in online search-based marketing. In addition to banners, Internet users are offered wallpapers and screensavers produced by advertising agencies. Advertising in chat programmes consists of links and information about specific products. Another phenomenon known as "ghost chatting" is a way to generate buzz and thus advertise a product without revealing the source. Commercials are also spread on the Internet in a process called "seeding". The idea behind these commercials is that people who see the spot will like it and forward it to their friends. These marketing channels are joined by a variety of product-based games.

According to a 2008 report by the World Internet Institute on young Swedes and the Internet[2], Swedish families with children in the home are the most wired group in the population in terms of media technology. A full 94 percent of families with children in the home have access to the Internet.

The table shows that 20 percent of 3-year-olds and 50 percent of 5-year-olds used the Internet at least once in 2008. Among 9-year-olds, the share was above 90 percent, and from age eleven and up, virtually all Swedish children use the Internet.

Table 1. Internet usage among children and adolescents (age 3-16) in Sweden, 2008 (percent)

Age	Once or twice	At least once a week	Daily
3	21	15	3
4	28	15	4
5	51	30	7
6	70	55	14
7	73	55	15
8	75	56	20
9	92	68	30
10	94	88	54
11	98	92	69
12	98	93	74
13	99	98	81
14	99	99	86
15	99	99	86
16	99	99	89

Source: *Unga Svenskar och Internet 2008*, Olle Findahl & Sheila Zimic, World Internet Institute, December 2008.

In one recent study of adolescents and online advertising performed in Sweden,[3] the researchers conclude that young people are not particularly critical of modern advertising in general. Nor are they aware of or particularly critical of marketing methods, or of the fact that young consumers are being used to spread commercial messages among groups of friends.

Two characteristics of messages that can potentially trigger a desired action have been well-established within communication studies: simple content and delivery as close as possible to the action in time and space, in what is called a *point of action display*. Examples of this kind of marketing ploy include stickers and posters, as well as banners on websites.

As shown above, this strategy is already found on the Internet, and especially in online communities. In plain language, the strategy plays out as follows. If, for instance, I write to my online friends, "I'd love to go shopping this week, but I'm broke", one or more banners offering loans will instantly appear. There is no question that this is a gold mine for advertisers, because it makes it possible to tailor advertisements to each and every Internet user. In a nutshell: the sad see ads for anti-depressants, dieters are fed advertising for diet pills, the poor are offered text loans, etc. Whether or not this approach is an invasion of the privacy of citizens is an issue that should be kept at the forefront of debate, and most importantly, awareness of these strategies should be raised among consumers of all ages, young and old.

Notes

1. *Markedsføringskanaler til børn og unge i Norden, Kortlægning med fokus på nye markedsføringskanaler*, Henrik Busch, Steen Knudsen and Michael Thim, Initiative Universal Media, Copenhagen, Tema Nord 2006:572.
2. *Unga Svenskar och Internet 2008*, Olle Findahl & Sheila Zimic, World Internet Institute, December 2008.
3. Sandberg, H (2010) (Tema Nord report series 2010:502) *"Reklam funkar inte på mig…" Unga, marknadsföring och Internet"* ["Advertising doesn't work on me…" Young people, marketing and the Internet"].

Fandom, New Media, Participatory Cultures

Irma Hirsjärvi

Fandom – a special interest in something, being a fan of something – is simply put an intense relation to something: a poet or poems, the artist or an artwork, an athlete or a sport, a historical time period such as the Middle Ages, a style, a band or a certain musical style, a star or a media figure. Surprisingly, these relationships have their beginning in early childhood and they include ethical and ideological choices on many levels. From these relationships stem intellectual, emotional, and social commitments and movements. When this kind of activity is combined with the multiple uses of new media in the lives of children and young adults, we see the rise of new kind of strategies in participatory cultures. The multiple possibilities for individual activities have created revolutionary ways of participation in the everyday life of children and young people.

American media researcher Henry Jenkins (2006), in his extensive research on fandom and converging media cultures, has pointed out how fandom activities are created by national and international networks. These networks present completely new kinds of intellectual networks that employ media for both individual and social purposes and that use media convergence greatly to their advance. These networks are available to and also widely participated in by children and young adults.

The background for the present article is in the research on networks of Finnish science fiction fans, the transcultural influences connected to them, fans' relationship to science fiction culture and their membership in a fan network. Originally this group, which in the 1970s consisted of a few adults and teenagers, has become a nationwide network of fans: in other words, a fandom. Among diverse other activities, it provides writing courses and competitions to referee practices and multiple publication opportunities. The network has affected the Finnish literary culture in a visible way; the change can be followed through the past five decades. It demonstrates the power of participatory cultures on the levels of production and personal expression. Furthermore, it presents other alternative actions, for example the use of traditional marketplaces (Hirsjärvi 2009).

Similar processes are evident in the cultures of children and young people around the globe. The present article will concentrate on examples of networks of Finnish children and young adults. Four example networks are used: the first two are fandoms of literary genres, the third is a fandom of Japanese popular culture, and the last is a Finnish movie fan group, which has created a network of independent movie makers. All these networks are Finnish, and all have strong connections to international networks focused on similar interests. However, these networks represent a very small percentage of the world's children, and they are located in a Nordic welfare society; this is particularly evident when it comes to the availability of information and technology, and the opportunity to use them. The circumstances of these well-connected and well-situated children differ from those of the "disconnected and unequal" (Reguillo 2009) – children whose situation is less fortunate. The possibilities for international and transnational participatory cultures can be regarded as encouraging examples of the changes in store for the future culture of children and young adults. They offer insights into the organizing practices children use in their everyday lives, and may help us understand the dynamics of their uses of media.

Finnish fans of science fiction culture: two generations

The Nordic scale of this already international phenomenon, fandom – which is simultaneously a global, local, glocal and transcultural movement – was revealed in the previously mentioned research project concerning the networks of Finnish science fiction fans (Hirsjärvi 2009). The group in question was rather small, around 120 fans, out of whom twenty active members of fandom were interviewed. The purpose of the project was to study the personal experiences of fandom and the meaning-making processes of fan experiences, all in the larger context of the science fiction genre. In this case, it was again revealed how "personal is political" – and even a "matter of economy".

The network of Finnish science fiction fandom was created with considerable help from Sweden. Yet during the following decades, the great differences between the practices of Finnish and other Nordic SF fandom networks became evident. In Finland, new kinds of practices were created rapidly and efficiently. Whereas in Sweden the fandom could be described as a closed network of hardcore fans, in Finland the activities were open to everyone. As a result, through its openness and visibility in all media, Finnish SF fandom has in fact influenced Finnish publishing of fantasy and science fiction. This has resulted in a vast difference in the amount of publication and funding of fantastic literary genres between Sweden and Finland, as well as the international visibility of these genres. Since the 1970s, the cultural and economic impact of the small group of Finnish SF fans compared to the position of the fantastic literature in

Finland has been quite remarkable. The research shows that a network of fans – the fandom – with an ability to use new media is a powerful tool in the hands of young people (Hirsjärvi 2009).

During the research project, the focus was on the small network of fans, who were originally mostly schoolchildren and students networking in the communities of the biggest cities in Finland. The interviews showed how remarkably early the interest in these fantastic genres had began (often in the early teens or even before school) – and how passionate it had remained. It was also striking how lonely the children had felt with their own special interest, and how important it had been for them to find people with similar interests. Finding the fandom as a teenager or as a young adult had been a remarkable experience. Meetings of adult fans included social activities: chatting in the regular pub meetings, publishing fan magazines and arranging multiple science fiction events and conferences, as well as writers' workshops and writing competitions. Children evolved from individual lonely fans into a group of organized and specialized people who were strongly connected by their similar interests, and who worked with innovative enthusiasm.

These facts, together with the research of Henry Jenkins, help us to ask questions regarding the Finnish field of science fiction and fantasy fandom from a totally new viewpoint, and to rethink the age factor in fandom research. It appeared that the childhood factor was mostly missing from fandom research. The early interest in a genre that was simultaneously connected to a scientific worldview and a fantastic imagination seemed to be something very important. The key issue appeared to be that in SF fandom, motivation for participating in fandom activities arises from one's childhood experiences, and that the social, productive, and ideological spheres cannot be separated in the meaning-making processes (Hirsjärvi 2009).

This idea was only developing, and at the beginning of 2003, it was unclear how these research results gathered from a small group of Finnish hardcore SF fans would and could be generalized. At that point, a brand-new website, Risingshadow.net, was opened for the fans of fantastic literature. On average, 94 people joined the site every month. Currently (in March 2010), Risingshadow.net has 2379 registered, regular users; 2.5 users join the site every day, and 73 new messages are sent daily. The site offers hundreds of reviews of Finnish and translated books, and information on their authors. The front page lists current literary events in SF and fantasy fandom as well as the publication dates of upcoming books. This was a new kind of fandom in both science fiction and fantasy.

The striking aspect was the age structure of the site's users. Even though their age varies between seven and seventy, the average age has been around 14–16 years, even lower. The users of Risingshadow.net came from all over the country, from small villages and the countryside, the east, west and north of Finland, not only from densely populated Southern parts and larger cities. These web pages have become a center of a literary culture, created by librarians, but updated, enhanced and co-built by young SF and fantasy fans.

Risingshadow.net offered – and continues to offer – children and young adults from all over the country the possibility to meet and to network with those who

135

share the same interests. The website is a platform for organizing, analyzing, and spreading information; it provides a space for discussions among people of all ages, and it offers visibility to young writers, artists, and knowledge seekers. It comments, criticizes, advises and supports. It is a place of participation on the social, emotional, and organizational level and on the level of artistic and intellectual expression. Including this new fandom in my research by making additional interviews, I was able to verify that many of the basic themes found in research results on fandom experiences of the "old" fandom were suited to this younger fandom as well.

Children and young people in the Anime and Manga Network

Three years later, a totally new 'fantastic' fandom – the network of anime and manga fans – had become the most influential new wave of youth culture since the rock culture in Finland. The Finnish anime fans were even younger than the people in Risingshadow.net – seldom over eighteen years old, on average in their early or mid-teens. They adopted their specialized organizational practices from the fans of Japanese popular culture abroad (Valaskivi 2009).

The cultural interaction between these three fandoms is intriguing: the people of Risingshadow.net created the site totally independent of the "old SF fandom". Conversely, the anime and manga culture was actually introduced in Finland largely through major science fiction magazines as well as the SF events. The Finnish Anime society was founded by the very same SF people, and the first national anime event Animecon was organized by the science fiction society of Turku. Nevertheless, anime fans have created their own culture. The multiple forms of anime fan culture that have flourished around the country during the past ten years – manga series, J-rock (Japanese popular music) events, or Lolita meetings, as well as the publishing of the hugely successful Anime magazine – have been produced entirely without the help of the 'old' SF fandom (Valaskivi 2009).

As Katja Valaskivi observes, the fandom of Japanese popular culture changes drastically the ways in which an anime fan uses media (Valaskivi 2009). In the interviews conducted in Finland in 2009 for the Global Comparative Research on Youth Media Participation project (www.jyu.fi/ymp), it was possible to verify her findings (Hirsjärvi & Tayie 2010). Whereas the people of the "old fandom" of Finnish science fiction were interested in social matters, scientific explora-tion, gender and mind games and literature, the interests of the 'anime children' focused on the body, sexuality, experience, and visual culture. This does not mean that anime and manga fandom cannot be a political, personal experi-ence. Especially the anime fandom in Finland – as well as abroad – could be described as the biggest queer project in history. Anime and manga websites and events create a special space of expression and freedom. The fandom has strong connections to the "multisexual" experiences of SF fandom, which can be analyzed in terms of performativity, as suggested by Judith Butler (Butler 1993), or as an overall rewriting of the conventions of sex and gender in fantastic cultures (Butler & Delany 2008, Valaskivi 2009). All these could also be regarded as "heterotopias" in a Foucauldian sense: places that are private but not closed, spaces that offer exceptional Utopian experiences surrounded by an everyday world with its rules, in slices of time like weekend conventions, moments of writing in discussion groups, listening, creating to or adding anime music videos to Youtube (Foucault 1967).

Connecting kids and adults

What connects these networks – the 'old' Finnish SF fandom, members of Risingshadow.net, and the Finnish anime fandom – are their intense relations to certain cultural phenomena. All these cultures are based on foreign – not Finnish – culture, and thus they have become transcultural phenomena. Each network employs new media as a platform for their new ideas and practices. The interest in each of these cultural phenomena arises (in plural) from each child's personal interests. The fans use fandom for their individual needs and as a tool for their identity work. In this process, the children and young adults are truly motivated because their participation in the fandom activities arises from personal interests; they learn more efficiently than through traditional educational organizations. They learn by doing – by editing and creating homepages and documents, publishing and translating and building international relations.

Resistance and overriding

The network operates with a speed and passion commercial companies could never manage. They discover how to affect people. Fan fiction – stories distributed mostly through the Internet, based on existing movies, TV series, or other types of fiction and assimilating new storylines or characters – is a good example of this kind of activity. Fan fiction is a form of literature that is written and produced both by challenging and overriding the traditional production lines of literature. It is a huge intercultural phenomenon – as is shown on websites like Fanfiction.net, which provides, among other things, novels or series of novels based on Harry Potter storylines, Jane Austen's novels, Star Trek or anime and manga stories, not to mention multiple other sources. The language is usually English, and the networks are international and Internet-based. Thus the writers have an online connection to each other. Together they are also strong.

In his book *Media Convergence* (2006), Henry Jenkins introduces Heather Lawver, who became an editor of the internationally distributed Internet journal *The Daily Prophet* (www.dprophet.com) in her teens. She is one of the millions of Harry Potter fans, and one of many who act as writers or producers, challenging copyright laws and publishing companies. For example, eager Chinese fans translated the 600 pages of the sixth Harry Potter novel, *Harry Potter and the Half-blood Prince* (2005), in two weeks from English into Canton Chinese and distributed it online. Fans have also banded together to fight big corporations for their rights to read and write the texts they love – with success. It is no wonder that, in the research on markets and culture politics, the gift economy structure of fandoms as networks has become a hot topic, as they are also the most innovative area of hybrid economy and the third sector. This campaign – one of many – made the publishing company check their policy of copyright and marketing, and also apologize for their actions and cancel the pending lawsuits (Jenkins 2006, Taalas & Hirsjärvi 2004, Taalas & Hirsjärvi 2008).

A Finnish example of fan fiction is *Star Wreck*, which has its origins in the American TV series Star Trek (later also a series of movies, cartoons, animation etc.) created by Gene Roddenberry. This innovative project was originally an action animation story created by using simple computer graphics designed by a couple of schoolboys. *Star Wreck* subsequently grew into several digital film projects. The group continued their work, creating new versions of the story, learning and seeking information about computer graphics and blue screen technology. Finally, after seven years of explorative work of "five students and unemployed people", together with 300 extras, created a full-length motion picture called *Star Wreck* by using "a bit of blue linoleum and few home computers" – practically without funding (StarWreck 2010). Without the intense enthusiasm for Star Trek and other science fiction, this project probably would not have survived for so long.

The organizing practices of the production of *Star Wreck* created an entirely new method of movie making, which was the subject of remarkable interest from international film companies and filmmakers – and brought funding for the production of a new movie. The project begun by Finnish school kids and later students created a way of filmmaking that employs homemade special effects and blue screen technique in a revolutionary manner. It produced the most internationally successful Finnish movie ever. This fan production has spread through the Internet and commercial DVD releases around the world. Success was followed by the largest international funding ever to a Finnish production, for the next movie, *Iron Sky* (Star Wreck 2010).

Why should this particular project have any repercussions for discourses on children and media? Is it simply because it reveals the potential and organizing practices of children's media use – and the meaning-making processes behind them? Yes, it truly is an interesting field of media participation. Moreover, in and through fandoms, young people and children learn to use the global possibilities of new media, which override the formal education and traditional practices: because their special interests drive them to do it. These changes in organizing practices are important areas of research regarding children and media, in examining the individual processes of meaning-making and identity formation while being strongly connected to empowering processes the new media may offer.

Fandom in the everyday life of children

The special interests have arisen from the local, national and international organizational practices of transcultural fandoms and the individual meaning-making processes of fans. The intercultural fan practices are scrutinized as part of the comparative research on Global Comparative Youth Media Participation project, run by Finnish media researcher Sirkku Kotilainen. In this project, both qualitative and quantitative data on the media participation of young people between 11–18 years will be gathered in six countries from different continents. The special focus is on children's own choices and activities. Information about the meaning-making processes, similar to those described in earlier examples of SF, fantasy and anime fans, will be collected and participation with the media, through the media and by the media will be examined.

Fandom practices teach children and young adults to use new media. In this position, they are consumers (using, purchasing, etc.), on the one hand, and producers (writing, editing, etc.), on the other; however, they are also connected to many other positions through their fandom. These positions are described in the picture below, which is based on the ideas of Abercrombie and Longhurst (1998) concerning fandom in relation to the different aspects and levels of consuming and producing, and combined with Lacy's (1995) idea about the differing but many times simultaneous positions of an artist of public art: the artists roles of activist, experimenter, analyzer and reporter in her work. In this picture, all the spheres are on the move, as the fan uses the different positions for different purposes.

Picture 1. Fandom positions

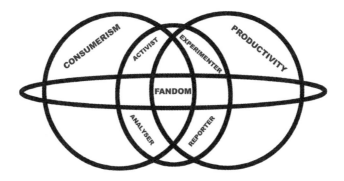

This picture also connects some of the questions of fandom research (basically questions about participation, media uses, community, and productivity) to the basic questions of children and young adults' participation and civic actins with media. It can be said that the present article discusses "Youth, communication and social change", which is the subtitle of Rossanna Reguillo's article "The Warrior's code" (Reguillo 2009). In the article, she reminds us of the essential understanding of the diversity of the lives, expectations, and possibilities of children around the world, and presents three examples of media participation, resistance, and political activity among young people. She describes the new possibilities of negotiating with the elite power, and the possibility of great refusal: "no". The three examples she uses are the so-called student's Penguin Revolution in Chile in 2006, the blogosphere that offers an alternate space for communication, and youth participation in political moments like the War in Iraq.

In her discussion on bloggers, Reguillo observes that, first of all, being visible in the world of Internet strengthens the self as author, gives a voice to independent speakers and meaning to their names, making the writing personally relevant. Second, she shows how the blogosphere brings "subjective, personal, emotional, everyday matter shaping politics", when everyday life and the public world emerge. She also discusses how the global, transcultural, and multicultural nature of the blogosphere expands our understanding of local issues (Reguillo 2009). Furthermore, in these blogospheres, the organizational practices of fan networks themselves create new politics. Reguillo's examples come from Latin American countries, where the diversity and the political situation, including the life of children, differ drastically from life in the Nordic countries. In both worlds, the diversity of the life of children and young adults is visible, but the organizational practices include similarities in meaning-making processes.

Studying children's and young adults' relationships to and in fandoms is important for many reasons. As fandom is essentially about processes in the psychological, aesthetic, and ideological spheres of personal experience and is usually formed at an early age (Hirsjärvi 2009); we need to look at it in order to understand the possibilities for participatory cultures among children and young adults. Being a member of a fandom means being a critic; it means opportunities for self-expression, social networking, and identity work. It provides pleasure, togetherness, and joy in a heterotopia. All of these factors are strongly connected with the ideological spaces or "ideoscapes" that are not independent of the economic or political factors of everyday life (Appadurai 1990). I strongly emphasize Reguillo's thesis about the ways in which children and young people use media in negotiations with the power elite, and the ways in which the new media help to create tools for political activity. In these negotiations, fandom is a link between the personal and the political – also when it comes to children – and combined with new media, it has considerable power.

References

Abercrombie, Nicholas & Longhurst, Brian (1998) *Audiences. A Sociological Theory of Performance and Imagination*. London: Sage.

Acker, Joan (1990) Hierarchies, Jobs, Bodies: A Theory of Gendered Organizations. *Gender & Society* 4: 2, 139-158.

Acker, Joan (2004) Gender Capitalism and Globalization. *Critical Society* 30: 1, 17-14.

Appadurai, Arjun (1990) Disjuncture and Difference in the Global Cultural Economy. *Public Cult* 1 (2), 21-24.

Butler, Judith (1993) *Bodies that Matter. On the Discursive Limits of "Sex"*. New York: Routledge.

Butler, Octavia & Delany, Samuel R. (2008) Women, Art and Culture. An Introduction to Women's Studies. Butler & Delany Teach Us how to Read and Use sf." http://wac250spr08.blogspot.com/2008/03/how-we-read-sf-women-in-sf-histories.html

Gherardi, Silvia (1994) The Gender we Think, the Gender We Do In Our Everyday Organizational Lives. *Human Relations* 47: 6, 591-610.

Hirsjärvi, Irma (2009) *Faniuden siirtymiä. Suomalaisten science fiction fanien verkostot* (Mediations of fandom. The networks of the Finnish sf fandom). Jyväskylä: Research Centre for Contemporary Culture.

Hirsjärvi, I. & Tayie, S. (2010, forthcoming) Youth Media Participation. Notions of the Methodological Approach of the Interviews in an International Comparative Project.

Jenkins, Henry (2006) *Convergence Culture. Where Old and New Media Collide.* New York: New York University Press.

Lacy, Suzanne (1995) Debated Territory: Towards a Critical Language for Public Art. Teoksessa Suzanne Lacy (toim.) *Mapping the Terrain. New Genre Public Art*, p. 171-188. Seattle, Washington: Bay Press.

Reguillo, Rossana (2009) The Warriors Code? Youth, Communication and Social Change. In Thomas Tufte & Florencia Enghel (eds.) *Youth Engaging with World. Media Communication and Social Life*, 21-39.

Suoninen, Annikka (2003) Harmillisen loistava sarja. Babylon 5 nuorin silmin. Teoksessa Tuija Modinos ja Annikka Suoninen (toim.) *Merkillinen media. Tekstit nuorten arjessa.* 205-204. Jyväskylä: SOLKI. [Annoyingly Glorious TV-series. Babylon 5 Through the Young Eyes]. In Tuija Modinos and Annikka Suoninen (eds.) Peculiar Media. Texts in the Everyday Life of Young People.

Taalas, Saara & Hirsjärvi, Irma (2008) Fanit ja seuraajat. Tieteiskirjallisuuden kuluttamisen organisoituminen. [Fans and followers. The Organizing of the Consuming of Ccience fiction]. In Kaarina Nikunen (eds.) *Fanikirja. Tutkimuksia nykykulttuurin fani-ilmiöistä.* (Fan book. Research on contemporary fandom). 200-224. Jyväskylä: Reseach Centre for Contemporary Culture.

Taalas, Saara L. & Hirsjärvi, Irma (2004) Risingshadow. Notes on the Fantastic Literature Fans and the Organizing of Consumption. Proceedings of the 22nd Standing Conference on Organizational Symbolism. Halifax, Canada.

Tufte, Thomas & Enghel, Florencia (2009) (eds.) *Youth Engaging with World. Media Communication and Social Life*, Yearbook. Göteborg: Nordicom, The International Clearinghouse on Children, Youth and Media.

Valaskivi, Katja (2009) *Pokemonin perilliset. Japanilainen populaarikulttuuri Suomessa.* [The Heritage of Pokemon, Japanese Popular Culture in Finland].University of Tampere, Department of Journalism. Publications A. 110 / 2009http://tampub.uta.fi/tiedotusoppi/978-951-44-7617-4.pdf

Internet sources

Star Wreck (2010) http://www.starwreck.com/introduction.php

Michel Foucault (1967) Of Other Spaces. Heterotopias. http://foucault.info/documents/heteroTopia/foucault.heteroTopia.en.html

Playfulness in Children's Media Usage

Pål Aarsand

Media usage is often described as fun, exciting and joyful. But when it comes to children's consumption of media, we see descriptions that follow two other lines of reasoning. First, media are presented as problematic and in need of restrictions and guidelines, which renders children's media usage negative and something to avoid. Second, when children and media are discussed in relation to education, media usage is viewed in terms of learning and education. For instance, it has been argued that by playing digital games, the child develops competence in terms of how to cooperate, think strategically, and manoeuvre in virtual landscapes (cf. Prensky 2001; Tyner 1998). Along this line, the status of children's media usage has been upgraded by describing the competences needed to handle media, such as digital literacy, computer game literacy, or new media literacy. In this way, learning and knowledge are introduced as aspects of media practices, while some media are considered edutainment. Such a view indicates that children's media usage is considered a tool with which one can gain something beyond the activity itself (cf. Dormann & Biddle 2009).

Common to both lines of reasoning is the tendency to forget or ignore children's playfulness in media practices. For instance, there is reason to believe that a media activity such as game play is something that children participate in because they find it fun, interesting and/or enjoyable. Claiming that media usage is fun and enjoyable does not mean it is not a serious activity, or an activity that is always good and fair. In the present text, I argue that fun and playfulness are important aspects of children's media practices. The present paper investigates children's use of new media in play *in situ* from the children's perspective and with a particular focus on playfulness.

Play, game play and interaction research

To be seen as play, participation in an activity has to be voluntary (e.g., Caillois 2001 [1958]). This means that one cannot be forced into play if the activity is to be considered play by all participants. Recent research on play and interaction emphasizes that play is an activity guided by locally negotiated and developed rules (Evaldsson 2004; M.H. Goodwin 1995). The interactional perspective on children's play has highlighted the relevance of aspects such as social hierarchies, gender, age, ethnicity, language use, and playfulness in relation to language use. Playfulness, which is of particular interest in the present paper, is usually discussed in terms of speech play and the poetics of language, where rhymes, repetitions, singing, format tying and rhythm have been discussed. Research on children's play has been carried out on playgrounds, in the schools as well as at home (e.g., Thorne 1993, Evaldsson 2004, Goodwin 1990, Sutton-Smith 1997). Play is also an important concept in the study of children's use of digital games (e.g., Ito et al. 2008; Linderoth 2004). But game research often underlines that play and playfulness differ from games and game play because the latter, it is argued, are governed by the rules of the game. Game studies have largely focused on the tension between game design (the game) and the player (e.g., Juul 2005 2010; Pearce 2006; Salen & Zimmerman 2004) and in such studies, the relation between agency and game structure has been a central topic. Studies inspired by anthropology tend to highlight game play as communities of practice, where questions concerning how to enter, learn and handle the practice are of importance (Pearce 2009). When children's play is discussed with regard to digital technology and new media, whether we talk about it as dangerous or as necessary, it often becomes very serious (cf. Dormann & Biddle 2009; Pearce 2006). For instance, in research on game play and digital games, the notion of *serious games* has become a research field (cf. Buckingham & Scanlon 2003; Charsky 2010).

Serious games emphasize phenomena such as learning, health and social change. 'Serious games appropriate the medium of games, used initially to entertain, as a way to educate, persuade, or change behaviour' (Kafai, Heeter, Denner and Sun 2008, p. xxi). Research on serious games and children focuses mainly on what children learn when they are gaming and how this knowledge is related to school knowledge (Charsky 2010). The main idea is to make use of mechanisms similar to those used in digital games to encourage children to spend more time on schoolwork to improve their school performances and develop their knowledge (cf. Buckingham & Scanlon 2003; Kim, Park, & Baek 2009).

Related to this discussion is the idea that games are natural learning environments for children, which are thought to motivate them (e.g., Gee 2003; Prensky 2001). Serious games can also be seen as part of what has been called *edutainment*, which is a combination of education and entertainment, where learning is supposed to take place and be fun. For instance, successful digital games manage to keep the player playing. Put differently, the overall purpose within the field of edutainment has been to motivate the player by combining education with elements from entertainment. However, common to much of the research on edutainment is the emphasis put on the educational aspect, which has resulted in less focus on fun and playfulness in these practices (cf. Dorman & Biddle 2009; Charsky 2010). The notions of edutainment and serious games underline the importance of studying children's use of media in their everyday lives. But, in this connection, the notion of children's playfulness seems to be lacking in studies of children's media activities.

Theoretical stances

Three theoretical concepts are central in the present study of playfulness in children's media practices: participation framework, positioning and intertextuality. First, to study how play with media is accomplished, I have used the notion of *participation framework* (C. Goodwin & Goodwin 2004). The notion of participation framework moves beyond the individual and focuses on what is produced in the activity. Here, participation is described as 'actions demonstrating forms of involvement performed by parties within evolving structures of talk' (Goodwin & Goodwin 2004, p. 222). The main idea of participation framework builds on Goffman's (1974, 1981) work on activity frames. Activity frames can be described as a common understanding among the participants concerning what activities are taking place. Thus, the concept of participant framework implies a user perspective on how participants see and create a common understanding of the situation, for instance play. Activity frames are not to be seen as static, rather they are blurred, dynamic, and they change during the course of the interaction (Tannen & Wallat 1999 [1987]). Within activities, certain positions are established in relation to both participants and the activity as such. We can differentiate between ratified participants, who are part of the activity, and bystanders, who are not a legitimate part of the communication frame (Goffman 1981). The next concept, *positioning,* is an ongoing activity in which persons and objects are placed and enter, in relation to the main activity, for instance game play, and is used to understand the accomplishment of playfulness. Analytically, participation framework and positioning can be used to understand how activities are accomplished with regard to the participants' contributions and what consequences this has for the main activity.

Activity frames guide the participants in their actions, which means that positioning as well as actions are understood in light of these frames. For instance, yelling at adult men who are running around on a field is allowed and sometimes even expected when the activity is framed as football. This does not mean that activity frames exclude the outside world, rather they tell us that experiences from other activities may be treated differently within other activity frames. The last concept that is central in the present study is *intertextuality,* and it has been used to describe how a text incorporates and responds to other texts, or how one activity incorporates and responds to other activities. For analytical purposes, it is useful to differentiate between what have been called the horizontal and the

145

vertical dimensions of intertextuality (Fairclough 1992; Kristeva & Roudiez 1980). Horizontal intertextuality refers the fact that utterances exist in a dialogue with and relation to other utterances, in the same act, as can be seen in dialogues among the participants. In the present text, *vertical intertextuality,* which can be explained as relations between texts across time and space, has been used to explore the relation between different media activities. The concept of intertextuality has been debated when it comes to phenomena other than written words, for instance remediation (Bolter and Grusin 1999).

Playing with media

The use of media, digital games and the Internet is central in the media landscape of children in the Nordic countries (e.g., Medierådet 2006; Medietilsynet 2010). To understand children's use of digital media in their everyday lives, I will investigate how media are used with a particular focus on situations in which playfulness is displayed. The present study of children's playful use of media has been carried out on data from one week of videotaped observation of two first grade classrooms, two after-school centres and four homes. The focus children were 7-8 years of age. I have chosen examples that show variation in terms of media, place, time of the day and social constellations in children's use of new media. The examples have been transcribed according a modified version of conversation analysis (Heritage 1984) (see Appendix 1) and translated into English.

Throughout my data, children's playful use of new media seems to reoccur at home, school as well as after-school centres. In the present text, playfulness has been studied in detail in three different media practices. First, two boys game playing at home; second, four boys on the school playground playing Star Wars; third, two children using Skype at home.

Play and digital games

Playing digital games is one of the most popular media activities in Nordic children's lives. In the first example, I will study how playfulness is made a part of children's game play. We will meet two boys, Justus and Tobias, who are playing Lego Star Wars on Playstation 2 in Justus's living room. The boys have just customized their avatars, as 'Stormtroopers', and are now about to move into a hall while shooting at the enemy.

Excerpt 1. Game play

Participants: Justus (7) and Lukas (7)
Game: Lego Star Wars

1	Lukas	"Ple:::[:ase" ((Shoots against the enemy in a crowded corridor))
2	Justus	[OKAY I WILL <u>CON</u>TINUE (.) ATTACKING ((runs after the enemy))
3		(6) ((the boys continue to shoot))

4	Lukas	U:::rg
5		(1)
6	Lukas	No Justus they are not allowed to be there
7	Justus	Yes (.) but (.) I have dressed up (.) I'm only pretending
8	Lukas	I have also dressed up
9		(2)
10	Justus	But you dressed up naked you forgot the other clothes ((they both enter
11		a new area in the game))
12	Lukas	Ye:s
13		(2)
14	Lukas	You you are supposed to say "why have you forgot to put on your
15		clothes?"
16	Justus	Why have you forgot to put on your trouser and jumper?
17		(2)

Lukas starts out by changing his voice and begging for mercy, which is done on behalf of the enemy he is attacking (line 1) (cf. Aarsand & Aronsson 2009). In this way, he displays his own success in a crowded area. Justus responds by telling Lukas that he will continue the attack, thereby joining Lukas in the fight against the enemies. After a seven-second-long attack, Lukas suddenly claims that the enemy are in the wrong place (line 6). In this way, he is also telling Justus to get them out of there. Justus, who looks like a Stromtrooper, says he is dressed up and just pretending to be a Stormtrooper. Lukas, who also looks like a Stormtrooper, claims that he is also dressed up. Thus, Lukas aligns with Justus both by shooting at the same group of Stormtroopers and by stating that he has done the same as Justus, got dressed up. The talk about dressing up in the game comes right after the enemies have run away and the boys have got control of the area. Then, they walk through a door and enter another level in the game. At the same time as this happens, Justus says that Lukas forgot to put his clothes on, thereby he continues the talk on the topic of dressing up (line 10). The comment seems rather absurd because the avatar on the screen is all dressed in white armour. Lukas plays along and accepts Justus's description of the situation (line 12). After a second's pause, Lukas even elaborates on the formal scenario when he takes Justus's perspective and says 'You you are supposed to say "why have you forgot to put on your clothes" ' (lines 14-15). Justus slightly changes the format and says 'why have you forgot to put on your trouser and jumper?' (line 16). He repeats the words and the structure while he makes minimal changes in the utterance. This format tying (M. H. Goodwin 1990) becomes an elaboration of the topic, in which the description of the episode becomes more descriptive.

The activity is framed as game play both through their orientation to the game and how they are occupied with the task they are about to solve. When the boys have managed to chase away the enemies and gain control of the situation, Justus initiates a pretended situation, a role play, within the game. It could be claimed that this is an example of how activity frames are established within

147

other activity frames (Tannen & Wallat 1999 [1987]). The boys start to play with the idea of being dressed up, pretending to be a different character than they really are in the game. The boys are not only playing with their avatars, but they even pretend that the avatars are dressed up to look like somebody else and, thereby, cannot be identified by the enemy. In addition, Lukas is unsuccessful in dressing up in this play scenario, which causes reactions from the co-avatar controlled by Lukas, who wonders why he has no clothes on (lines 14-16). Here, the boys develop the story of their game play, which goes beyond the game setting of the scene. The playfulness takes place within an activity that is framed as a game with relatively strict rules guiding the players in what to do and how to act. The new activity, which takes place within the ongoing game play activity, deals with the primary activity frame. This has to be done; otherwise, the game will break down. There is reason to believe that it is no coincidence that the playfulness takes place in this calm part of the game, where the players do not need to give their full attention to the screen (cf. Aarsand & Aronsson 2009).

Media usage on the playground

Media saturate people's everyday lives and are used across geographical locations, social groups, age, ethnicity and gender. Media, such as digital games, are usually related to use of hard- and software, but several studies show that this is only part of the practice. For instance, it has been shown that talk about games is a central aspect of game play (Aarsand & Aronsson 2009). In the next excerpt, we will meet four boys who spend a great deal of time discussing computer games, particularly Star Wars.

In the next example, we will meet boys at a school called West. During the fieldwork, the boys used digital games at home (as we could see in Excerpt 1), at the after-school centre, in the classroom as well as on the playground. The school and the after-school centre were located next to each other, which meant that they shared playgrounds. Behind one of the school buildings, there was a large playground with a small forest, wood stocks, sand, stones, and hills where the children spent time between classes during the school days. When we enter Excerpt 2, the boys have been playing for almost 20 minutes. Konrad has just joined the group.

Excerpt 2. Media in play

Participants: Justus (7), Samuel (7), Konrad (7) and Robin (8)

1	Konrad	What are we playing?
2	Robin	We're playing Star Wars
3	Samuel	Who are you?
4	Konrad	I'm Chewbacca
5	Samuel	You may also be xxx (0.5) or some gorg? I will be=
6	Konrad	=xxx
7	Samuel	Obi-Wan Kanobi

8	Robin	Uhm:: I am Cody ((they all start walking))
...		
9	Samuel	Clone troopers I need to get a Clone trooper Clo::ne
10		troo::pers ((sings))
11	Justus	No xxx ((sings))
12	Samuel	Otherwise I won't have a cool time ((singing)) now I want to kill
13		(.) come and we have not had a mission in three months
14	Justus	Okay then
15	Samuel	Ye:::s ((claps his hands)) now we go
16	Justus	But we did not get a mission ((the boys run up the hill))
17	Samuel	No I know

Konrad starts by asking what they are playing and receives an answer that they are playing Star Wars (lines 1-2). Samuel immediately asks what character Konrad is, who answers Chewbacca (line 4). Samuel tries to come up with other and less central positions within the Star Wars universe (line 5), but no one supports his attempt to bring forward alternatives. In this way, Konrad enters the play, and he even gets a central character, Chewbacca, in the Star Wars universe. Then, the other boys also present themselves as important characters in Star Wars, Samuel as Obi-Wan Kanobi (line 7), Robin as Cody (line 8) and Justus has already claimed the position as Luke Skywalker before we enter the episode. Every time someone new enters this constellation of boys, Justus, Samuel and Robin, or asks what they are playing, they tell them that they are playing Star Wars before they present themselves with names of characters in Star Wars. The distribution of positions within the play seems to be of particular importance to the participants. This means that in order to obtain a name that works within the local practice of Star Wars on the playground, one needs to know what characters can be chosen. Knowing the Star Wars games and/or movies becomes a precondition and a resource in participating in play on the playground.

A minute later, Samuel states that he needs clone troopers, and even sings this out loud. Clone troopers are the main army within Star Wars. Justus aligns with Samuel by singing along (lines 11). Samuel keeps on singing, now that he needs soldiers, Clone troopers; otherwise he wants to have a good time. Note that Samuel talks from his position as Obi-Wan Kanobi when he complains that they have not had a mission in three months. The time aspect of three month signals that a long time as passed since they have done anything of interest (line 13). A central part of the narrative in Star Wars consists of a war between good and evil, where fighting and killing are part of the activity. Samuel's 'I want to kill' (line 12) can be seen as part of the script of how to behave like a Star Wars hero. Justus agrees that it is time to do something, which Samuel sees as support and he starts walking up the hill (line 15). Justus responds by saying that they still have no mission, thereby indicating that the situation actually has not changed before he follows the others. Samuel agrees with the fact that they do not have a mission, but still he follows the others.

Media, games and movies are used as resources in these children's play on the playground. The characters and stories from Star Wars work as resources in organizing and structuring the boys' play. Negotiations about identity positions within the Star Wars universe are the start of the play, and this matters when it comes to establishing a power structure and how the play will evolve. Central characters are more attractive to the participants and seem to have more influence on how the game is accomplished. It is no coincidence that Justus and Samuel have claimed two of the central characters in the movies, Luke and Obi-Wan, as they are the two who usually organize this kind of play on the breaks. Robin and Konrad seldom offer suggestions that have implications for how the play develops The playfulness can also be seen in how Samuel enters the position of Obi-Wan Kanobi and develops this character by singing like an actor in a musical. It could be claimed that Samuel not only makes intertextual references to movies and digital games, but also to other genres such as musicals or music videos. In Excerpt 1, we saw how the participants give their avatar life within the game; here, something similar occurs when they develop their characters and the play story beyond the movies and the games. While the subject positions that are available to the players are accurate with regard to the films and games, the accomplishment of the activity is playful and open to local initiatives and developments.

Exploring Skype in play

The Internet is an object of discussion among researchers as well as policy makers (Bolter & Grusin 2000, Jenkins 2006, Pearce 2009, European Commision 2006). It consists of a huge number of media phenomena in which children participate to varying degrees. In the next example, I will study how three children use the online phone program Skype. Skype allows users to talk while seeing each other on the computer screen. To use Skype with moving pictures, you need a computer with a camera and an Internet connection. The software is free to download and use.

Before we enter the next excerpt, the mother has logged on to Skype and phoned her brother's family. She has adjusted the camera so that people in front of the other computer are able to see those who are located in their living room. When we enter the excerpt, Nisse, the cousin, is located on the 'other side' of the phone, or on the screen. The mother, Anna (7) and Jon (5) are located in the living room where the video camera is located, and they have been talking to Nisse for about ten minutes. Anna has a pair of tongs in her hands and Nisse has a hammer. They both hold the tools up in the air in front of the camera.

Excerpt 3.

Participants: Jon (5), Anna (7), Mother, and Nisse (on the screen)
Place: Living room

1	Anna	I take yo:u (0.5) Nisse do you want me to pinch you ((clicking with a tongs))
2		(1.5)
3	Nisse	Hi hi a:::

4	Anna	I'm gonna pinch u:h [you ((Nisse reaches both hands into the air))
5	Jon	[I'm GONNA HIT YOU= ((hits in the air with the hammer))
6	Anna	Hands up or I shoot you ((holds the tongs to the screen))
7	Jon	Hands up or I will hi:t you ((holds the hammer up to the screen))
8	Anna	Down with your hands or I will shoot ((Nisse takes his hands down))
9		(3)
10	Anna	I'm gonna shoot now
11		(5)
12	XXX	Xxx ((Noise on the screen. Jon puts the hammer down))
13	Mother	Be very careful so that you don't hit anybody because they are very heavy=
14		((walks out of the room))
15	Nisse	=Hands up ((Anna raises her hands into the air))
16	Nisse	Take your hands down ((Jon and Anna raise their hands into the air))
17	Nisse	Down with your hands [down with your hands ((keep their hands up in the air))
18	Jon	[He he he ((Anna and Jon move their hands down and up while laughing))

Picture 1: lines 7-8   Picture 2: line 16   Picture 3: line 18

Anna shows her tongs to Nisse on the screen at the same time as she says she will pinch him (line 1). Nisse, who does not react to what Anna said, says hello before Anna once again says that she will pinch him (line 4). The timing of these turns may be due to the fact that the voice seems to be delayed, which often happens when using Skype. This means that persons talking on Skype have to talk one at the time and sometimes even wait for answers. In any event, Jon follows and tells Nisse that he is going to hit him with a hammer (line 5). Both Anna and Jon hold up the tools in front of the screen so Nisse can see them. The distance as well as the quality of Anna and Jon's voices indicates that these threats are not to be taken seriously, rather they are playing and using the possibility to interact across space. Anna continues with this play when she says 'hands up or I will shoot you' as she points to Nisse on the screen (line 6). Jon follows his sister and points with the hammer at the screen and says 'hands up or I will hit you' (line 7, picture 1). While Anna's tongs have turned into a gun, Jon's hammer still remains a hammer. Anna continues to use the tongs as a gun, and forces Nisse to put his hands down (line 8). Before the mother leaves the room, she tells the children to be careful with the tools because they may hurt each other. Suddenly the interaction pattern changes and Nisse shouts 'hands up' (picture 2) and 'hands down' (picture 3), which both Jon and Anna do (lines 15-16). Jon laughs while he and Anna try to follow the instructions given by Nisse, who is given control of the situation. If one of the children had found the situation unpleasant, there is reason to believe that s/he would have moved out of the camera's range, or even shut down the program.

What differentiates Skype from an ordinary phone are the moving pictures in real time. When using a camera, this kind of interaction becomes both possible and meaningful for the participants. Anna and Jon can see what Jon is doing and vice versa, which makes it possible for them to use their bodies in phone calls. In the present example, Skype is not only a medium for talk, but also a communication tool in which the children include other modalities such as bodies, gazes and objects. We can see that, through their playful use of Skype, the children test how the medium can be used in their everyday lives. We can also see that play and laughter are central ingredients of the present activity.

Children's use of media in play

The present article focuses on playfulness in three different media practices in Nordic children's lives: playing digital games, using media in play on the playground and using Skype. The main argument is that playfulness has several different functions in children's media practices. Digital games are an example of media that have often been described as an activity guided by strict rules that are part of the game design (Juul 2005, Salen & Zimmerman 2004), which means that how one should act and play is largely determined by game designers.

In the first example, we see how the participants, through jokes and role-play, elaborate on game play in a way that affects how they play the game. The boys have chosen avatars and have dressed these avatars up so that they could not be identified as the avatars they actually were, according to the player. It could be argued that when they play with the identity of their avatars, they do this with reference to the storyline of Star Wars, where the main characters on missions sometimes try to melt into the surroundings by dressing up. But, it could also be argued that use of the words 'dressing up', and not working 'under cover', shows how they handle and understand the game by making references to a well-known activity outside the game. Their playfulness develops the game play story by making richer descriptions of the avatars, their agenda, and the mission they are about to accomplish. Moreover, it could be argued that experiences from other media, as well as other play activities, are used to elaborate game play.

In the example from the playground, the opposite movement can be seen when the boys framed their play as Star Wars, using characters and tools with intertextual references to digital games and movies in their play. The boys usually discussed possible characters and weapons, and they distributed positions within the play. Sometimes they remained in discussions and jokes about the different characters, at other times they made up stories independent of the game and the movies. This playful way of using media in everyday interaction underlines how media work as a resource in peer groups on the playground. It also indicates that having experience of popular media is of importance to participating in play. It has been argued that we are facing a media mix (Ito 2008), a notion that describes how products are found across different media, such as movies, books, games and websites. The idea of media mix also shows that media phenomena are no longer to be seen as activities located in one place. On the playground, children's playful use of the media phenomenon Star Wars shows how they mix experiences from different practices, as well as how they develop the Star Wars culture within the peer group (cf. Jenkins 2006). Playfulness seems to be of importance when it comes to how children accomplish play with media. Intertextual references seem to be central in this playfulness.

Playfulness has long been related to games and playgrounds. While playing digital games has been considered a problem, play on the playground has been considered positive and almost part of children's nature. With regard to children and digital media, play is not a concept that usually occurs in descriptions of such practices. Despite this, children have often been presented as early adopters: unafraid, natural and more competent users than adults are (Tapscot 1998, Gee 2003).

In Excerpt 3, we saw how children used Skype as a mediator in play. Skype with the camera made it possible to play in front of the screen while being seen, which is completely different from a regular phone conversation. This means that a new arena for play has been created, an arena that transgresses local space as the only place where face-to-face play may occur. Skype offers other possibilities for communication than other media such as phones, TV, and magazines, in that it is a multimodal communication environment. The joy and playfulness displayed in the children's use of Skype underline the activity as nonserious, as pretend and not for real. Playfulness is not only about showing tools and interacting with relatives and friends, but also a way for children to learn how to use the medium in meaningful ways in their everyday lives. In addition, playfulness can be seen as an aspect of media practice, in that the restrictions and possibilities of the media are learnt, for instance, when to talk and where to stand/sit in order to be seen.

In sum, playfulness is a central aspect of children's media practices, hands-on as well as hands-off media practices, and it takes place and is created irrespective of the media producers' intention. Playfulness, as part of media practices on the playground, shows how media serve as resources in accomplishing play. Moreover, media work as a tool that is modified, developed and explored through playful activities. Playfulness becomes a way of trying out media on the playground, in the peer-group, as well as in families. Playfulness is an aspect of children's media practices in which their agency and creativity are displayed. As such, in children's media practices, media are integrated into children's own situations.

References

Aarsand, P., & Aronsson, K. (2009) Response Cries and Other Gaming Moves: Toward an Intersubjectivity of Gaming. *Journal of Pragmatics*.

Bolter, J.D., & Grusin, R. (1999) *Remediation: Understanding New Media*. Cambridge, Mass.: MIT Press.

Buckingham, D., & Scanlon, M. (2003) *Education, Entertainment, and Learning in the Home*. Cambridge: Open University Press.

Caillois, R. (2001 [1958]) *Man, Play and Games*. Urbana and Chicago: University of Illinois Press.

Charsky, D. (2010) From Edutainment to Serious Games: A Change in the Use of Game Characteristics. *Games and Culture, 5*(2), 177-198.

Dormann, C., & Biddle, R. (2009) A Review of Humor for Computer Games: Play, Laugh and More. *Simulation & Gaming 40*(6), 802-824.

European Commision (2006) *The Ministerial Declaration on e-Inclusion*. Paper presented at the ICT for an Inclusive Society Conference, Riga.

Evaldsson, A.-C. (2004) Shifting Moral Stances: Morality and Gender in Same-Sex and Cross-Sex Game Interaction. *Research on Language & Social Interaction, 37*(3), 331-363.

Fairclough, N. (1992) *Discourse and Social Change*. Cambridge: Polity.

Gee, J.P. (2003) *What Video Games have to Teach us about Learning and Literacy*. New York: Palgrave Macmillan.

Goffman, E. (1974) *Frame Analysis: An Essay on the Organization of Experience*. New York: Harper and Row.

Goffman, E. (1981) *Forms of Talk*. Philadelphia: University of Pennsylvania Press.

Goodwin, C., & Goodwin, M.H. (2004) Participation. In Duranti, A. (ed.) *A Companion to Linguistic Anthropology* (pp. 222-244). Malden, MA: Blackwell Publishing.

Goodwin, M.H. (1990) *He-said-she-said: Talk as Social Organization among Black Children*. Bloomington, Ind.: Indiana University Press.

Goodwin, M.H. (1995) Co-Constructing in Girls' Hopscotch. *Research on Language & Social Interaction, 28*(3), 261.

Heritage, J. (1984) *Garfinkel and Ethnomethodology*. Cambridge: Polity.

Ito, M., Horst, H., Bittanti, M., Boyd, D., Herr-Stephenson, B., Lange, P.G., et al. (2008) *Living and Learning with New Media: Summary of Findings from the Digital Youth Project*. Berkley: The John D. and Catherine T. MacArthur Foundation Reports on Digital Media and Learning.

Jenkins (2006) *Convergence Culture*. New York and London: New York University Press.

Juul, J. (2005) *Half-real: Video Games between Real Rules and Fictional Worlds*. Cambridge, Mass.: MIT Press.

Acknowledgments

The article is based on data from the LINT project financed by The Knut and Alice Wallenberg Foundation, The Bank of Sweden Tercentenary Foundation and The Swedish Research Council programme for the study of Learning and Memory in children and young adults.

Juul, J. (2010) *A Casual Revolution: Reinventing Video Games and their Players*. Cambridge, Mass.; London: MIT Press.

Kafai, Y.B., Heeter, C., Denner, J., & Sun, J.Y. (2008) *Beyond Barbie and Mortal Kombat : New Perspectives on Gender and Gaming*. Cambridge, Mass.: MIT Press.

Kim, B., Park, H., & Baek, Y. (2009) Not Just Fun, but Serious Strategies: Using Meta-cognitive Strategies in Game-based Learning. *Computers & Education, 52*(4), 800-810.

Kristeva, J., & Roudiez, L.S. (1980) *Desire in Language: A Semiotic Approach to Literature and Art*. Oxford: Blackwell.

Linderoth, J. (2004) *Datorspelandets mening: bortom idén om den interaktiva illusionen*. Göteborg: Acta Universitatis Gothoburgensis.

Medierådet (2006) *Fakta om barns och ungas användning och upplevelser av medier*. Stockholm: Medierådet.

Medietilsynet (2010) *Barn og digitale medier 2010*. Oslo: Medietilsynet.

Pearce, C. (2006) Productive Play: Game Culture From the Bottom Up. *Games and Culture, 1*(1), 17-24.

Pearce, C. (2009) *Communities of Play: Emergent Cultures in Multiplayer Games and Virtual Worlds*. Cambridge, Mass.: MIT Press.

Prensky, M. (2001) *Digital Game-based Learning*. New York: McGraw-Hill.

Salen, K., & Zimmerman, E. (2004) *Rules of Play: Game Design Fundamentals*. Cambridge, Mass. ;London: MIT.

Sutton-Smith, B. (1997) *The Ambiguity of Play*. Cambridge, Mass.; London: Harvard University Press.

Tannen, D., & Wallat, C. (1999 [1987]) Interactive Frames and Knowledge Schemas in Interaction: Examples from a Medical Examination/Interview. In A. Jaworski & N. Coupland (eds.) *The Discourse Reader* (pp. 346-366). London and New York: Routledge.

Tapscott, D. (1998) *Growing up Digital. The Rise of the Net Generation*. New York: McGraw-Hill.

Thorne, B. (1993) *Gender Play: Girls and Boys in School*. New Brunswick, N.J.: Rutgers University Press.

Tyner, K.R. (1998) *Literacy in a Digital World: Teaching and Learning in the Age of Information*. Mahwah, N.J.; London: Lawrence Erlbaum.

Appendix 1. Transcription key

Sign	Meaning
?	Inquiring intonation
=	Contiguous utterances
:	Prolongation of preceding vowel
…	Lines left out
(2)	Pause 2 seconds
(.)	Pause shorter than 0.2 second
xxx	Something was said but the transcriber could not hear it
no	Underlined means stressed word (or part of it)
°no°	Quiet speech
((no))	Comments made by the researcher
that [was	
[yes it was	The bracket indicates the onset of over lapping speech

Addiction and Randomness

A Comparative Analysis of Psycho-structural Elements in Gambling Games and Massively Multiplayer Online Role-playing games[1]

Faltin Karlsen

A highly-debated subject among the public during recent years has been the possibility of becoming addicted to online games. A common response from game researchers is to describe this as unlikely by referring to the complexity of the games in question. Nick Yee, for instance, has stated that:

> Online games are social worlds with their own geography, culture, dialect, and social rules ... They are places where people meet and then get married face-to-face. And to the extent that they are social places, asking whether someone can be addicted to an MMO is like asking whether someone can be addicted to the United States. (Yee 2006)

Edward Castronova uses a similar argument, and, in this case, he contrasts computer game playing with being an alcoholic, as, allegedly, his mother was:

> Now suppose she instead had been addicted to EverQuest. To me, that sentence, in comparison to alcohol addiction, sounds like someone suggesting: What if your mother was addicted to France instead of alcohol? I would reply, Fine! She likes France. Let's move to France. End of problem. (Castronova 2005: 65)

The basis for this argument is a view of online games as complex spaces where the player has a vast number of avenues of exploration available. In their arguments, Yee and Castronova seem to imply that the many possibilities that exist in the game universe will automatically generate an equally varied form of use. An interesting aspect of this argument is that, in contrast to more traditional media types where the complex social and cultural context of the user is seen as mitigating the impact of the media, the complexity has now moved inside the medium itself. It is unclear what kind of empirical support Yee and Castronova have for their arguments, and it might be pertinent to ask whether their descriptions are slightly idealistic. It would, for instance, be easy to turn their argument around and point to the fact that people get addicted to things in the real world as well, although, arguably, *this* world has a higher level of complexity to offer the 'users'.

I read Yee and Castronova's claims partly as a response to sensationalistic and imprecise use of the concept of addiction among the general public. Their emphasis on the social and cultural complexity of these games reminds us that the players often experience them as socially fulfilling and as a varied and engaging pastime activity – which explains some of the time and effort they spend on them. In this capacity, Yee and Castronova's perspective is representative of a certain focus on social elements in game studies and media studies. In game studies, a large body of research describes how players of online games organize different activities within the confines of the games (Ducheneaut et al. 2006; Karlsen 2009; Kendall 2002; Mortensen 2003; Taylor 2006). Several studies focus more discretely on how the elements of competition and cooperation conjointly contribute to excessive use, for instance in connection with organized group play like *raiding* (Taylor 2003; Karlsen 2008b; Linderoth & Bennerstedt 2007). These studies show that social demands related to regular group play cause players to invest much more time than initially indented, which is an important finding. However, by focusing primarily on social elements, these studies do not explain whether there are also particular structural elements in this genre that cause players to play excessively.

Psychologists have occasionally made the argument that computer games share many of the same structural elements with gambling games and, therefore, may be subject to some of the same psychological mechanisms with regard to excessive playing (Fisher & Griffiths 1995; Griffiths 1991). Gambling is the only play activity that is currently recognized as a pathological disorder. Regardless of whether or not players of computer games can be categorized as addicted in a strictly pathological sense, there is general acceptance that some players show a level of involvement in computer games that can be characterized as problematic (Griffiths & Davies 2005; Wan & Chiou 2006). One research group has addressed the lack of 'rigorous attempts to classify and organize the psycho-structural elements of video games in a similar way to gambling' (King et al. 2009). One of the reasons for this lack is because computer games are structurally more complex and heterogenic than gambling games are and, therefore, not as straight forward to categorize. Despite this, they have created a tentative taxonomy of structural features and psychological mechanisms in computer games, inspired by similar structural analysis of gambling games. The explicit aim with their taxonomy is for it to 'act as a catalyst for future research into excessive video game play, particularly in those areas that the psychological literature has not explored in detail' (King et al. 2009).

Methods and materials

The present article is an analysis of online game addiction, based on the assumption that this phenomenon, however marginal, deserves a more thorough empirical investigation than has been conducted so far. In accordance with the above-mentioned wish for structural research within psychology, as well as the lack of adequate structural analyses within game studies, my analytical approach has been to isolate different structural playing elements in MMORPGs in order to analyse whether they encourage problematic playing behaviour. Empirically, I will compare structural elements from World of Warcraft with elements from gambling games that are closely linked to addictive behaviour. I have also interviewed twelve heavy users of World of Warcraft in order to evaluate whether similar structural features are used in the same manner, and to investigate how structural and societal elements interrelate. Ethnographical observations from World of Warcraft will also inform this analysis. The interviews were conducted during the spring of 2009 using a 'snowball' approach. The informants had all been playing World of Warcraft and had experienced some, but not necessarily serious, problems related to their playing. The informants were all young adults, ranging from 20 to 27 years. They lived in different urban areas in the eastern part of Norway.

The main criterion for choosing informants was that they had been playing World of Warcraft excessively. Most of them reported that, during certain periods, they had played almost every waking hour, or up to 16 hours a day. The length of the period varied from a few weeks to more than two years, and the informants had experienced everything from mild to serious problems related to their playing. Of the milder, self-reported effects of this, players said that, during such periods, they were less socially active than usual and sometime skipped meals, neglected household chores or suffered from mild sleep deprivation. At the more severe end of the spectrum, the excessive playing had resulted in informants losing jobs, flunking out of school, being thrown out of their home, and being abandoned by their partners. At the time of the interview, they had either quit playing or played much less than before.

Before I begin the analysis of what motivated the players to play excessively, I will present relevant research from gambling addiction.

Types of gambling

Gambling can be defined as 'a monetary transaction between two parties based on the outcome of an uncertain event' (Walker et al. 2008: 11). The presence of money and the element of randomness are two of the most significant aspects of gambling, in addition to the element of at least two competing parties. In modern, commercial gambling these are normally represented by a gambler and a house. The house will have a so-called *house edge*, which is the percentage the house will, on average, make money. The size of the house edge varies from game to game. In electronic gambling machines it is usually about 10 per cent; in European roulette it is as small as 2.6 per cent (Turner 2008: 57).

Gambling games can be sorted with regard to temporal qualities. At one end of the spectrum we find games with very short intervals between each round, like blackjack, roulette and electronic gambling machines. These are often referred to as continuous games or games with high event frequency (Turner & Horbay 2004). At the other end, we have games with much longer intervals between each bet, like Lotto and different sport-betting games. These games are often run on a weekly basis, and are referred to as games with low event frequency, or as discrete games (Walker et al. 2008: 19).

Gambling games can also be sorted along a spectrum from games of pure chance, like roulette and lotto, to games where skills also play a part, like poker. Also, in games where skills play a role, the house will win in the long run, regardless of how skilled the player is. Most commercial gambling games are games of pure chance, and the most popular of these are lotteries like Lotto and electronic gambling machines.

The problem with randomness

The element of randomness we find in games of pure chance is something that challenges many people's cognitive abilities. Several psychological phenomena are described in connection with this. One of the most common is the phenomenon of *chasing*, where a gambler is trying to recoup his or her losses by continuing gambling. Over time, this can have devastating economic results for the gambler. Another phenomenon is known as the *gambler's fallacy*: a belief that, after a gaming event has occurred, it is less likely that the same event or outcome will happen again. Similarly, a gambler might perceive a row of losses as strong evidence of an imminent success and bet more heavily (Rogers 1998). This reasoning can be explained by the fact that the player fails to understand that each round in the game is a separate event without any connection to previous or future events. They would rather believe that chance is self-correcting and fair (Kahneman et al. 1982). Despite popular belief, an electronic gambling machine is never 'due' to win, and every combination of numbers has an equal likelihood to win in a round of Lotto.

Both these psychological phenomena are caused by gamblers relying on heuristics or mental 'rules of thumb' rather than on a proper understanding of how randomness works. An example of this is the common belief that some combinations of numbers are more likely to win than others. In a survey conducted by a group of researchers, only 51 per cent of the general public correctly answered 'false' to the statement: 'A random series of numbers, such as 12-5-23-7 is more likely to win than a series of numbers in sequence, like 1-2-3-4' (Czerny et al. 2008: 73). Among gamblers who played excessively, only 38 per cent answered this question correctly. The reason for this misconception is that people think that a random range of numbers should 'look' random. A complicating factor is that many game designers also intentionally confuse the level of randomness involved. It is, for instance, common in roulette casinos to show a list of the last winning numbers, even though each game is a separate event where future or past outcomes have no impact on the result. This might lead gamblers to believe that there is some sort of system behind this game, and that they are about to uncover this system (Turner 2008).

Pathological gambling

Gambling addiction or pathological gambling entered the Diagnostic and Statistical Manual of Mental Disorders in 1980. In the latest edition of this manual (DSM-IV), pathological gambling is listed as an 'impulse control disorder' (American Psychiatric Association 1994). Research on problematic or pathological gambling has shown that there are certain structural characteristics in games that are most likely to lead to problematic gambling habits. Dickerson and O'Conner list eight different criteria, of which accessibility and continuous forms of gambling are regarded as the most important criteria for people in developing problematic gambling habits (Dickerson & O'Connor 2006: 17). Turner states that the most problematic types of gambling are electronic gambling machines and blackjack, due to the fact that they are 'fast, continuous, have relatively small minimum bets, and are widely available' (Turner 2008: 62). The high likelihood of problems related to electronic gambling machines has even earned them the dubious nickname: 'crack cocaine of gambling' (Mandal and Doelen 1999). The gambling forms with high event frequency are regarded as especially dangerous because of the psychological reward mechanisms on which they are based, as they reward the players with small wins at variable intervals. According to operant conditioning theory, behaviour that is rewarded on a variable, rather than a fixed, ratio schedule is most likely to be reinforced (King et al. 2009). Variable intervals are, again, created by randomness, which is a core element in all types of gambling games.

Gamblers are playing for different reasons, including the excitement of the game and as an escape from life (Spunt et al. 1998). A study of Australian gamblers states that being in 'the zone' was a central motivational factor among problem gamblers. The same study also found that big payouts, frequent payouts and free games were features that the general gambling public found highly attractive (Livingstone & Woolley 2008: 79).

Studies of online games show that there is a wide range of factors that influence how people play, including the possibility of exploring the game universe, mastering the gameplay, cooperating with fellow players and pestering other players' lives (Bartle 1996 2003; Karlsen 2004; Yee 2007). With regard to World of Warcraft, it has been argued that one of (possibly many) gaming goals is 'to keep developing an avatar so that the player can make further accomplishments within the game space' (Karlsen 2009: 79). While the overall goals for playing World of Warcraft may be different from gambling, World of Warcraft has some of the same structural features as gambling games, especially if we look at electronic gambling machines. As already mentioned, these games are characterized by being fast, continuous and widely available (Turner 2008: 62). The activity demanded of the gambler is repetitive – mainly consisting of deciding between a few possible actions by pressing buttons. The gambling game rewards the gambler on a varying ratio schedule. Online games like World of Warcraft are also continuous and widely available but, unlike electronic gambling machines, consist of both fixed and variable reward schedules. In World of Warcraft, the general design scheme is a fixed level structure where the avatar gradually grows in abilities while constantly being ushered towards areas that match the difficulty level of the avatar. The main activities while developing, or *levelling*, an avatar are to kill monsters and to solve so-called quests. The outcome of a monster fight is easily deduced by the level of the avatar, and rewards the avatar with a consistent number of experience points. How many experience points the monster will give the avatar is based on the difference in level between the monster and the avatar, but the amount is not subject to randomness. Also the *questing* activity has an overall fixed structure, designed as missions with explicitly-stated objectives, usually involving killing a set number of monsters or finding a set number of items (Karlsen 2008a; Rettberg 2008; Sullivan 2009).

In the following analysis, I will focus on an activity in World of Warcraft that has a variable reward structure comparable to gambling, namely raiding. This will be analysed in light of two psycho-structural phenomena known from gambling that are linked to problematic playing behaviour: *entrapment* and *near miss*. My aim is to evaluate whether these phenomena are also present in World of Warcraft.

Entrapment

Entrapment is a phenomenon known from gambling, especially in connection with lottery games like Lotto. According to Rogers, 'entrapment is related to the point at which, despite mounting losses, players feel obliged to continue betting ("investing") both time and money through some internal sense that they have gone too far to give up now' (Rogers 1998: 120). Lotto gamblers are described as entrapped when they feel obliged to keep betting week after week. This is often caused by the gamblers betting on the same row of numbers every week and being afraid that 'their' row of numbers will come up if they stop betting (Walker 1992). This is again connected to a superstitious belief that they have chosen a particularly lucky set of numbers, or simply that they have chosen a specific set of numbers, like birthdays, instead of choosing numbers at random every week. A similar effect is observed in connection with electronic gambling machines where players hold on to the machines for hours, because they think they are 'due' to win and are afraid to miss the jackpot if they stop playing (Turner 2008: 46). This phenomenon is also connected to the gambler's fallacy described earlier.

The phenomenon I found from World of Warcraft that most closely resembled entrapment was connected to raiding. At first glance, World of Warcraft has few structural similarities with a game like Lotto, since World of Warcraft is a continuous, persistent game. However, the raiding activity in World of Warcraft shows some resemblance to the slow, repetitive pattern we find here. Raiding in World of Warcraft is currently done in groups of different sizes, with a maximum of 10 players in the smallest or 25 players in the largest groups. The maximum size prevents the players from overpowering the monsters by sheer numbers. The object of raiding is to conquer so-called *bosses* that drop particularly valuable items that can equip the avatars. The basic structure of raiding is a chain of goals that are spread out in time. The raiding takes place inside special dungeons, so-called *instances*. These consist of a varying number of bosses, from one single boss to around 15. Normally, the deeper inside the dungeon you enter, the harder it will be to kill the bosses. Every week, and sometimes more often, the raiding dungeons reset. This means that the monsters and bosses in the instances *respawn* and the progress you have made the previous week is erased. But it also means that the raiders are able to kill the same bosses over again and get a new chance at the loot they drop. The instances are further designed with different difficulty levels, so that the players will normally focus on one or a few instances at a time, slowly moving towards more challenging ones. Dedicated raiding guilds have, as their ultimate goal, to kill every boss in this game. Players will usually raid several nights each week with the prospect of getting loot and progressing further inside the dungeons. Raiding is a type of playing that requires a specific set-up of avatar types, which again demands player accountability over longer periods of time. Raiding guilds, therefore, often demand a certain level of commitment from members and can, for instance, require members to raid four or five evenings each week. Players with avatars that are scarce, such as healers, may also be asked to raid when they have not signed up for raids (Karlsen 2009: 111).

As part of my ethnographic research, I was a member of several raiding guilds in World of Warcraft. My participant observation here suggested that some kind of entrapment mechanism was involved. After raiding for some months, a guild would normally have *cleared* the instances several times and got most of the items they needed from the place. At this stage, I sometimes observed how players would get some sort of fixation on a specific item they were still in need of. They could sign up week after week for raids in order to get this particular item. Some of them were convinced that, if they did not participate in the raid, an item was certain to drop and they displayed a noticeable level of distress if they, for some reason, were unable to participate; as with the Lotto players, they were frightened of not being present when 'their' item dropped. During my interviews I asked the informants about this phenomenon. The general finding was that few of them currently had this kind of fixation on items, but some told me they had experienced this earlier in their playing career. Keen attention to gear was evident in most of the interviews. For instance Geir, who had his most intense raiding period a couple of years before the time of the interview, described the interest like this:

> In Blackwing Lair, yes it was that sword that dropped from that Chrono something. Cromatic Blade, which I was very, very keen to get. Before that it was the dagger from Ragnaros and then different item pieces. You need your armour set or ... it is always something. Gear was something that, when you had beaten the content, gear was what you were farming for. (M, 27)

When the bosses no longer represent a challenge, they are *farmed* for their drops in order for the players to get hold of items that are especially powerful for their class. This informant also told me that items had been even more important when he played a different online game, EverQuest, around five or six years earlier:

> In EverQuest, items were very, very much more powerful than in World of Warcraft. I remember leading a raid on a drake called Nagafen and got a cloak called Cloak of Flame, which was the dream item for all melee characters because it gave 36% haste. This was the real big deal and an incredibly valuable item. If you were to buy it, it would have cost thousands of in-game cash. (M, 27)

This informant described, with passion, for how many months and how many Nagafen raids he had been on in order to get hold of this item. In this final successful event, the player had to wager against 21 other melee players, and was ecstatic when he won. An interesting aspect of this recount is how vivid the memory still is for the player, many years after the incident. This might bear some resemblance to problem gamblers who can recount a large win early in their playing career. This is a subject on which I unfortunately have no reliable data and, therefore, will pursue no further. This intense recollection of getting a specific item, however, illustrates the importance that gear or items may have for the players.

One of the reasons my informants now had a more relaxed attitude towards items, compared to earlier, can partly be explained by the fact that the development company, Blizzard, has made it easier to get hold of high quality (epic) loot than earlier. As Andreas explains:

> *Researcher:* So you sort of have enough equipment?
> *Informant:* Yes, nowadays so much of it just drops. On a Naxxramas run, in 25-man mode, it drops like a hundred epics. Earlier when we ran around in Molten Core we were 40 players and the bosses dropped 1 or 2 epics each. It was quite different then. (M, 27)

The current Naxxramas instance is, regarding length of play, somewhat comparable to the earlier Molten Core instance, but the loot to player ratio is currently many times better. Despite the noticeable inflation in epics over the years, some of my informants also gave me enthusiastic accounts of much more recent gear acquisitions. Ivar for instance told me that:

> Well, the best thing about WOW is when you have been in a raid for seven hours and then finally the gear you are waiting for drops, and you get it. That has to be the best thing about WOW, the best feeling. It happened to me on Sunday about a week ago when I had been in a raid for seven hours without getting anything. Then my tier 8.5 leggings dropped, and I got it. Yes! Then I ... I screamed a bit, I have to admit. I was happy. I was very happy. (M, 24)

He further explained that he was currently after an item called *Leviathan Fueling Manual*, which he actually had seen drop 12 times without being able to get. This illustrates an important difference between World of Warcraft and Lotto: the much higher chance of achieving goals in World of Warcraft. While players might have a dry spell and get no loot for a period of time, they will, if they keep raiding, acquire the items they are after. The dedication to keep on raiding is, in this respect, a rational choice, while to keep betting on the same row in Lotto, in the great majority of cases, will not lead to the desired outcome. The relative abundance of high-quality items will generally weaken the potential for an entrapment effect to occur in World of Warcraft, as this makes 'winning' individual item pieces less special.

Dragon Kill Points

As we see above, to Ivar, acquiring gear was an important motivation to raid. However, he told me that of equal importance was gaining so-called *Dragon Kill Points* or DKP. DKP is a player-invented distribution system based on effort, and the most common method for distributing items during raids (Fairfield & Castronova 2006; Karlsen 2008b). There are many different DKP-systems, but most of them have in common that the players earn points by participating in raids: points that, later, can be used to 'buy' items that drop during raids. The player with the highest number of points will then have first-right to take the item. The distribution system developed by Blizzard is, in contrast, based on chance. Here the players *roll* on items with the /roll command, which will randomly distribute numbers between 1 and 100 to each player. The highest roller wins the item. This is still the normal way of distributing items in smaller groups.

The use of DKP is interesting, as it shows that players are taking measures to reduce the level of randomness connected to loot distribution – they simply prefer loot distribution based on effort rather than luck. This makes distribution of resources acquired through raiding more predictable for the players, but also influences their playing habits. To my question, about whether he often raided more than intended because he is after specific gear, Ivar answered:

> Well, that might happen. Sometimes. But mostly, not because I am after gear but because of the DKP. So that on bosses later on I can get gear. I do that quite often. (M, 24)

Most of my informants who had been in a raiding guild told me that DKP made them more likely to participate in raids. The main reason was that they needed more DKP to be able to outbid other players for especially popular items. Geir for instance said that:

> It was a really hard competition among the rogues to acquire items you were interested in. Of course you needed to have max DKP, which you can only acquire by farming, which you only get by participating in raids. It was a lot of raids you didn't really bother about but which you still went on only because of the DKP, that's for sure. (M, 27)

The DKP system allows the players to minimize the element of luck. They are not able to change the basic reward structure of raiding, which is the likelihood the items have for dropping, but they are trying to eliminate the randomness in loot distribution as designed by the game developers. From the perspective of the leaders of the raiding guild, DKP ensures that the most active players obtain gear before the more casual players. This is a rational way to make certain that the most active players have the best gear and, in effect, to ensure optimal raid progress. The irony is that the players get 'trapped' by their own rationality, as they will fight to get on top of the DKP list in order not to fall behind fellow guild members in getting gear. Rather like Lotto players who bet on the same row each week, these players feel obliged to keep raiding. While this behaviour in the Lotto setting is based on a misconception about the randomness involved, or an irrational fear of missing out on a win should the numbers come up, in World of Warcraft the repetitive behaviour is based on sound reasoning combined with a strong focus on gear, accentuated by the competitive environment of the game.

In sum, there seems to be some, albeit weak, entrapment mechanism present in raiding, as players are sometimes afraid of missing out on opportunities to acquire specific items. However, what seems to be of greater importance is the competitive environment of the raiding guild and, especially, how this is expressed through the DKP system. DKP is a method for dealing with randomness, which indirectly contributes to a higher level of dedication. As such, the structural elements of the game represented by the reward system are only partly accountable for players' dedication to excessive play. The social, competitive component seems to be just as important, as well as each player's focus on their individual achievements. The element of randomness, important in gambling, is of less importance in online games in this respect.

In the next section I will take a closer look at another psycho-structural phenomenon known from gambling: the so-called *near miss* principle, which might potentially increase the involvement of the player.

Near miss

A near miss is a losing situation which the gambler interprets as being close to winning. The excitement the player feels in this situation can lead to more dedicated play. Near miss in a slot machine setting will be two winning symbols out of three on the payout line. It has been argued that a slot machine gambler is not constantly losing, but rather constantly 'nearly winning' (Griffiths 1999). Applied to Lotto, near miss is said to occur when the gambler, for instance, gets four out of six winning numbers and wins a small prize (Rogers 1998). King et al. have recently argued that near miss is also a common experience for computer game players. Here, they mention failing to kill a difficult boss at an end of a level as being one incident where the player might experience a near miss situation (King et al. 2009: 4). In World of Warcraft, this is quite a common experience, especially in raids. All of my informants who had been raiding seriously had examples where they had exceeded normal raiding hours in order to defeat a boss. As Frank explained, in response to the question: Did you sometime play longer, or extend the raid in order to achieve something?:

> Yes, that happened quite often actually. We had a slogan: 'We'll wipe 'til it's clean.' So we run over and over again until we made it. But at some point it had to end because the players had work or something the next day. So, if we were frustrated over something we didn't accomplish, we kept going as long as we had the resources and players for it. (M, 21)

The experience of failing at something they should accomplish, or are close to accomplishing, in this case, led to an increased dedication to continue playing. Another of my informants, Ivar, had been raiding late the night before the interview:

> *Researcher:* How long do the raids last?
> *Informants:* Um, last night I sat up until four o'clock and we began at eight, so I was in bed at about four or half past four.
> *Researcher:* Wow, is that common? Is it common that the raids take that long?
> *Informant:* No, we usually try to limit it, till about half past eleven or twelve. But we had a progressing raid and we wanted to get down Mimiron who is one of the last Keepers in Ulduar. And you have to do it in something called hard mode in order to get to Yogg-Saron and the last boss Observer. And we tried that last night, but we struggled a bit. (M, 24)

To describe the prolongation of a raid by four hours as 'to struggle a bit' may be considered an understatement. However, this is an example of how difficulty in accomplishing a goal may extend play considerably. Getting a boss down was generally described as important, especially getting it down for the first time. Geir for instance stated that:

> When our guild took down Ragnaros for the first time, the boss in Molten Core, it was very, very big. We had been working hard on it, we had wiped several times and people started to get annoyed. But then we focused, started again and then made it. And that was great! We played Queen's: *We are the Champions*, and, like, virtually opened the champagne, and … We lived long on that feeling, the good feeling in the guild. It was very rewarding. (M, 27)

Four of my informants actually stated that getting this particular boss down was the best memory they had from World of Warcraft. Celia described a similar experience on a different boss:

> I think the best experience was when our guild had spent two months trying to get Kael'thas down and we finally managed it, and I was there. It was … it is one of the most challenging things we have worked for. That one particularly. It was before nerfs and everything. And then to finally succeed after working on it for two months, I think that was great fun. There were 25 people there and being able to work together as a group in that manner, when you finally accomplish what you have been working for, is just great. (F, 21)

In this case, however, the joyful moment was partly spoiled by her boyfriend being unable to participate:

> It was also a slightly bitter experience because my boyfriend, who should have been in that raid, got ill and had to cancel on that very day. So, he became a bit grumpy when the rest of us managed to kill him. (F, 21)

The near miss experience of almost getting the boss down may increase the dedication of the players but, unlike in gambling, this is something they actually have a fair chance of accomplishing. It might be a rational choice to keep trying on a hard boss if, for instance, you may have a particularly good group set-up that evening. In contrast, a near miss situation in Lotto gives the player the illusion of almost having won, while in reality there is still a one-to-several-million chance of winning the next time you hand in a ticket.

Another interesting aspect of conquering bosses, illustrated in the quotes above, is the special value of getting the boss down for the first time. The first kill on a particularly hard boss is an important happening in a guild, as it demonstrates their success as a group and creates a common reference point for the members – contributing to the lore of the guild. There will always be new chances for getting loot from the bosses, but the feeling of accomplishment and success of a first kill is not possible to recreate. This might actually be regarded as a specific type of entrapment found in raiding guilds: the fear of losing out on a great occasion. Performing a first kill on a boss is, structurally speaking, similar to any other boss kills in World of Warcraft, but the players regard this as a very special achievement – an added value that can, in part, be related to the social aspects of the game. A combination of reward structures, competition between the raiding guilds and the social life inside the raiding guild contributes to the existence of the concept of first kill. While the ordinary entrapment mechanism connected to rewards is relatively weak, this socially-embedded entrapment mechanism seems to have a stronger impact.

Conclusion

One general finding of the present study, which confirms earlier studies, is that excessive playing of online games is closely linked to socially-based motivation factors. The game arena is highly competitive and a place for rewarding cooperation. However, these social elements are also closely linked to structural elements of the game, especially the reward system. Psycho-structural elements known from gambling, like entrapment and near miss, are observable in World of Warcraft, but their impact seems comparatively weaker.

As far as near miss goes, several of my informants reported playing longer than planned when struggling with bosses in raids. It seems that being near to defeating a boss or clearing an instance collectively increases the dedication to play. This might increase considerably the time spent on an already quite time-consuming activity. This phenomenon is also emphasized by some kind of group pressure on those who want to stop playing, as this might ruin the other group members' chances of achieving the goal. This illustrates the higher level of complexity of MMORPGs compared to gambling games, and how overall game goals, the reward structure and social obligations all influence each other.

The entrapment phenomenon observed in World of Warcraft is linked to rewards, represented by items of high quality that the bosses drop. Players report that, occasionally, they have been preoccupied with getting hold of specific items, but a gradual inflation of high quality items seems to diminish this effect. The much higher possibility of acquiring such items compared to winning a big prize in gambling also makes the dedication to play more of a rational choice than a cognitive misconception. For this reason, the entrapment mechanism here must be regarded as weak. However, another phenomenon that resembles entrapment seems to exist, namely that players are afraid of missing out on big events in the guild, like killing a hard boss for the first time. This is an event that cannot be recreated and the players will therefore have to be raiding constantly in order not to miss it. This phenomenon has less to do with the reward structure of the game and has, rather, a strong social component. A first kill has a uniqueness that bears some resemblance to winning a big prize in gambling, but the reward is indirect and socially-constructed, rather than a direct outcome of the encounter itself.

An important finding in both the entrapment and near miss analyses is that randomness has a much less prominent place in World of Warcraft than in gambling games, even when the reward structure is based on randomness. Interestingly, the players are also taking measures to eradicate the randomness that exists in the game, especially in connection with loot distribution in raids. This is expressed by the player-invented DKP system, where players are going out of their way to reduce randomness connected to loot distribution. The DKP system is based on effort rather than luck and ensures that the most frequent raiders will acquire loot before others. The side effect of this is that the players may get trapped by their own rationality, as several informants report raiding routinely in order to keep up with the DKP race in the guild.

For some players, the game goals and social commitments reach such a level of importance that they overshadow every other obligation. While this indicates that the players easily identify with game goals and get satisfaction from accomplishing them, it is also possible that rational choices within the game universe may seem irrational outside it. An important question for further research is to achieve a better understanding of how some players manage to balance game goals with other requirements in their lives, while, for others, commitment to game goals and social obligations within the game reach a level of importance that causes all other priorities to be ignored.

Note

1. The present article is a shorter version of the article Entrapment and near miss: A comparative analysis of psycho-structural elements in gambling games and massively multiplayer online role-playing games in *International Journal of Mental Health and Addiction*, Springer New York, online May 4, 2010, with a permission to reprint.

References

American Psychiatric Association. (1994) *Diagnostic and Statistical Manual of Mental Disorders DSM-IV*. Washington DC: American Psychiatric Association.

Bartle, Richard A. (1996) 'Hearts, Clubs, Diamonds, Spades: Players who Suit MUDs'. Retrieved from http://www.mud.co.uk/richard/hcds.htm.

Bartle, Richard (2003) *Designing Virtual Worlds,* Indianapolis: New Riders.

Castronova, Edward (2005) *Synthetic Worlds: The Business and Culture of Online Games*, Chicago and London: The University of Chicago Press.

Czerny, Ewa, Koenig, Stephanie, & Turner, Nigel E. (2008) 'Exploring the Mind of the Gambler: Psychological Aspects of Gambling and Problem Gambling', in Massod Zangeneh, Alex Blaszczynski, & Nigel E. Turner (eds.) *In the Pursuit of Winning: Problem Gambling Theory, Research and Treatment*, New York: Springer.

Dickerson, Mark, & O'Connor, John (2006) *Gambling as an Addictive Behaviour: Impaired Control, Harm Minimisation, Treatment and Prevention*, Cambridge: Cambridge University Press.

Ducheneaut, Nicolas, Yee, Nicholas, Nickell, Eric & Moore, Robert J. (2006) 'Alone Together? Exploring the Social Dynamic of Massively Multiplayer Online Games', *Conference on Human Factors in Computing Games,* Montréal, Québec, Canada 407-416.

Fairfield, Joshua & Castronova, Edward. (2006) 'Dragon Kill Points: A Summary Whitepaper', *Rational Models Seminar,* University of Chicago.

Fisher, Sue, & Griffiths, Mark (1995) 'Current Trends in Slot Machine Gambling: Research and Policy Issues', *Journal of Gambling Studies* 11, 239-247.

Griffiths, Mark D. (1991) 'Amusement Machine Playing in Childhood and Adolescence: A Comparative Analysis of Video Games and Fruit Machines', *Journal of Adolescence* 14, 53-73.

Griffiths, Mark (1999) 'The Psychology of the Near Miss (revisited): A Comment on Delfabbro and Winefield, *British Journal of Psychology* 90, 441-445.

Griffiths, Mark, & Davies, Mark N.O. (2005) 'Video-Game Addiction: Does it Exist?' in, J. Goldstein & J. Raessens (eds.) *Handbook of Computer Game Studies,* pp. 359-268, Cambridge MA: MIT Press.

Kahneman, Daniel, Tversky, Amos, & Slovic, Paul (1982) *Judgment under Uncertainty: Heuristics and Biases*, Cambridge: Cambridge University Press.

Karlsen, Faltin (2004) 'Media Complexity and Diversity of Use: Thoughts on a Taxonomy of Users of Multiuser Online Games', in Miguel Sicart & Jonas Heide Smith (eds.) *Other Players*, Copenhagen: IT University of Copenhagen, Denmark.

Karlsen, Faltin (2008a) 'Quests in Context: A Comparative Analysis of Discworld and World of Warcraft', *Game Studies.*

Karlsen, Faltin (2008b) 'High-End Gaming in World of Warcraft', *The 13th Conference for Norwegian Media Researchers,* Lillehammer, Norway.

Karlsen, Faltin (2009) *Emergent Perspectives on Multiplayer Online Games: A Study of Discworld and World of Warcraft*, PhD thesis at Department of Media and Communication, Oslo: University of Oslo.

Kendall, Lori (2002) *Hanging Out in the Virtual Pub: Masculines and Relationships Online,* California: University of California Press.

King, Daniel, Delfabbro, Paul & Griffiths, Mark (2009) 'Video Game Structural Characteristics: A New Psychological Taxonomy', *International Journal of Mental Health and Addiction.*

Linderoth, Jonas, & Bennerstedt, Ulrika (2007) *Living in World of Warcraft – The Thoughts and Experiences of Ten Young People*, edited by The Swedish Media Council.

Livingstone, Charles, & Richard Woolley (2008) *The Relevance and Role of Gaming Machine Games and Game Features on the Play of Problem Gamblers*, report for the Independent Gambling Authority South Australia.

Mandal, Veronique Perrier & Chris Vander Doelen (1999) *Chasing Lightning: Gambling in Canada.* Toronto: United Church Publishing House.

Mortensen, Torill Elvira (2003) *Pleasures of the Player: Flow and Control in Online Games*, PhD thesis at Department of Humanistic Informatics Faculty of Media and Journalism, Volda: Volda University College.

Rettberg, Jill Walker (2008) 'Quests in World of Warcraft: Deferral and Repetition', in Jill Walker Rettberg & G. Hilde Corneliussen (eds.) *Digital Culture, Play and Identity: A World of Warcraft Reader*, Cambridge: The MIT Press.

Rogers, Paul (1998) 'The Cognitive Psychology of Lottery Gambling: A Theoretical Review', *Journal of Gambling Studies,* 14, 111-134.

Spunt, Barry, Dupont, Ida, Lesieur, Henry, Liberty, Hilary James & Hunt, Dana (1998) 'Pathological Gambling and Substance Misuse: A Review of the Literature', *Substance Use and Misuse,* 33, 2535-2560.

Sullivan, Anne (2009) 'Gender-Inclusive Quest Design in Massively Multiplayer Online Role-Playing Games', in *Foundations of Digital Games Doctoral Consortium*. Florida.

Taylor, T.L. (2003) 'Power Gamers Just Want To Have Fun?: Instrumental Play In A MMOG', in 1st Digra Conference: Level Up, The University of Utrecht.

Taylor, T.L. (2006) *Play between Worlds: Exploring Online Game Culture,* London: The MIT Press.

Turner, Nigel E. (2008) 'Games, Gambling, and Gambling Problems', in Massod Zangeneh, Alex Blaszczynski & Nigel E. Turner (eds.) *In the Pursuit of Winning: Problem Gambling Theory, Research and Treatment.*

Turner, Nigel & Horbay, Roger (2004) 'How do Slot Machines and Other Electronic Gambling Machines Actually Work?' *Journal of Gambling Issues.*

Walker, Michael B. (1992) *The Psychology of Gambling.* Oxford: Pergamon.

Walker, Michael, Schellink, Tony & Anjoul, Fadi (2008) 'Explaining Why People Gamble', in Massod Zangeneh, Alex Blaszczynski & Nigel E. Turner (eds.) *In the Pursuit of Winning: Problem Gambling Theory, Research and Treatment*, New York: Springer.

Wan, Chin-Sheng, & Chiou, Wen-Bin (2006) 'Why Are Adolescents Addicted to Online Gaming? An Interview Study in Taiwan', *CyberPsychology and Behavior* 9, 762-767.

Yee, Nick (2006) 'The Trouble with "Addiction".' In The deadalus project: http://www.nickyee.com/daedalus

Yee, Nick (2007) 'Motivations of Play in Online Games', *CyberPsychology and Behavior* 9, 772-775.

Influences of Mediated Violence
International and Nordic Research Findings

Cecilia von Feilitzen

The subject of children's and adolescents' relations to media has been on the agenda as long as media – books, press, recorded music, film, radio, television, etc. – have existed. With each new medium come both hopes and fears. In the public debate, the hopes have been for better opportunities for information/ education, culture/entertainment and social relations – even peace – between persons, groups, cultures and countries. The fears have concerned the possible injurious influences of media contents as well as of using the medium *per se*.

Considering the possible offensive and harmful influences of *film* and *television*, many kinds of risks have been under intensive discussion. However, it is no exaggeration to say that the issue given most attention internationally both in the public debate and in the research, especially regarding children and young people, is the consequences of watching media violence.

With regard to digital *video/computer games* as well, violent content is one concern in the forefront in both public debate and research. However, the hopes and fears – and the direction of research – have not been altogether the same for all media, but depend on the contents and character of the medium, as well as on the role of the media user. Therefore, apprehensions about *the Internet* and *mobile phones* are partly different.

This article[1] deals with research findings on the influences of mediated violence and will have little to say about research on other possible offensive or harmful influences – or the plentiful research on the media's potentially positive and desired influences. The article also limits itself to the screen media – film and television, digital games, and the Internet (mobile phones included) – because at present, the risks of these media are the most debated issues in relation to young people.

International and Nordic research

It must be stressed that research on children, young people and media has been much more exuberant and has a longer tradition in richer countries, such as Australia and New Zealand, Europe (mostly Northern and Western Europe), Japan and other well-to-do countries in Asia, as well as North America, while in other countries such research is often less common and sometimes non-existent. The knowledge we have about the influences of media violence originates, thus, from relatively few countries with specific media situations – and research findings cannot be automatically generalized across borders. Consequently, in most countries there is a great need for research on children and media in the changing local and global media landscape. Such research should be carried out both on the countries' own social and cultural terms and through more international comparative investigations.

At the same time it is interesting to note that in the Nordic countries (Denmark, Finland, Iceland, Norway and Sweden), research focused on mediated violence specifically has, on the whole, been relatively sparse, at least compared to the many studies on this subject in the U.S. One historical explanation might be that films in the Nordic countries previously were censored, why many violent elements were cut away, and that the public service television channels (for a long time the dominating television) were restrictive as regards broadcasting violent programmes. The public debate on media violence was also intensive and might, at least partly, have functioned as a modifier of the violent output. Nordic public service television has also consistently been concerned about producing and sending children's programmes of high quality and diversity for different age groups at times suitable for them. Hence, researchers during the 1960s-1980s dealt more with children's programming and children's general use of television than with possible influences of media violence.

The expansive technical media development and the increasing global or trans-national media output, which occurred hand in hand with the so-called deregulation in the Nordic countries from the mid-80s onwards, have, as in most countries, changed the media landscape. Public service media in these countries now have competition from a large number of private, commercial radio stations and TV channels, both international and new local ones. Cinema films, TV series and music are largely supplied by the world's largest media corporations. Video and computer games are a 'new' medium used by most children. And the Nordic countries are among the world's most Internet-dense countries, entailing even more globalization of information and entertainment.

In the light of these media changes, the Nordic public debate on (the nowadays much more extensive) media violence in films and on television has abated. The debate is to a greater extent dealing with mediated violence in digital games, on the Internet and via mobile phones. Nevertheless, there is still more Nordic research on learning, competences, empowerment, identity, youth cultures and civic engagement than on risks of playing computer games and being on the Internet. In one way this focus fulfils the previous orientations during the 1960s-1980s concentrating more on the 'positive' influences on children of the media.

Simultaneously, we can notice that research in the Nordic countries since the 1980s has been influenced more by the cultural studies and reception traditions than by the media effects tradition that is still lively in the U.S. Whereas the effects tradition has 'a media perspective', asking what *the media (violence)* are doing with the individual, the cultural studies and reception traditions have, among other things, 'a user perspective', asking what *the individual* is doing with the media (violence). The latter research builds on the fact that different individuals generally experience excitement, violence, horror and power – and other media contents – very differently, need it to different extents and give it different meanings depending on the individuals' experience and context. It is important to understand the fascination that many persons (but by no means everyone) feel for media violence. Some violent portrayals of today also have their roots in historical myths, folk tales and ancient drama.

This article will, in brief, use both these perspectives when presenting research findings, and will also mention *examples* of empirical Nordic research findings in the text and notes. Even if the Nordic examples show a clear tendency to have moved from the 'media perspective' towards 'the user perspective' over time, the article does not claim to give a complete catalogue of the Nordic investigations on influences of mediated violence.

Film and television

The media perspective

The representations of media violence in film and television most often referred to in the public debate, as well as in research, are depictions of visible, manifest, physical violence, and the threat of such violence, intended to kill, hurt or inflict physical suffering on the victim(s), i.e., fights, shootings, murders, etc.

Because research on physical media violence predominates, we know in the media violence context little of other forms of symbolic violence – such as mental and structural oppression, and power relations – that are also represented in the media output. Furthermore, the research has been largely concentrated on depictions of violence in entertainment, fiction and drama as opposed to representations of violence in the news and other factual contents. The reason has been that we must know about reality, but if fictional violence is injurious it ought to be reduced.

Research on film and television violence has been conducted since the 1920s, and three to four thousand studies on influences of violent contents in these media are said to exist in the U.S. alone. Thus, we can base our conclusions concerning the influences of film and TV violence on many studies starting from different theories and using different methods, but with findings pointing in the same direction.

Imitation

There is considerable empirical research showing that portrayals of violent actions in film and television can lead to *imitation*, particularly among younger children. Parents in several early Nordic studies also gave a great number of examples of children's imitation of a range of elements in TV programmes, including violent ones, in their play after having watched television.

Aggression

However, imitation of violent elements does not necessarily mean *intentional* aggressive actions. The many more studies focused on *aggression* as a consequence of viewing film and TV violence do not support the notion that media violence is the *only* or *decisive* cause of violence (and violent crimes) in society – however, most studies indicate that media violence nevertheless play a role.

Media contents seldom have a *direct* or *sole* influence on our *actions*. We definitely get *mental* impressions – conceptions, feelings, etc. – from the media. But these are mixed with all the other conceptions, norms, values, feelings and experiences we have already acquired and are acquiring from our own practice and from our family, school, peers, etc. Our own experiences, as well as impressions from other persons, are generally of greater importance than impressions from the media. It is this melting pot of collected impressions that increases or decreases our propensity to act in a certain way.

The majority of studies on media violence and aggression in the U.S., as well as some studies in other countries, show that media violence – in an indirect and most often reinforcing way, in interaction with more significant impressions, both in the short and in the long run – *contributes* to increased aggression for certain individuals under certain circumstances. Which circumstances? An early Swedish study[2] showed, for example, that young children who often watchted the popular TV Western series *High Chaparal* and who had to go to bed immediately after the programme showed aggressive tendencies, but this was not the case among children who also were intensive users of the series and were allowed to play and talk with the family after having watched the programme.

The international longitudinal studies carried out during recent decades, in which the same individuals have been followed for several years, indicate, in sum, that viewing media violence seems to statistically explain 5-10 per cent[3] of children's and young people's increased aggression over time, whereas 90-95 per cent of that aggression is due to other factors. These 'other' factors include the child's personality and earlier aggression; insecure, tangled or oppressive circumstances in the family, school and peer groups; socio-cultural background; unfavourable societal conditions, etc. Included here are also factors such as youth unemployment, alcohol and drugs, access to weapons, ethnic segregation, adults' diminished control, and a consumer-oriented society that stimulates theft and other economic crimes for which violence can be a means. The two Nordic longitudinal studies, one Finnish[4] and one Swedish,[5] that have been conducted on long term influences of watching media violence support these findings.

At the same time, research indicates that children who have good relations with their parents, peers, etc., who do not live in a violent environment or a violent society, who have secure social conditions, who like school, and are not frustrated or aggressive for some other reason, will most likely not become more aggressive through exposure to media violence.

Fear and uneasiness

Although in most children, young people and adults media violence does not contribute to aggression, there are several other important types of influences of media violence that we should be aware of.

One such influence is *fear* (or uneasiness, discomfort, becoming upset). Many children and young people like to be a little afraid, in a way that is exciting, when they watch fictive films and programmes. And some young people consciously seek out horror films in order to feel the horror. However, several studies have shown that entertainment violence can also give rise to fear that is stronger than what one was seeking. Murders, shooting, fights, knives, mysterious environments, monsters, masks, darkness, horrid sounds, etc., can have an unexpectedly frightening effect. Children also often feel deep displeasure or horror when children or animals are hurt on the screen. Most young people say that they at some time, or several times, have been frightened or horror-struck by entertainment violence, not seldom for an extended period.

Several Nordic studies[6] have asked parents or the children themselves which programmes and elements on television that have frightened them. Laboratory experiments in Finland[7] and the above-mentioned Finnish longitudinal study[8] have also tried to study the relationship between fear and aggression in connection with watching TV violence.

Violence in news and factual programmes can also be frightening. We are all scared now and then by depictions of real violence. This is necessary; we have to be shocked sometimes by such representations of violence. Fear is a biological gift, something positive, a means of survival, of protecting ourselves and counteracting dangers and societal evils. But it is obviously undesirable if our anxiety becomes so strong that our inclination to act is blocked.

Much of what is shown on the news and other factual material is at a geographical, cultural and psychological distance from the child's everyday life. But *when* children identify with or experience a violent situation in news/factual programmes, *when* they feel that this can happen here or to me – then media violence about reality is *more* frightening. So even if entertainment violence more often gives rise to fear, depictions of real violence, when they are frightening, frighten more *intensively*. This is because you cannot brush away (portrayals of) actual violence, persuade yourself that it is only make-believe, as you can entertainment violence.

Conceptions of violence in reality

There are also indications that media violence provides erroneous *conceptions of real violence*. For example, research results indicate that too much TV viewing can give audiences exaggerated ideas about the amount and type of violence in society.[9] Thus, media violence can convey or reinforce ideas that there are more violent persons and more violence out there than is actually the case. Such erroneous conceptions, in turn, can give rise to fear within the viewer of personal encounters with violence, as well as to adopt a pessimistic view that one cannot trust other persons.

Not only fictive violence but also news violence can influence people's conceptions of violence in reality.

Habituation

A further kind of influence that some studies have dealt with is emotional and cognitive *habituation,* that is, decreased excitement, decreased fear, and lowered inhibitions in response to media violence, which means that the level of tolerance increases. According to a Swedish study, young people even say themselves that this happens to them.[10] Some people then seek other kinds of, and stronger, excitement and violence from the media. And because the media are competing for audiences, they spice films, programmes, etc., with more violence.

The user perspective

As mentioned, some research has a user perspective: Why do an individual watch media violence? For some people – but not at all everyone – media violence means *excitement*. For others, watching media violence may be a part of *play*, *identity seeking* and the *feeling of group belonging*.

For example, interviews with 15- to 16-year-olds in Sweden[11] show that watching certain selected violence and horror genres can be a way of measuring toughness, a test of manliness in the gang, as well as one of several expressions of a lifestyle that unites the group and a counter-cultural protest action against an adult world that, from the young people's viewpoint, is oppressing or indifferent. This is more likely to be true of young people whose identity is not strengthened in school and whose low marks are a sign of competence and creativity that are being wasted.

A Danish example[12] of the meanings of media violence for identity seeking and group belonging is the following: Among teenage boys, the competent interpreters of action films – those who are acquainted with the conventions and narrative structures of the films – maintain or create, through continuous commentary while viewing, their positions and relations in the group.

Working through problems, understanding, knowledge

Many studies show that people who are already aggressive have a tendency to be attracted to media violence. This may also be true of certain children who, e.g., have experienced violence at home, in war, or in other contexts. One of several possible explanations is that some persons use media portrayals in an attempt to *work through and understand* their situation, as well as factors that have contributed to the aggressive environment, or the fact that they feel anxiety, are oppressed, frustrated or aggressive. It might be that these children feel a kind of temporary relief – even though the relief does not solve their conflicts in the long run. It is equally likely that viewing media violence also reinforces their aggression.

The motives for watching media violence can be more conscious and intentional, as well. A Norwegian study[13] and a Swedish one,[14] both with juvenile delinquents, show that these young people, depending on their group belonging and lifestyle, seek out particular violent genres and view these specific programmes or films repeatedly. It is not the case that chiefly the films or programmes make these young people violent – as mentioned previously, other factors are more decisive for aggression and crime – but their life situations imply the desire to *learn special actions* in order to master a possible violent situation in the future, for example, if they are threatened by another gang.

Summary

In sum, it is clear that we all get impressions from and are influenced by film and TV violence – but in different ways based on our varying motives, intentions, wishes and life conditions. From the above-mentioned examples of undesired influences – imitation, aggression, fear, erroneous conceptions and habituation – it is also evident that we all, in one way or another, are negatively influenced by media violence.

Video and computer games

Digital games form a more *interactive* medium than film and television, since the player can steer, in several respects, the course and outcome of the game. And certain games, such as role-playing games online, can be said to allow *participation*, in that the player more or less creates the personality and actions of his/her avatar and contributes more profoundly to the narrative of the game.

Naturally, research on digital games is much more recent than research on film and television. This means that whereas studies on film and television violence number in thousands, studies on digital game violence number in hundreds, perhaps slightly more than a hundred if we single out those asking whether aggression could be a consequence of playing violent video/computer games.

Researchers also state that it is not possible to simply generalize findings on the influences of film and TV violence to those of violent digital games, as the contents, formats and narratives of the games mostly deviate from film and TV contents, and as the role of the player is not only to 'receive' or 'consume'.

Game playing has, as mentioned, more features of interactivity and play and perhaps also implies another kind of identification, not least when playing from a first-person perspective.

The media perspective

As regards the research findings on the influences of violence in digital games, studies show that small children have a tendency to *imitate* violent actions in digital games in their subsequent play.

The research on *aggression* has, however, till now showed different and partly contradictory findings. Thus, some international studies, often starting from social learning/social cognitive theory, indicate that digital game violence can contribute to increased aggression in the form of aggressive thoughts, emotions, attitudes and behaviour, particularly after repeated playing and over time. At the same time, other studies fail to support or contradict findings showing that playing violent video/computer games contributes to aggression. Still other studies show increased aggressive thoughts, feelings and behaviour while playing, but these phenomena do not linger and are not transferred to people or things outside the game.

Apart from imitation and aggression, a few studies on digital games have dealt with *fear*. According to a Danish study,[15] children say they can become scared and have nightmares after playing digital games, but that movies and fiction on television and in film are more anxiety-provoking. The researchers connect this finding with the type of identification. In the games, the characters do not react emotionally in the way they do in film and TV series, where the viewer feels and experiences along with the movie's or series' characters' development, which is why identification with film and TV violence is thought to be stronger.

Excessive gaming

Though not directly related to violent representations in games, it is worth mentioning that there is some agreement among researchers concerning one type of harm related to digital games – and that is the consequences of 'exaggerated', 'excessive' or 'problematic' gaming. In other words, a minority of those who play a lot, report that they to a varying extent neglect sleep, eating, family, hygiene, studies, work and other leisure activities – see, for instance, a Swedish in-depth study with ten gamers.[16]

The user perspective

When trying to understand the individuals' motives of playing video and computer games, it is important to bear in mind that the games are very variated – content analyses show that several game genres do not contain violence or only little violence. On the other hand, there are several games, especially those popular among boys, that are found within the genres 'action/combat' (including 'first person games/shooters' and 'fighting games'), 'sports/racing', 'strategy and 'adventure' and that more often contain violent representations.

Regarding findings from studies adopting a user perspective, empirical data have not especially discerned different genres. What has been found for the games generally is that what digital game players themselves find most motivating about the playing is not the violence itself, but *the challenge*, i.e., learning to master and advance in the levels of the game, overcoming difficult situations, solving problems, and competing. Essential is also the emotional *excitement and immersion* that the games give rise to (it is fun, exciting, a relief from everyday routines and demands, etc.). When playing with others, social motives are also important. Playing certain games in certain ways may also be an essential marker of one's social and cultural group belonging and lifestyle. However, *the violent elements* in the games have been shown to be a relatively motivating factor as well, primarily for boys.

Other researchers taking a user perspective have started from the hypothesis that the essence of digital games is precisely their relation to children's play, pleasure and fantasy. In the last-mentioned Danish study,[17] child players said that the fictive violence they engage in is just for fun and does not entail any desire or inclination to hurt (or kill) on their part.

There are also speculations that playing games might serve as a vent for inner aggression, or at least help satisfy desires that are not allowed to turn into behaviour in everyday life. For instance, one interpretation by a Danish researcher[18] of young men's interest in video/computer games is that young boys live in a subordinate and powerless societal situation. Thus, playing violent electronic games may signify exercising resistance, giving expression to one's masculinity, creating power and gaining control – on a symbolic level.

The Internet

Turning to the Internet, it should be emphasized at the outset how few studies exist that focus on the possible influences of representations of violence on the net. The research to date that is relevant in this context has tended to take a more holistic approach, studying opportunities and benefits of the Internet vs. *risks* of harmful influences and the Internet user's *experiences* of harm – but not harmful influences *per se*. Thus, in the studies, violence as pictured on the Internet is regarded as one of a multitude of risks.

As we know, the Internet is a platform, or a virtual space, for an almost limitless quantity of diversiform (mass) media and (inter)personal or social media, as well as their intermediary forms. These different mass and (inter)personal/social media, in their turn, allow the Internet user to take on many more roles than the film, television or game user can. On the Internet s/he can be a receiver – or on the contrary a producer, creator and sender – of mediated communication. And between these two extremes – the reception and sender roles – the user can be *interacting* or *participating* to different extents, e.g., in games and in communities owned, maintained and copyrighted by someone else. Furthermore, mass mediated and, especially, (inter)personally or socially mediated communication on the Internet can also turn into face-to-face communication in real life, when meeting friends or strangers whom one first or previously met on the net. Given this, the Internet is related to *all main forms of communication*

The many informative, entertaining, social and practical advantages of the Internet, in combination with the many different user roles, also means a greater spectrum of possible offensive and/or injurious influences of the Internet than of conventional media. For children and young people, these harms may be aggravated by the fact, supported by several studies, that many parents have little idea of what their children, especially their teenagers, are actually doing on the Internet.[19]

If we consider the traditional media, it is reasonable to believe that more or less similar desirable and undesirable experiences and influences may stem from using these media on the Internet as from using them on their old platforms (the TV or radio set, the DVD player, the printed newspaper or book, the CD, etc.).

However, with regard to websites, communities, newsgroups, chat rooms, etc., not all their originators reveal their identity – or the site, group, etc., may disappear and emerge again in another guise reachable via another link. Particularly on these anonymously offered but nevertheless often easily accessible sites and groups, the Internet user may intentionally find, or non-intentionally come across, contents that are less common or non-existent in the conventional media – e.g., severe violence, violent pornography, child pornography, racism, hatred, etc. This may entail risks of influences other than those related to identifiable media, producers and senders.

Additional risks of harm are connected with the (inter)personally or socially mediated communication that often addresses specific others – e.g., bullying, threats, violations of privacy and personal integrity, economic crimes, etc., which are often feasible due to the sender's anonymity.

Risks of harm may be even graver in subsequent face-to-face communication in real life.

The media perspective

In one study, Swedish 9- to 16-year-olds were asked: 'Is there any content on television, film, games and on the Internet, that you feel bad about?'. They could choose a maximum of five responses among the fixed response alternatives. Slightly more than 40 per cent (more girls than boys) chose 'shocking pictures on the Internet – real pictures or films with dead, bloody people and animals' as content they feel bad about.[20]

It is hard to say exactly how many children and young people who involuntarily have met with representations of coarse violence or harassments, since the way of asking and other methodological aspects have differed within and between countries. In the Nordic countries, repeated studies have been made on this subject by the governmental media councils.[21]

A European study summarised what the research had arrived at in 21 EU contries (Nordic countries included) by the end of 2008.[22] Bearing in mind that many risks have received little or no attention, the research suggests that some risks are more prevalent and/or more homogenous across countries than others are. The findings show an approximate ordering of online risks to teenagers as follows:

- Giving out personal information: the most common risk in the European studies – around half of online teens do it, with considerable cross-national variation (13% to 91%)

- Seeing pornography: the second most common risk, with around 4 in 10 online teens across Europe doing it, but again with considerable cross-national variation (25% to 71%)

- Seeing violent or hateful content: the third most common risk, with approximately one third of teens doing it (apart from a much higher figure in one country, a fair degree of consistency across countries)

- Being bullied/harassed/stalked: generally around 1 in 5 or 6 teens online experience this (though there is also a group of high-risk countries here and one low-risk country)

- Receiving unwanted sexual comments: ranging from 1 in 10 teens in certain countries to 1 in 2 in one country

- Meeting an online contact offline: the least common but arguably most dangerous risk; there is considerable consistency in the figures across Europe, with around 8 per cent of online teens going to such meetings (in two countries, however, the percentages were much higher). Some research also indicates, however, that many of these contacts are with peers and end up as positive experiences.

There are also gender differences in risk, according to the European summary.[23] Boys appear more likely to seek out offensive, violent and pornographic content on the Internet. They also more often tend to meet somebody offline that they have met online and to give out personal information. Girls appear more likely to be upset by offensive, violent and pornographic material, to chat online with strangers, to receive unwanted sexual comments, and to be asked for personal information. Both boys and girls are at risk for online harassment and bullying.

Patterns of relationships

During the latest years, research points increasingly at relationships between risky online behaviour, a troubled home and/or personal life, and corresponding risky offline behaviour. There are also Nordic examples of such studies.[24, 25]

The range of psychosocial difficulties and risk factors include in various studies emotional distress, school conduct problems, conflict-ridden home environment, engaging in violent behaviour, sexual solicitation, maybe use of alcohol and drugs and access to weapons.

Thus, these findings do not seem to contradict previous traditional media research showing that film and TV violence is more likely to contribute to aggression in children who are already aggressive, have a troubled home environment, poor peer and school relations, etc.

The research therefore points out that some young people are more likely to be at risk than others are. Since there is often a correlation between (risky) offline behaviours and (risky) online behaviours, it would seem that studies taking a multiple media approach – studying the overall media user profile in combination with the media users' life situations – would be important in the future. We also ought to broaden the traditional view of media violence and include all the mediated violent forms existing on the Internet, not least the mediated (inter)personal violence, such as bullying, harassment, etc.

The user perspective

Research on risks – just as research on the benefits and opportunities of the Internet – has partly taken a user perspective.

An example of such a study focusing on Internet violence is a Norwegian qualitative, in-depth study[26] with 40 children aged 12-13 and 14-15 years, about, among other things, their possible habit of and interest in visiting websites with violence, pornography and bizarre elements. The boys were consistently much more interested in sites with violence, pornography, etc., than the girls were. The boys had 'travelling sites' with controversial or shocking contents – hard-core porno, animal porno, sadism, morbid violence, mutilations, death, wounded persons, medical pictures of deformed or malformed persons or fetuses, etc.

According to the boys, their reason for visiting the sites was that they wanted to see the 'worst' things. The researchers concluded that for many boys these sites – which the boys themselves called 'unlawful' or 'forbidden' – function as a kind of manhood test and entrance ticket into the boy culture, a notion supported by the fact that the boys typically visited such sites in the company of other boys.

Another study with a user perspective,[27] interviewing Swedish children 11-13-years-old, found that although the media debate seems to display consensus regarding what threats the Internet poses to young people, children's views of the Internet in many ways differ from the media related adult view. The children were aware of many downsides and it turned out that many children had in fact well-developed counter strategies, often thought out by the children alone or together with peers. In some, but remarkably few, cases adults had been giving tips or teaching the children strategies.

A third study, from Sweden as well,[28] also stresses the fact that many worries about the Internet in the public debate and research reflect concerns from an adult point of view. In the analysis of children's spontaneous contacts via Children's Helpline (by mobile phone, e-mail or chat) to the non-governmental organization BRIS (Children's Rights in Society), children mentioned several of the 'adult' concerns, too. But a considerable number of child contacts to BRIS were instead about parents' use of IT: Some children had discovered that their fathers visited pornographic websites, in several cases sites with child pornography; that the father – despite an ongoing relationship with the mother – had contact with other women (or younger girls) through various sites; or that the parent/s was/were unfaithful in real life. Other examples of children's discomfort were when parents – owing to excessive use of the Internet generally or of gaming or gambling sites – did not devote enough time and attention to them.

Notes

1. The article consists of brief and revised excerpts from the booklet Cecilia von Feilitzen (2009) *Influences of Mediated Violence. A Brief Research Summary*. The International Clearinghouse on Children, Youth and Media, Nordicom, University of Gothenburg (63 pp.). In the booklet there are a number of explicit references to concrete international studies. In the current article, however, references to Nordic research have been prioritized.
2. Olga Linné (1969) *Barns reaktioner på våldsinslag i tv* [Children's reactions to violent elements on television]. Stockholm, Sveriges Radio informerar nr 6
3. The statistical explanation is the square of causal correlations, of which the latter range from 0.10 to 0.30 in different studies (and seldom are zero correlations).
4. Vappu Viemerö (1986) *Relationships Between Filmed Violence and Aggression*. Åbo Akademi, Department of Psychology.
5. Inga Sonesson (1989) *Vem fostrar våra barn – videon eller vi? TV, video och emotionell och social anpassning* [Who Brings Up Our Children – the Video or We? Television, video and emotional and social adaption]. Stockholm, Esselte Studium
6. Some early studies are:
   Olga Linné (1964) *Barn och etermedia* [Children and ether media]. Sveriges Radio, Publik- och programforskningsavdelningen nr 6
   Ingela Schyller & Leni Filipson (1979) *Tusen och en siffra om barns läggvanor, biovanor, tv-tittarsituation, rädsla vid tv-program, sagoläsning* [Thousand and one figures on children's bedtimes, cinema habits, TV reception situation, fear of TV programmes, fairy-tale reading]. Sveriges Radio, Publik- och programforskningsavdelningen nr 16
   Inga Sonesson (1979) *Förskolebarn och TV* []Pre-school children and television]. Malmö, Esselte Studium
7. Kaj Björkqvist (1985) *Violent Films, Anxiety and Aggression. Experimental Studies of the Effect of Violent Films on the Level of Anxiety and Aggressiveness in Children*. Åbo Akademi, Department of Psychology.
8. Vappu Viemerö (1986) *Relationships Between Filmed Violence and Aggression*. Åbo Akademi, Department of Psychology
9. These investigations were initiated by George Gerbner and colleagues in the U.S. and have been repeated in several other countries – sometimes but not always with the same results. A Swedish such study is Elias Hedinsson (1981) *TV, Family and Society. The Social Origins and Effects of Adolescents' TV Use*. Stockholm, Almqvist & Wiksell International
10. Keith Roe (1983) *The Influence of Video Technology in Adolescence*. Lund University, Department of Sociology, Mediapanel No. 27
11. Keith Roe (1983) *Mass Media and Adolescent Schooling. Conflict or Co-existence?* Stockholm, Almqvist & Wiksell International

12. Tove Arendt Rasmussen (1989) 'Actionfilm og drengekultur' [Action Films and Boys' Culture], in Lennard Højbjerg (red) *Reception af levende billeder.* København, Akademisk Forlag, pp. 221-234

13. Ragnhild T. Bjørnebekk (1998) "Violence Against the Eye", *News on Children and Violence on the Screen*, No. 2-3, 1998, p. 5

14. Gudrun Uddén (1998) *"You Want to Be a Hero" – Young Criminals' Thoughts about Real Violence and Film Violence.* Stockholm, The Council on Media Violence/The National Council for Crime Prevention

15. Birgitte Holm Sørensen & Carsten Jessen (2000) 'It Isn't Real. Children, Computer Games, Violence and Reality', in Cecilia von Feilitzen & Ulla Carlsson (eds.) *Children in the New Media Landscape. Games, Pornography, Perceptions.* Yearbook from The UNESCO International Clearinghouse on Children and Violence on the Screen. Göteborg University, Nordicom, pp. 119-122

16. Jonas Linderoth & Ulrika Bennerstedt (2008) *Living in World of Warcraft – the thoughts and experiences of ten young people.* Göteborg University, Department of Education & Stockholm, The Media Council, http://www.medieradet.se/upload/Rapporter_pdf/World_of_Warcraft_eng. pdf (December 2008)

17. Birgitte Holm Sørensen & Carsten Jessen (2000) "It Isn't Real. Children, Computer Games, Violence and Reality", in Cecilia von Feilitzen & Ulla Carlsson (eds.) *Children in the New Media Landscape. Games, Pornography, Perceptions.* Yearbook from The UNESCO International Clearinghouse on Children and Violence on the Screen. Göteborg University, Nordicom, pp. 119-122

18. Jens F. Jensen (1993) "Powerplay – maskulinitet, makt och våld i datorspel [Powerplay – masculinity, power and violence in computer games]", in Cecilia von Feilitzen, Michael Forsman & Keith Roe (red) *Våld från alla håll. Forskningsperspektiv på våld i rörliga bilder.* Stockholm/ Stehag, Symposion, pp. 151-173

19. E.g. Medietilsynet (2010) *Barn og digitale medier 2010. Fakta om barn og unges bruk og upplevelse av digitale medier* [Children and digital media 2010. Facts on children and young people's use and experience of digital media], http://www.medietilsynet.no/Documents/Trygg%20bruk/ Rapporter/Barn%20og%20digitale%20medier/Barnogdigitalemedier_72dpi.pdf

20. *Ungar och medier 2008. Fakta om barns och ungas användning och upplevelser av medier* [Kids and Media 2008. Facts about children's and young people's use and experience of media]. Stockholm, Medierådet, http://www.medieradet.se/upload/Rapporter_pdf/Ungar_&_Medier_2008. pdf (November 2008)

21. See, for example (February 2010):
    (Denmark) Medierådet for børn og unge (2009) *Digitalt børne- og ungdomsliv anno 2009* [Digital child and youth life in 2009], http://andk.medieraadet.dk/upload/6_summary_med_grafer_og_kommentarer.pdf
    (Norway) Medietilsynet (2010) *Barn og digitale medier 2010. Fakta om barn og unges bruk og upplevelse av digitale medier* (Children and digital media 2010. Facts on children and young people's use and experience of digital media), http://www.medietilsynet.no/Documents/ Trygg%20bruk/Rapporter/Barn%20og%20digitale%20medier/Barnogdigitalemedier_72dpi.pdf
    (Sweden) Medierådet (2008) *Ungar & Medier 2008. Fakta om barns och ungas användning och upplevelser av medier* [Kids and Media 2008. Facts about children's and young people's use and experience of media], http://www.medieradet.se/upload/Rapporter_pdf/Ungar_&_Medier_2008.pdf

22. 'Growing body of research on online risk in Europe', the 4th Alert from EU Kids Online, March 2008, http://www.eukidsonline.net (September 2008). The project was led by Sonia Livingstone and Leslie Haddon at the London School of Economics and Political Science.

23. Uwe Hasebrink, Sonia Livingstone & Leslie Haddon (eds.) *Comparing Children's Online Opportunities and Risks across Europe: Cross-national Comparisons for EU Kids Online*, a report for the EC Safer Internet Plus Programme, 2008, http://www.eukidsonline.net (December 2008)

24. David Shannon (2007): *Vuxnas sexuella kontakter med barn via Internet. Omfattning, karaktär, åtgärder* [Adults' Sexual Contacts with Children via the Internet. Extent, Character, Measures]. Rapport 2007:11. Stockholm, Brottsförebyggande rådet

25. Carl-Göran Svedin & Ingrid Åkerman (2006) 'Ungdom och pornografi – hur pornografi i media används, upplevs och påverkar pojkar respektive flickor' [Youth and Pornography – How Pornography in Media is Used and Experienced and Influences Boys and Girls], in *Koll på porr – skilda röster om sex, pornografi, medier och unga*. Stockholm, Kulturdepartementet, Medierådet, pp. 87-100

26. Taran L. Bjørnstad & Tom Ellingsen (2002) *Nettsvermere. En rapport om ungdom och internett* [Net Swarms. A report on youth and the Internet]. Oslo, Statens Filmtilsyn http://www.medietilsynet.no/Documents/Selvbetjening/Bestilling/Nettsvermere.pdf (December 2008)

27. Elza Dunkels (2007) *Bridging the Distance: Children's strategies on the Internet*. Umeå University, Department of Interactive Media and Learning

28. Thomas Jonsland & Peter Irgens (2008) *The Children, BRIS and IT. A study of young people's contacts with BRIS about the Internet, IT and mobile telephony 2008*. Stockholm, BRIS (Children's Rights in Society), http://www.bris.se/upload/Articles/it_rapport_300dpi.pdf (December 2008)

The Kids are Alright
Perspectives on Children's Online Safety

Elza Dunkels

There is a contradiction in the rhetoric about young people and the Internet, namely, that while many adults admit they haven't "kept up with the times", they have no trouble at all expounding all the dangers lurking on the internet and what needs to be done to combat them. It is an interesting phenomenon. How can people express such firm opinions about a subject they say they don't know very much about? I think it may have a lot to do with our ideas about children and young people, and it is that notion that I would like to develop in this chapter.

Different ways of looking at children's activities on the web

When I have interviewed children about the Internet (Dunkels 2007), I have noted a fundamental ambivalence in our Western society concerning openness. On the one hand we encourage ingenuousness; we urge our children to confide in grown-ups when they are worried or sad, to tell the teacher if someone has been mean to them. On the other hand, we warn them to be cautious, to not reveal too much about themselves – on the Internet, for example. One of the most common pieces of advice that young people hear is that they should not give out information about themselves (Lüders et al. 2009). The notion of "too much" is interesting; it suggests two things: (1) that we have a pretty good idea of what an appropriate amount of information would be, and (2) that there is some form of consensus about where the line should be drawn. The ambivalence to openness is latent and general, I would say, and the Internet may be the catalyst that causes it to surface.

Take, for example, adults' reactions to the much-discussed "Pro Ana" and "Pro-Mia" websites. These are meeting-places where anorexia and bulimia, respectively, are discussed not as disorders, but as lifestyles. Most of those who go to these sites, mostly girls, have these disorders and wish to share their experiences and ideas with like-minded.

It might be a good idea to try to look at these sites from a young person's point of view, to try to understand what it is all about for them. Most of the participants do not consider themselves sick, and they perceive the non-anorectic/non-bulimic people around them as hostile. Part of the ailment is to perceive the behavior as a lifestyle, as part of one's personality. If there is no one in her surroundings that accepts her behavior as part of her personality – not to eat is simply the way she is – then all those who try to persuade her to eat are The Enemy. They are trying to make her abandon her innermost convictions. In a situation like this, an opportunity to meet and talk to like-minded "sisters" about the things that mean a lot, a place where she can escape the constant surveillance of a hostile world, must be very welcome; a breathing space in a chaotic existence.

For the rest of us, the sites might be sources of information and insight – to the extent we can gain access to them. We might learn more about these complex ailments that we know far too little about. There has been some research on these phenomena, and the sites give us an interesting, albeit frightening, insight into a world many of us otherwise would never come in contact with (cf. Palmgren 2007).

Our ideas about children

In my doctoral research, much of the information and data that at first puzzled me were suddenly clarified when I added conceptions of children into the equation. Why weren't children more vociferous? Why were adults the only ones to speak out on children's use of the web? There was something wrong with the picture, and when I began thinking about how we conceive of children and childhood, some pieces fell into place. Nowadays, we no longer look on children as incomplete, as being on the way to becoming people. Today we tend to see them as competent individuals, as young citizens (see Eriksson 2008, i.e.). James and Prout (1997) describe an emerging research perspective where childhood is conceived of as a social construction. There is no universal state that is childhood; instead we have constructed it, decided that such a state exists and defined its characteristics. Another important aspect of this perspective is that childhood is always linked to other social parameters like class, gender and ethnicity. James and Prout relate examples showing that constructions of children and childhood are so strongly linked to the social context that attempts to export ideas about children to other cultures have proven much more complicated than was initially believed. One such example comes from the 1960s, when the phenomenon of "Fanta babies" in developing countries was widely debated. "Fanta babies" were undernourished because they were brought up on Fanta, the soft drink, which was a luxury, but was devoid of nutrients. The phenomenon may be interpreted as a case of the collision of different contexts surrounding the construction of the child. Advertisements for Fanta showed a rosy-cheeked, chubby little child drinking Fanta. What the pictures didn't show was that the child survived thanks to a daily intake of nutritious meals his parents could afford to provide alongside the drink. The image of the foreign child did not communicate the whole picture to third-world parents, nor was it intended to.

A history of how children have been perceived in relation to their Internet use might look something like this:

Frontier days

The first wave of reactions to children's ventures into cyberspace was characterized by wonderment and fear. Both scientific studies and media reporting focused on what was new and different and portrayed the young as a new kind of human being. Epithets like "Homo zappiens" – coined, albeit in jest, by Professor Wim Veen in The Netherlands (Veen & Vrakking 2006) – suggest differences amounting to the evolution of a new species. A preoccupation with differences and oddities is referred to as *exoticizing* a phenomenon, in this case young people and their culture. As a result, the phenomenon appears more different than it is. Reports from the frontier days of the Internet were often seasoned with lurid anecdotes, presented as typical. *"Suspected rape after meeting on chat-site"* (*Aftonbladet*, 2003) and *"SMS-terror drives child to suicide attempt"* (*Dagsavisen*, 2003) are a couple of examples culled from Nordic tabloids of that day.

In the wake of these sensationalist reports came a wave of profiteers, one is tempted to say charlatans. They lectured on all the terrible things that could befall children on the web. Some even showed pictures, even though the act of showing them may in itself have broken the law. Another group that sought to make money off the phenomenon were those who proferred solutions to the problems. When the Internet had become a common household fixture, there were many who spoke of a "Wild West out there", and I find the likeness apt – but perhaps not exactly in the sense intended. In many old Western films there was a comical character, a traveling purveyor of "snake oil", tonics that cured blisters on your feet, baldness on your head, and just about every conceivable ailment in between. Similarly, at the end of the twentieth century there were any number of people claiming to have simple solutions to complicated problems. One set of simple solutions were the many software products that promised to keep inappropriate content out of households' and schools' computers. Also in this category are various products designed to prevent cheating in school.

The "do-gooders"

The next wave of reactions resembles ideas and behavior in the Western world in the heyday of colonialism. Idle individuals with too much money on their hands began to devote themselves to charitable projects for the benefit of "the poor natives". They identified the problems the natives were suffering from, devised solutions to those problems, and then provided them. They taught the poor souls to read and to practice good hygiene. Although their intentions were good, their efforts often failed, the reason being a fundamental imbalance in the power relations between those who defined the problems and the objects of their good will. Similarly, many of the initiatives taken to bolster children's safety on Internet a decade ago suffered from the same fundamental imbalance. Adults defined the problems and came up with the remedies: children are at risk when they are online; therefore, they should be barred from posting pictures and personal information on the web.

Seldom were any children's views heard. The research that guided policy was strictly quantitative: How often do you...? Have you ever....? Studies of this sort should be preceded by interviews with young users so as to get some idea of how they use the web and what dangers they, themselves perceive. Otherwise, there is the risk that the survey only confirms one's a priori assumptions. Many of the early studies of this kind were exoticizing and clearly had a grown-up perspective. In many cases, studies focused on differences between children today and children in the pre-Internet era, with a view to showing the enormity of the change. Words like "virtual" and "cyber" were frequently used – "the virtual classroom", etc. These novel words tended to underline the newness of what was happening on the web. Originally, "virtual" meant, "in effect, though not in fact". Today we know that most young people hardly distinguish what happens online from in real life in any deeper sense. Of course, they can differentiate between the two, but Internet is perceived as simply another space, in addition to the many other spaces in real life. Internet has a number of specific characteristics, as do most other spaces offline. In a way it is unfortunate that we use the word "virtual" for what takes place online. It leads us to believe that online phenomena are somehow less real than anything that happens offline. Virtual friends are less real than a friend we meet face to face; virtual reality cannot be experienced in the same way as real life. For that reason I think we should use "web-based" when that is what we are referring to.

In time, titles like "New bottle but old wine: A research of cyber bullying in schools" (Li 2007) began to appear in the research literature. It can be taken as signaling a change. In my dissertation (Dunkels 2007) I conclude that inasmuch as most adults find it very difficult to understand young people's relation to the Internet, we should be very attentive to young people's views on the subject.

Charitable actions are hard to criticize since they almost invariably are based on a will to do good. A critical standpoint is easily mistaken for criticism of the good intent. It is equally important, however, to question actions taken for altruistic reasons as it is to question clearly unethical behaviors. A charitable initiative can do as much harm if it is based on a spurious analysis; in fact, it can do even more harm, as the dangers are hidden behind good intentions. If a respected person or organization sends a message, the receivers are less critical of it; one might say that the reputation of the sender rubs off on the message, lending it greater credence than it deserves.

A civil rights movement

The next period may be likened to a civil rights movement. It is a period of gradual awakening; more and more people became aware of a structural imbalance. Where are children's views about Internet? Shouldn't children have equal rights? Are there forces in society that oppress children? Increasingly, young people's perspectives are being sought out, and the tone is less lordly when people offer advice about how to use Internet safely.

One way of describing this development is the term, *childism* – an analogue of sexism, racism and so forth. Childism is about identifying power structures in society that are based on age, just as there are structures based on gender and ethnicity. "Childism" may be defined as

> [...] *prejudice or discrimination against the young. Also, childism refers to systemic conditions that promote stereotypes of the young* (Dunkels 2007).

Serious exploration of this structure might lead to the discovery that some members of society are discriminated against only because they are young. One who has written about childism is psychoanalyst and researcher Elisabeth Young-Bruehl (2005), who argues that one of the factors behind this form of discrimination is parents' notion that they own their children. There is also a primitive conception, even today, of children as wild creatures that need to be "civilized" and disciplined in order to qualify as full-fledged members of society.

What led me into this line of inquiry was a television interview with the Canadian poet, Leonard Cohen, who was asked what he felt about the fact that many members of his audiences these days were not even born when he composed and recorded his classic songs. The question was asked in a way that suggested that the interviewer thought the young girls in the audience foolish. Cohen responded coolly, in a totally different vein: At the age of twelve human beings are equipped with a full range of emotions and are thus perfectly capable of appreciating cultural expressions. If anything, our sensitivity dulls with age. He is right, of course. But where in our society is that insight reflected? Hardly anywhere, I'd say. Instead, there are all too many throwbacks to an era when children were regarded as human-beings-in-the-making, unable to think for themselves or to feel.

Childism is a little more complicated than sexism or racism, however. Sexism and racism are power structures that we have learned to spot; we know that they have no foundation in reality. For example, we no longer accept the notion that women are less competent at various occupations and should therefore be paid less for their labor. When it comes to the young, the situation is slightly different. The power structure is to some extent natural and desirable. Adults must take responsibility for their children, and experience sometimes justifiably gives mature people the upper hand. But there authority is not always justifiable. The power we have over young people can be both used and abused, which makes childism tricky.

It is easy to fall into the knee-jerk reaction, "So, you say; now kids should decide *everything*?" This is the same kind of reaction one heard when racism and sexism were first identified as issues. Anyone who has the upper hand finds it difficult to see that the status quo is no good, and that some of the privileges they enjoy thanks to prevailing structures have to be given up. There is nothing abnormal about this; it seems to be human nature. But, since we consider ourselves a civilized society, we have no choice but to root out unjust practices – no matter what our position in the power structure may be.

A second problem that attempts to develop theories of age and power run up against is that everyone entitled to express themselves is on the same side of the issue. We all, by definition, have "come of age" and are none too eager to let go of the power age confers. And, just as in the discussion of sexism, we can expect to hear, "But what about old people? Aren't they just as oppressed?".

In the "civil rights" phase, where we are just now, the rights of children and adolescents have begun to be recognized as an issue. Internet facilitates the process in that it offers a forum that is open to many more people. Some debatteurs will attract a lot of attention; you no longer have to be on television to become a national or international "personality". All it takes is for a few people to start circulating a funny video clip, and the characters in it become household names – and may end up on television after all.

The first two phases – "Frontier days" and "Do-gooders" – have the drawback that all the initiatives are put forward by volunteers and organizations that have commercial or ideological motives. This might be considered a boon to society since things get done without the expense of public revenue, but the problem is that the underlying motives of the actors are reflected in the questions posed and, not least, the solutions arrived at.

Shifman and Versano (2007) analyzed websites that offer "clean jokes", i.e., sites that have been vetted for offensive humor. The vetting is done so that parents can be assured that their children will not be exposed to anything inappropriate. The researchers, however, came to the conclusion that there are even greater risks involved in letting one's children visit censored websites. For one thing, it is impossible to weed out "offensive" or "inappropriate" jokes because there is no consensus about what is offensive or inappropriate. Humor is in the eye and ear of the beholder, and what is funny to some may well be offensive to others. Shifman and Versano come to the conclusion that parents are given a false sense of security when they rely on the judgment of a website; as a result, they may be less watchful concerning what their children are consuming.

Attitudes to adolescent youth

As regards adults' views on adolescents the situation is perhaps even more complicated than is the case with children, for here we have to add the fact that adults often perceive a challenge to their position of power in their relations with youth. It is an inherent feature of all hierarchies that those who have reached the top, who finally occupy positions of influence, may feel a threat from below. People at the top are reluctant to let those beneath them rise, and adults' relationship with youth may well be interpreted in those terms.

Concern is often expressed over the level of young people's knowledge nowadays, but there is no historical evidence of any decline having occurred. On the contrary, the overall level of knowledge in society has steadily climbed, but it is not clear to the group that wields power. Danish sociologist Kirsten Drotner (1999) speaks of "historical amnesia" to describe the fact that we as a collective never learn from past experience, i.e., history. There is a quotation sometimes attributed to Socrates that is often brought up in discussions of relations between the generations:

> The children now love luxury; they have bad manners, contempt for authority; they show disrespect for elders and love chatter in place of exercise. Children are now tyrants, not the servants of their households. They no longer rise when elders enter the room. They contradict their parents, chatter before company, gobble up dainties at the table, cross their legs, and tyrannize their teachers. (Quotationsbook 2007)

We laugh, of course, at an ironic reminder that some things never change, but the quotation is also a very poignant illustration of how members of the elder generation sometimes fail to appreciate the contributions young people make to social development.

We often hear warnings that democratic processes face a coming crisis inasmuch as young people of today show so little interest in political activity. The conclusion is drawn on the basis of the fact that membership in the parties' youth organizations is dwindling. We do well to stop and think about why this might be. In many countries, everyone under the age of 18 is legally excluded from political life – or at least the actual point of getting involved in politics, namely, influencing society around us. You have to wait until you are old enough to vote; until then, there are no formal channels by which to exert influence. So, the parties' youth groups may be seen as remnants of an era when those who stood outside the system were content to sign up and prepare themselves for the glorious day when they would be reckoned among the full-fledged. The upbringing children are given today renders them more critical of existing hierarchies. Consequently, fewer young people choose to sign up. It is interesting to think along these lines, anyhow, and not simply put their behavior down to lack of involvement or interest. We might, for example, see young people's discussions on the web as alternative ways to contribute to democracy.

Technical solutions to social problems

Filtering software is a good example of technical solutions to *social* problems. Now, what kinds of websites do we want to remove? Typical categories are sexual content, sadistic violence, and jokes about religion. The advertisements for these filters emphasize the families' or school's freedom of choice, but in practice customers don't have much freedom to speak of, for practical reasons. The software wouldn't be very useful if every customer had to define in detail what he or she wants kept out, as researchers Price and Verhulst (2005) observe. Instead the programs are designed on the basis of a priori values and norms, which usually include the conviction that children and youth should be protected from all material that has any sexual undertone whatsoever. This is just one example of how absurd attempts to filter content can be.

A modern family or school would hardly agree that children are harmed by information about sex or by exposure to images of naked skin, while at the same time they may strongly oppose sexism, pornography and exploitation of sexuality. But here we encounter a problem: it proves impossible to define sexism, pornography or exploitation as parameters for filter algorithms – no matter how much we might wish it were possible. This kind of technology is not particularly sophisticated, but even if it were, we could hardly reach agreement on the definitions of sexism, pornography or exploitation. There is no indication that any contemporary society can reach consensus on these crucial issues other than perhaps at the level of the lowest common denominator. We can be agreed about slavery, cruelty and physical abuse, but beyond that our opinions differ. Take, for example, the American photographer, Sally Mann, who has been accused of child pornography in her homeland for a photo of her little daughter squatting to piss on a stone cliff on a hot summer day. The same photo is applauded here in Sweden for depicting a girl in the same way as boys have been depicted for centuries. How might a "family filter" have reacted to the image?

There are any number of filter solutions, but all have the following in common:

- The aim is to steer minors' use of computers and perhaps especially the Internet.

- Tools like these are often too blunt. They eliminate good sites because they contain words that trigger the filter mechanism. Sites offering sex education and web-based health clinics for youth are examples of beneficial websites that many programs filter out.

- The programs give rise to a false sense of security. Adults feel comfortable, knowing that their children's school has a filter, but there is still the need for conversations about personal ethics. And how do children who have been sheltered by a filter react when confronted with content on an unfiltered computer? Awareness has to be won every day; no software can change that.

- The ideological foundation of the software – i.e., the reasons why some pages are censored, but not others – are not transparent. Users have to live with the values of those who created the filter.

We human beings have a general tendency to look for shortcuts to fill our needs. Had we not been essentially lazy, we might never have invented the wheel. Marketing professionals are well aware of this trait and are quick to exploit it to sell us products that we really don't need. Human problems, social problems, take time and energy to solve, whether or not there are technical products that offer a quick fix. To put an end to cheating, bullying or pupils' exposure to inappropriate material on Internet will always require hours and hours of work with the pupils. The only party who gains by our buying technical solutions is the company that seeks to profit from our uncertainty. Howard Rheingold (2007) goes so far as to say that anyone who censors Internet is not fostering a good relationship with his child.

We have considered several examples of how adults react to young people's use of the Internet and shown that remedies are not always as simple as they may at first seem. What seems revolting at first glance can seem reasonable when we have had a chance to think it over – and vice versa. We have to let our normal values be our guide, when it comes to the Internet, even though it may seem like other rules apply whenever the Internet is involved. Few of us would consider reading our child's diary without permission; still, many so-called "family filters" offer tools that allow parents to see which websites their child has visited.

References

Aftonbladet (2003) Misstänkt våldtäkt efter träff på chatt [Suspected rape after meeting on chat-site]. www.aftonbladet.se/vss/nyheter/story/0,2789,269827,00.html

Dagsavisen (2003) SMS-terror driver barn til selvmordsforsøk [SMS terror drives child to suicide attempt]. www.dagsavisen.no/innenriks/article948433.ece

Drotner, Kirsten (1999) Dangerous Media? Panic Discourses and Dilemmas of Modernity. *Paedagogica Historica 35*(3): 593-619.

Dunkels, Elza (2007) *Bridging the Distance – Children's Strategies on the Internet*. Umeå University. (Dissertation)

Eriksson, Maria (2008) *Barns röster om våld: att tolka och förstå* [Children talk about violence: to interpret and understand]. Malmö: Gleerups.

James, Allison & Prout, Alan (1997) *Constructing and Reconstructing Childhood: Contemporary Issues in the Sociological Study of Childhood*. London: Routledge.

Li, Qing (2007) New Bottle but Old Wine: A Research of Cyberbullying in Schools. *Computers in Human Behavior 23*(4), 1777-1791.

Lüders, Marika, Bae Brandtzæg, Petter och Dunkels, Elza (2009) Risky Contacts. In Livingstone, Sonia & Haddon, Leslie (red.) *Kids Online*. London: Policy Press.

Palmgren, Ann-Charlotte (2007) Idag är jag ingenting annat än en kropp [Today I am no more than a body]. In Lindgren, Simon (red.) *Unga och nätverkskulturer – mellan moralpanik och teknikromantik*. Stockholm: Ungdomsstyrelsen.

Price, Monroe & Verhulst, Stefaan (2005) *Self-regulation and the Internet*. The Hague: Kluwer Law International.

Quotationsbook (2007) Socrates http://quotationsbook.com/quote/44998/

Rheingold, Howard (2007) Sack the Nanny, Talk to Your Kids. *The Sydney Morning Herald,* 2007-09-25.

Shifman, Limor, & Varsano, Hamutal Ma'apil (2007) The Clean, the Dirty and the Ugly: A Critical Analysis of 'Clean Joke' Web Sites. *First Monday.* www.firstmonday.org/issues/issue12_2/shifman/index.html

Veen, Wim & Vrakking, Ben (2006) *Homo Zappiens – Growing Up in a Digital Age.* London: Network Continuum.

Young-Bruehl, Elisabeth (2005) Discovering Child Abuse, *The American Journal of Psychoanalysis,* Vol. 65, No. 3, 293–295.

The Authors

Pål Aarsand, Ph.D, Senior Lecturer, Department of Education, Uppsala University, Sweden, pal.aarsand@ped.uu.se

Thorbjörn Broddason, Ph.D., Professor, Department of Sociology, Faculty of Social and Human Sciences, University of Iceland, Reykjavík, Iceland, tbrodd@hi.is

Ulla Carlsson, Ph.D., Professor, Director, Nordicom, University of Gothenburg, Sweden, ulla.carlsson@nordicom.gu.se

Kirsten Drotner, Dr.phil., Professor, Institute of Literature, Culture and Media Studies, University of Southern Denmark, Odense, Denmark, drotner@dream.dk

Elza Dunkels, Ph.D., Senior Lecturer, Department of Interactive Media and Learning, Umeå University, Sweden, elza.dunkels@educ.umu.se

Ola Erstad, Dr.polit., Professor, Institute for Educational Research, University of Oslo, Norway, ola.erstad@ped.uio.no

Cecilia von Feilitzen, Professor, Scientific Co-ordinator, The International Clearinghouse on Children, Youth and Media, Nordicom, University of Gothenburg, Sweden and Media and Communication Studies, Södertörn University, Sweden, cecilia.von.feilitzen@sh.se

Ingunn Hagen, Dr.polit., Professor, Department of Psychology, Norwegian University of Science and Technology / NTNU, Trondheim, Norway, ingunn.hagen@svt.ntnu.no

Irma Hirsjärvi, Ph.D., Coordinator of the Global Comparative Research on Youth Media Participation at The Research Centre for Contemporary Culture, University of Jyväskylä, Finland, irma.hirsjarvi@jyu.fi

Gunilla Jarlbro, Ph.D., Professor, Communication and Media, Lund University, Sweden, gunilla.jarlbro@kom.lu.se

Sólveig Margrét Karlsdóttir, Research Assistant, Department of Sociology University of Iceland, Reykjavík, Iceland, smk10@hi.is

Faltin Karlsen, Ph.D., Associate Professor, The Norwegian School of Information Technology / NITH, Oslo, Norway, fk@nith.no

Sirkku Kotilainen, Ph.D., Senior Researcher, The Finnish Youth Research Network, University of Jyväskylä, Finland, sirkku.kotilainen@jyu.fi

Kjartan Ólafsson, Lecturer, Social Sciences, University of Akureyri, Iceland, kjartan@unak.is

Ingegerd Rydin, Ph.D., Professor, Media and Communication Studies, School of Social and Health Sciences, Halmstad University, Sweden, ingegerd.rydin@hh.se

Ulrika Sjöberg, Ph.D., Senior Lecturer, Media and Communication Studies, School of Social and Health Sciences, Halmstad University, Sweden, ulrika.sjoberg@hh.se

Birgitte Holm Sørensen, Ph.D., Professor, Director of the Research Programme, Media and ICT in a Learning Perspective, Danish School of Education, Aarhus University, Denmark, birgitte@dpu.dk

Tapio Varis, Dr., Professor of Vocational and Professional Education and UNESCO Chair in Global e-Learning, Faculty of Education, University of Tampere, Finland, tapio.varis@uta.fi

Part III.

Statistics – Young Peoples' Media Use

Compiled by Catharina Bucht

About the statistics

The statistics presented is selected to give an image of the media landscape in the Nordic countries, today and the development over the last decade. Under each section the aim has been to present time series with statistics on access and use, but also to include ad hoc figures or findings from recent surveys in each country. Availability of data varies among the Nordic countries and some countries have longer traditions of collecting data than others. Different survey methods have been used, which impairs comparability between countries and years. Data should therefore be taken as indicators of the trend and level of e.g. use.

Nordicom's statistics document developments in the media sectors in Denmark, Finland, Iceland, Norway and Sweden. The data are compiled and processed in collaboration with Statistics Finland (www.stat.fi), Statistics Iceland (www.statice.is), medianorway (www.medienorge.uib.no) and Nordicom-Sweden (www.nordicom.gu.se).

Tables and Figures

All Media

Internet

Mobile Phone

Games

Television

Video/DVD

Radio

Newspapers

Books

All Media

Finland: Media Equipment at Home in the Population Aged 10+ 2008 (%)

	%
TV	92
Video	54
DVD-player	60
PC	79
Access to Internet	76
Broadband connection	68
Mp3-player	45
Video game consol	26
Mobile phone	98

Source: Statistics Finland, 2010.

Norway: Media Equipment at Home Among Children and Youth 2009 (%)

	9-12 years	13-15 years	16-19 years	20-24 years
Daily newspaper (subscribed)	66	79	72	35
TV				
No. of TV-sets	2.3	3.5	3.2	1.6
Teletext	87	92	98	91
Video/DVD/PVR				
Video	70	66	65	35
DVD-player	94	95	98	85
PVR	31	29	32	17
PC	98	98	100	99
No. of PCs	2.6	3.2	3.2	2.4
Access to Internet	98	98	100	98
Broadband connection	74	90	97	92
CD-player	99	98	97	90
Mp3-player	74	91	87	90
Video game consol	90	82	84	68
Own mobile phone	87	93	98	100

Source: Statistics Norway, 2010.

Sweden: Media Equipment at Home Among Children and Youth 2009 (%)

	9-14 years	15-24 years
Daily newspaper (subscribed)	55	55
Radio	99	99
via Internet	51	77
via mobile phone	63	70
via ipod/mp3	32	35
TV-set	100	97
three or more	54	47
Access to TV		
in mobile phone	5	6
in ipod/mp3	1	2
Tele-text	90	94
Video/DVD/PVR	98	96
Video	66	53
DVD-player	97	94
PVR	15	16
PC	96	98
two or more	79	78
with access to Internet	96	98
with broadband connection	79	80
Internet access via other equipment than computer	32	39
Portabel computer	70	77
Mp3-player	68	81
Video game consol	85	68
Portable game consol (e.g.PSP)	24	17

Source: Nordicom-Sweden, 2010.

Finland: Daily Media Use Among Youth 10-24 years 2008 (%)

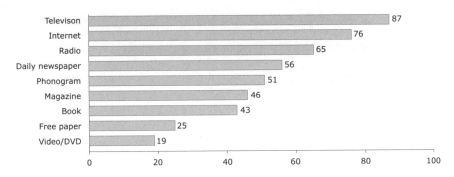

Source: Statistics Finland, 2009.

Norway: Daily Media Use Among Children 9-15 years 2009 (%)

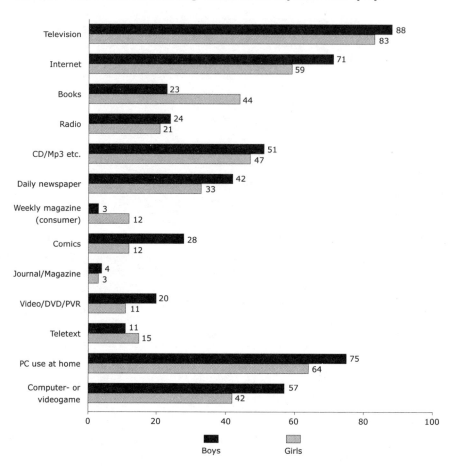

Note: Media use refers to share of the population who have used each medium an average day.

Source: Statistics Norway, 2010.

Norway: Daily Media Use Among Children 16-24 years 2009 (%)

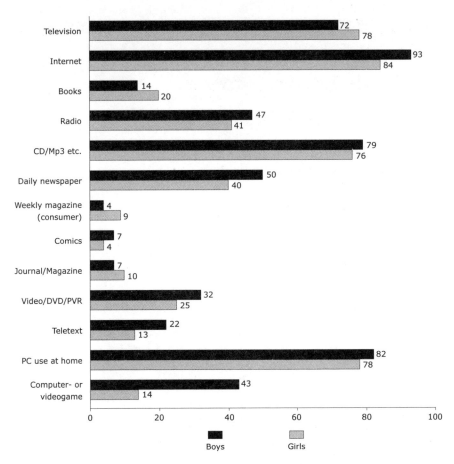

Note: Media use refers to share of the population who have used each medium an average day.

Source: Statistics Norway, 2010.

Sweden: Daily Media Use Among Children 9-14 years 2009 (%)

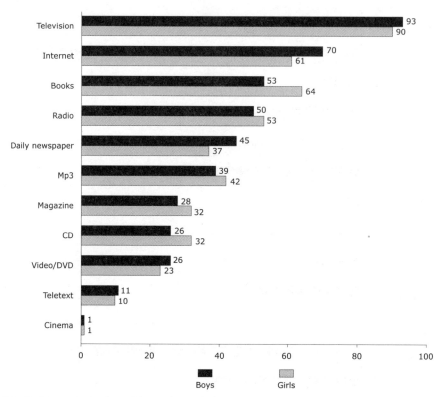

Television: Boys 93, Girls 90
Internet: Boys 70, Girls 61
Books: Boys 53, Girls 64
Radio: Boys 50, Girls 53
Daily newspaper: Boys 45, Girls 37
Mp3: Boys 39, Girls 42
Magazine: Boys 28, Girls 32
CD: Boys 26, Girls 32
Video/DVD: Boys 26, Girls 23
Teletext: Boys 11, Girls 10
Cinema: Boys 1, Girls 1

Boys ■   Girls ▨

Note: Media use refers to share of the population who have used each medium an average day. Daily newspaper and magazine refers to both printed and online, books refers to printed, audio- as well as e-book, radio and television refers to regular listening or viewing as well as via Internet and/or other media player.

Source: Nordicom-Sweden, 2010.

Sweden: Daily Media Use Among Children 15-24 years 2009 (%)

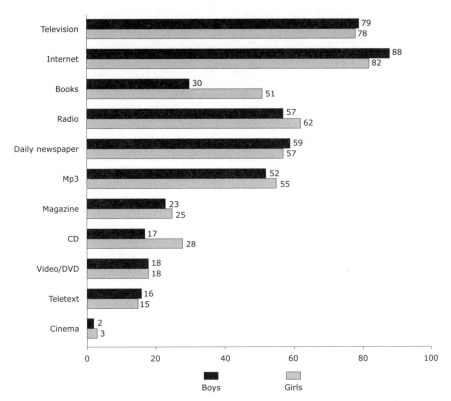

Note: Media use refers to share of the population who have used each medium an average day. Daily newspaper and magazine refers to both printed and online, books refers to printed, audio- as well as e-book, radio and television refers to regular listening or viewing as well as via Internet and/or other media player.

Source: Nordicom-Sweden, 2010.

Sweden: Popular Media Activities an Average Day Among Children 9-14 Years 2009 (%)

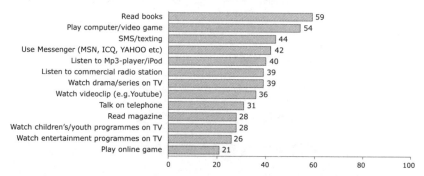

Read books — 59
Play computer/video game — 54
SMS/texting — 44
Use Messenger (MSN, ICQ, YAHOO etc) — 42
Listen to Mp3-player/iPod — 40
Listen to commercial radio station — 39
Watch drama/series on TV — 39
Watch videoclip (e.g.Youtube) — 36
Talk on telephone — 31
Read magazine — 28
Watch children's/youth programmes on TV — 28
Watch entertainment programmes on TV — 26
Play online game — 21

Source: Nordicom-Sweden, 2010.

Sweden: Popular Media Activities an Average Day Among Youth 15-24 Years 2009 (%)

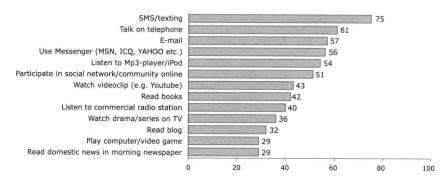

SMS/texting — 75
Talk on telephone — 61
E-mail — 57
Use Messenger (MSN, ICQ, YAHOO etc.) — 56
Listen to Mp3-player/iPod — 54
Participate in social network/community online — 51
Watch videoclip (e.g. Youtube) — 43
Read books — 42
Listen to commercial radio station — 40
Watch drama/series on TV — 36
Read blog — 32
Play computer/video game — 29
Read domestic news in morning newspaper — 29

Source: Nordicom-Sweden, 2010.

Denmark: Time Spent with Popular Media Activities Among Youth 15-25 years 2009 (min/day)

	Medium	Minutes/day
TV 2	television (public service)	37
P3	radio (public service)	31
Games/DVD/etc.		21
Facebook.com	web site	21
TV3	television	18
P4 total	radio (public service)	18
DR1	television (public service)	15
TV3+	television	10
Radio 100	radio	10
Bazoom.dk (photosharing)	web site	10
Google.dk	web site	9
TV 2 Zulu	television	8
Youtube.com	web site	7
Disney Channel	television	6
Nova FM	radio	6
Kanal 5	television	5

Source: TNS Gallup TV-Meter/DR, 2009.

Norway: Share of Time Used with Different Media Among Children and Youth 2009 (%)

9-15 years

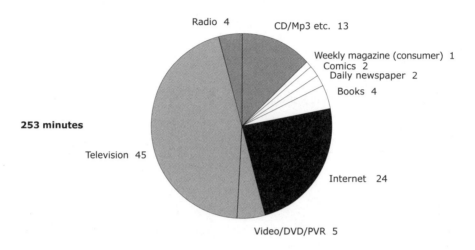

Radio 4
CD/Mp3 etc. 13
Weekly magazine (consumer) 1
Comics 2
Daily newspaper 2
Books 4

253 minutes

Television 45

Internet 24

Video/DVD/PVR 5

16-24 years

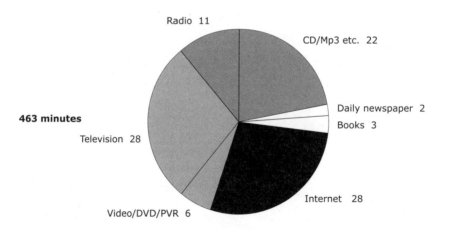

Radio 11
CD/Mp3 etc. 22
Daily newspaper 2
Books 3

463 minutes

Television 28

Internet 28

Video/DVD/PVR 6

Note: Time used refers to the total amount of time used to media consumption and does not account for consuming two or more different media simultanously.

Source: Statistics Norway, 2010.

Sweden: Share of Time Used with Different Media Among Children and Youth 2009 (%)

9-14 years

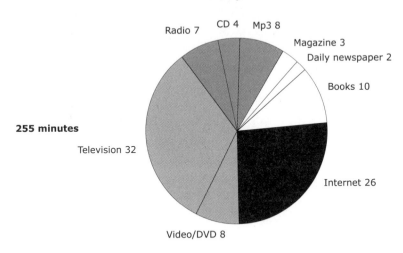

255 minutes

Radio 7
CD 4
Mp3 8
Magazine 3
Daily newspaper 2
Books 10
Television 32
Internet 26
Video/DVD 8

15-24 years

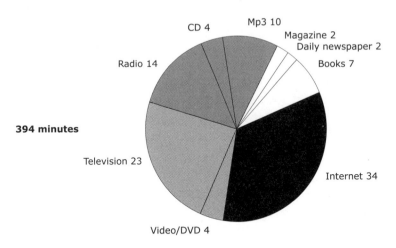

394 minutes

CD 4
Mp3 10
Magazine 2
Daily newspaper 2
Books 7
Radio 14
Television 23
Internet 34
Video/DVD 4

Note: Time used refers to the total amount of time used to media consumption and does not account for consuming two or more different media simultanously.

Source: Nordicom-Sweden, 2010.

Internet

Access to Internet at Home in the Nordic Countries 2000-2009 (%)

Year	Denmark[1] (Population)	Finland[2] (Households)	Iceland[3] (Pop./Households)	Norway[4] (Population)	Sweden[4] (Population)
2000	..	32	65	52	52
2003	71	47	78	64	71
2006	83	65	83	79	80
2009	86	73 [5]	90	91	89 [6]

.. Data not available
[1] Share of population aged 16+.
[2] Share of households.
[3] 2000 share of population; from 2003 on, share of households. Figures are not strictly comparable between years due to different survey methods and wording of questions.
[4] Share of population 9-79 years. Annual averages.
[5] Broadband access only.
[6] Access via PC.

Source: Nordicom, 2010 (processed), see www.nordicom.gu.se/eng.php?portal=mt

Finland: Daily Use of Internet Among Children 2009 (%)

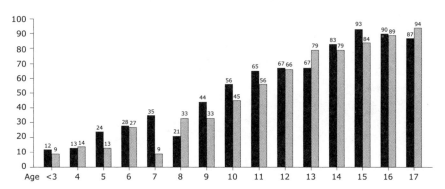

Source: Finnish Communications Regulatory Authority, 2009.

Internet Use the Average Day in Norway and Sweden 2000-2009 (%)

Norway	2000	2003	2006	2009
All	27	42	60	73
Sex				
Men	33	49	67	78
Women	21	34	54	67
Age				
9-15	**23**	**37**	**56**	**66**
16-24	**38**	**58**	**80**	**89**
25-44	34	54	73	87
45-66	21	35	53	67
67-79	4	4	17	38
Sweden				
All	32	33	62	65
Sex				
Men	36	38	68	69
Women	28	29	57	61
Age				
9-14	**26**	**28**	**63**	**65**
15-24	**48**	**42**	**84**	**85**
25-44	46	43	73	78
45-64	29	34	62	63
65-79	5	9	26	34

Note: Annual averages.

Sources: Statistics Norway, Nordicom-Sweden, 2010.

Sweden: Most Frequent Internet Activities Among Children 9-14 years 2009 (%)

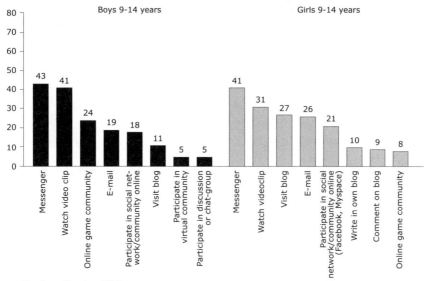

Source: Nordicom-Sweden, 2010.

Finland: Restrictions Used by Parents Regarding Children's Use of the Computer 2009 (%)

Time spent using the computer	64
Time of day	62
Content used	59
Other rules	17
Let children decide themselves	16
Not able to say	11

Note: Parents with children < 18 years.

Source: Finnish Communications Regulatory Authority, 2009.

Norway: Trust in Internet Among Children 9-16 years 2003-2010 (%)

To what extent do you believe Internet content is true/correct?

	2003	2006	2008	2010
Everything	2	3	1	2
Most of it	47	34	31	35
Only some	36	47	51	49
Nothing	1	2	1	1
Don't know	13	11	7	13

Note: Children 9-16 years.

Source: Norwegian Media Authority, 2010.

Norway: Children 9-16 years Talking to Parents About Internet Activities 2010 (%)

To what extent do you talk to your parents about what you do on the Internet?

	To my mother	To my father
A lot	15	13
Some	33	29
A little	36	37
Not at all	11	15

Note: Children 9-16 years.

Source: Norwegian Media Authority, 2010.

Norway: Learning about Internet Among Children 9-16 years 2010 (%)

Where did you learn most about Internet?

Learned my self	49
From my parents	47
Friends my own age	40
Older brothers/sisters	31
My teachers	25
Elswhere	9

Note: Children 9-16 years.

Source: Norwegian Media Authority, 2010.

Norway: House Rules for Internet Use at Home Among Children 9-16 years 2010 (%)

Which of these rules do you follow at home?

Not allowed to meet someone I only know online	54
Not allowed to leave mean comments on MSN/e-mail	53
Not allowed to give out personal information on web sites or when chatting	50
Not allowed to buy anything	50
Tell my parents if I find something unpleasant	43
Not allowed to talk to strangers online	39
Not allowed to download music/movies which are not paid for	35
Not allowed to copy images/videos without permission	34

Note: Children 9-16 years.

Source: Norwegian Media Authority, 2010.

Denmark: Comments on Others Internet Profiles 2009 (%)

Do you leave comments on other people's Internet profiles,
e.g. guestbooks, pictures, status on e.g. Facebook or Arto?

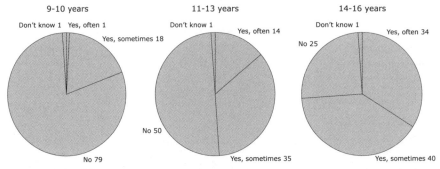

9-10 years

Don't know 1 Yes, often 1
Yes, sometimes 18
No 79

11-13 years

Don't know 1
Yes, often 14
No 50
Yes, sometimes 35

14-16 years

Don't know 1
Yes, often 34
No 25
Yes, sometimes 40

Source: Danish Media Council & Zapera.com A/S, 2009.

Denmark: Youth Participation in Debates and/or Groups on Internet 2009 (%)

Do you participate in debates and/or groups on the Internet,
e.g. Arto Debat, Facebook Groups or similar?

9-16 years

Don't know 1   Yes, often 8

Yes, sometimes 26

No 65

Source: Danish Media Council & Zapera.com A/S, 2009.

Denmark: Children and Youth with Own Internet Profile, 2009 (%)

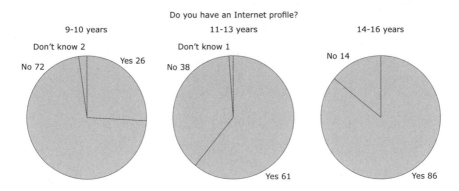

Do you have an Internet profile?

| 9-10 years | 11-13 years | 14-16 years |

Source: Danish Media Council & Zapera.com A/S, 2009.

Denmark: Where Do Youth Have Their Internet Profile? 2009 (%)

Name of site	Type	%
Facebook	SNS	73
MSN	SNS	59
Arto	Web community	41
YouTube	Photo/video sharing	25
Habbo Hotel	Virtual world	20
Game sites		17
GoSupermodel	Game/creativity	17
Skum (DR)	Web community	9
MySpace	SNS	8
Netstationen	Web community	3
NationX	Web community	3
Vix	Photo/video sharing	1
Other		20
Don't know		0

Base: Respondents 9-16 years old who have their own Internet profile

Source: Danish Media Council & Zapera.com A/S, 2009.

Mobile Phone

Children Using Own Mobile Phone 2008 (%)

	Yes	With access to Internet	No
Finland	87	22	13
Denmark	79	17	21
Sweden	76	21	23
EU 27	64	11	37

Source: European Commission, 2008.

Norway: Daily Telephone Use among Children and Youth 2009

	9-15 years Boys	9-15 years Girls	16-24 years Boys	16-24 years Girls	9-79 years All
Private telephone call					
%	58	71	85	91	83
No.	1.9	2.2	5.7	4.1	3.8
Private mobile phone call					
%	46	60	84	91	74
Private SMS					
%	35	49	83	94	64
No.	3.7	5.8	9.9	14.4	4.7
Access to Internet via mobile phone					
%	8	1	15	10	7

Source: Statistics Norway, 2010.

Sweden: Access to Mobile Phone Functions Among Children 9-14 years 2009 (%)

Boys 9-14 years		Girls 9-14 years	
SMS/text messages	95	SMS/text messages	97
Games	87	Games	92
Camera	84	Camera	89
MMS	81	MMS	88
Mp3-files	73	Mp3-files	75
FM-radio	62	FM-radio	66
Internet	61	Internet	60
Video phone call (3G)	36	E-mail	35
E-mail	25	Video phone call (3G)	34
Messenger/MSN	22	Messenger/MSN	23
Mobile TV	9	GPS-navigator	6
GPS-navigator	6	Mobile TV	6

Note: Among children with own mobile phone. In the age group 9-14 years 85% of the boys and 93% of the girls have access to their own mobile phone.

Source: Nordicom-Sweden, 2010.

Sweden: Mobile Phones and Purpose of Use Among Children 9-14 years Average Day 2009 (%)

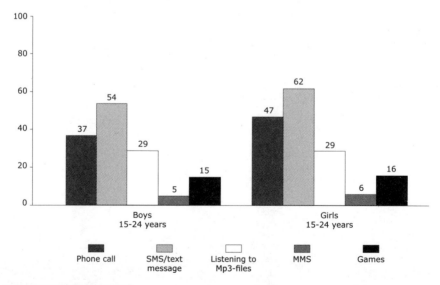

Note: Among mobile phone users.

Source: Nordicom-Sweden, 2010.

Sweden: Access to Mobile Phone Functions Among Youth 15-24 years 2009 (%)

Boys 15-24 years		Girls 15-24 years	
SMS/text messages	99	SMS/text messages	99
Games	93	Games	92
MMS	92	Camera	96
Camera	90	MMS	91
Mp3-files	84	Mp3-files	83
Internet	77	FM-radio	72
FM-radio	76	Internet	75
E-mail	52	E-mail	51
Video phone call (3G)	51	Video phone call (3G)	47
Messenger/MSN	30	Messenger/MSN	24
GPS-navigator	25	GPS-navigator	15
Mobile-TV	14	Mobile-TV	7

Note: Among children with own mobile phone. In the age group 15-24 years 92% of the boys and 96% of the girls have access to their own mobile phone.

Source: Nordicom-Sweden, 2010.

Sweden: Mobile Phones and Purpose of Use Among Youth 15-24 years Average Day 2009 (%)

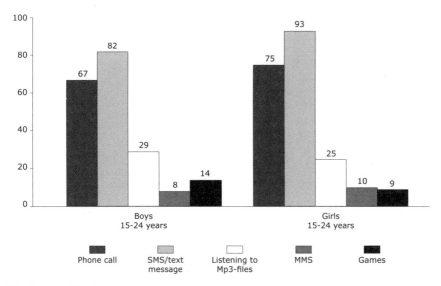

Note: Among mobile phone users.

Source: Nordicom-Sweden, 2010.

Games

Norway: Use of Computer/Video Games an Average Day 2005-2009 (%)

	Age			
	9-15 years		16-24 years	
Average Day	boys	girls	boys	girls
2005	57	23	27	9
2006	59	33	32	7
2007	61	32	29	8
2008	53	30	41	8
2009	57	42	43	14

Source: Statistics Norway, 2010.

Sweden: Use of Computer/Video/Online Games an Average Day 2007-2009 (minutes)

	Age	
Year	9–14	15–24
2007	95	109
2008	77	103
2009	75	96

Source: Nordicom-Sweden, 2010.

Norway: Electronic Game Playing Among Children 9-16 years 2010 (%)

When you play electronic games/computer games, who do you usually play with?

Family or friends in the same room	57
Alone	54
Family or friends over Internet	28
With online contacts	18
Don't know	6
Do not play electronic games/ computer games	4

Base: Children 9-16 years.
Source: Norwegian Media Authority, 2010.

Norway: Favourite Game Genres Among Children 9-16 years 2010 (%)

Sports- and racing games	44
Party games	43
Shooting- and action games	42
Humour-/cartoon games	38
Other	34
Strategic games	28
Roleplaying games	18
Adventure games	13
Don't know	4

Base: Children 9-16 years. Games on- and offline.
Source: Norwegian Media Authority, 2010.

Sweden: Top 15 Games Sold 2009

Place	Title	Format	Genre	PEGI[1]	Publisher
1.	The Sims 3	PC	Simulator	12	Electronic Arts
2.	New Super Mario Bros Wii	Wii	Platform	3	Nintendo
3.	Modern Warfare 2	PS3	Action	18	Activision
4.	Modern Warfare 2	XB360	Action	18	Activision
5.	Wii Sports: Resort	Wii	Sport	7	Nintendo
6.	Modern Warfare 2	PC	Action	18	Activision
7.	New Super Mario Bros	DS	Platform	3	Nintendo
8.	Mario Kart Wii	Wii	Racing	3	Nintendo
9.	World of Warcraft: Wrath of the Lich King	PC	Online	12	Blizzard
10.	FIFA 10	PS3	Sport	3	Electronic Arts
11.	FIFA 10	XB360	Sport	3	Electronic Arts
12.	Wii Fit	Wii	Party	3	Nintendo
13.	Assassin's Creed 2	PS3	Action	18	Ubisoft
14.	Singstar Abba	PS2	Music	3	SCEE
15.	World of Warcraft	PC	Online	12	Blizzard

[1] Pan-European Game Information age rating system.
Note: The list is based on reportings from 300 retailers.
Source: Swedish Games Industry, 2010.

Television

Number of TV Channels Available in Denmark, Finland and Sweden 2009

Country	Children's Channels	Foreign Channels	Total
Denmark	11	214	411
Finland	11	184	254
Sweden	8	179	328

Note: Estimates. Free to air channels on satellite have been counted only in their country of establishment, even if they are, in practice, available in most European countries.

Source: European Audiovisual Observatory, 2010.

TV Programming for Children and Young People by Public Service Channels in the Nordic Countries 2005-2008 (hours)

Country	Channel	2005	2006	2007	2008
Denmark	DR 1	834	844	..	1 407
	DR 2	2	5	..	51
Finland	YLE TV1	207	243	129	4
	YLE TV2	876	836	794	1 187
Iceland	RÚV	584	552	554	552
Norway	NRK1	965	1 002	1 055	..
	NRK2	18	13	30	..
Sweden	SVT 1	777	784	930	685
	SVT 2	6	22	11	97

.. Data not available.

Note: The tables include programming for children and young people in various categories such as "entertainment", "education" and "animation".

Source: European Audiovisual Observatory, 2010.

TV Channel Families Market Shares in Denmark, Finland, Norway and Sweden 2009 (%)

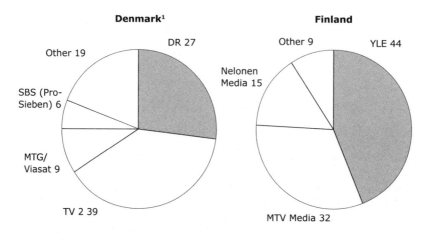

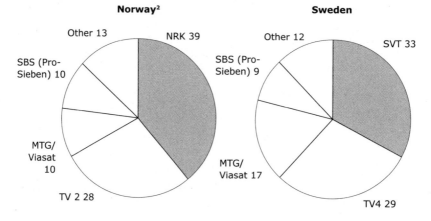

[1] MTG/Viasat: Data include TV3, 3+ and TV3 PULS. MTG pay-tv channels TV1000 and other Viasat-channels not included. MTG and TV 2 / Denmark: TV 2 Sport, a joint venture between MTG and TV 2 / Denmark, is not included.

[2] Pay-tv channel TV 2 Sport is not included. MTG/Viasat: Data include TV3 and Viasat 4. MTG pay-tv channels TV1000 and other Viasat-channels are not included. SBS (ProSieben): Data refer to main channels TVNorge and FEM.

Note: Share of daily viewing time. Public service television in grey.

Source: Nordicom, 2010 (processed), see www.nordicom.gu.se/eng.php?portal=mt

Total Daily TV Viewing Time 2000-2009 (minutes)

Year	Denmark				Finland[1]				Iceland[2]	Norway[1]				Sweden		
	(Age 3+)	(3-10)	(11-19)	(20-25)	(Age 10+)	(4-9)	(10-14)	(15-24)	(Age 12-80)	(Age 12+)	(3-6)	(7-11)	(12-19)	(Age 3+)	(3-14)	(15-24)
2000	149	..	..	..	168	75	105	111	149	163	83	103	114	150	96	106
2003	157	82	98	165	173	74	95	106	153	164	83	89	109	150	89	104
2006	150	82	96	158	169	68	88	105	149	156	85	91	88	154	96	101
2009	189	111	120	202	176	74	89	93	158	184	107 [3]	114	108	166	98	100

.. Data not available.

[1] Timeshift within 7 days included in Finland and Norway from 2008 on.

[2] TV-meter rating figures from 2007 on. With the introduction of TV-meter measuring, catch-up-channel viewing was included.

[3] 2009: Population aged 2-6.

Note: TV-meter rating figures, except for Iceland 2000-2006.

Source: Nordicom, 2010 (processed), see www.nordicom.gu.se/eng.php?portal=mt

Daily Reach TV Viewing[1] 2000-2009 (%)

Year	Denmark				Finland				Iceland	Norway				Sweden		
	(Age 3+)	(3-10)	(11-19)	(20-25)	(Age 10+)	(4-9)	(10-14)	(15-24)	(Age 12-80)	(Age 12+)	(3-6)	(7-11)	(12-19)	(Age 3+)	(3-14)	(15-24)
2000	71	..	..	..	77	63	72	65	88	72	67	65	62	76	73	61
2003	71	59	55	60	77	65 [2]	68	62	91	71	64	62	59	73	65	56
2006	72	61	54	65	75	62	64	61	87	69	62	61	55	71	63	54
2009	74	66	57	65	73	..	..	..	..	71	69 [3]	66	56	70	62	50

.. Data not available.

[1] Definition of daily reach: Denmark and Sweden: share of viewers who have watched at least 5 consecutive minutes; Finland and Norway: based on one minute's viewing; Iceland: share of respondents who tuned in to the stations per day on average.

[2] 2003: population aged 3-9.

[3] 2009: population aged 2-6.

Note: TV-meter rating figures, except for Iceland.

Source: Nordicom, 2010 (processed), see www.nordicom.gu.se/eng.php?portal=mt

Public Service TV Market Shares 2000-2009 (%)

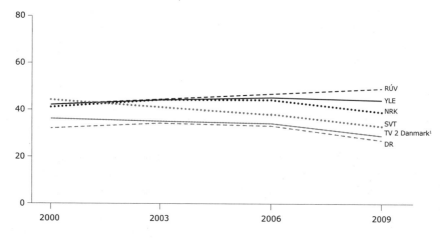

¹ TV 2 main channel only.

Note: TV-meter rating figures, except for Iceland 2000-2006. Timeshift within 7 days included in Finland and Norway in 2009.

Source: Nordicom, 2010 (processed), see www.nordicom.gu.se/eng.php?portal=mt

Denmark: Children's Viewing on Domestic Public Service vs Foreign TV Channel's (% of viewingtime)

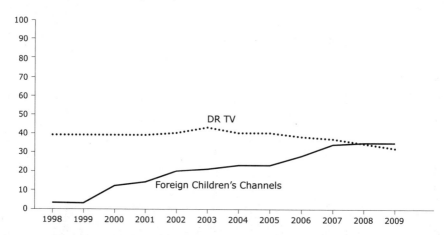

Note: Children 3-10 years.

Source: TNS Gallup TV-Meter/DR, 2009.

Finland: Restrictions Used by Parents Regarding Children's TV-Viewing 2009 (%)

	%
Programme content	79
Time in the evening	77
Time spent viewing TV	52
TV channels	22
Let children decide themselves	17
Other	6
Not able to say	2

Note: Parents with children < 18 years.

Source: Finnish Communications Regulatory Authority, 2009.

Nordvision's Programme Cooperation Among the Nordic Public Service TV Broadcasters 2009

About Nordvision

Nordvision is a television and media partnership involving the five Nordic public service broadcasting organizations funded by license fees. Nordvision was established in 1959 by the public service broadcasting companies in Denmark (DR), Finland (YLE), Norway (NRK) and Sweden (SVT). Iceland (RÚV) joined Nordvision in 1966. Sweden's Utbild-ningsradio (UR) Greenland's national broadcasting company (KNR) and Faroe Island's Sjønvarp Føroya (KVF) are associated members of the Nordvision partnership.

The nucleus of the Nordvision partnership is co-production of programmes and web projects, programme exchange, and the sharing of professional expertise and experience in expert groups.

Source: www.nordvision.org

Hours/programmes generated by co-production and exchange in total 2009

	Hours	Programmes
Co-productions	570	1 340
Programme exchange	1 059[1]	2 049
Total hours	1 629	3 389

[1] Number of generated programme hours is based on the average programme length (31 minutes) for exchange programmes in the three factual programme screenings in 2009 (2049x31 min/60=1059 hours)

Note: In total among Nordvision public service broadcasters: DR, YLE, RÚV, NRK, SVT and UR.

Source: Nordvision, 2010.

Co-production Hours per Broadcaster 2009

		Hours
YLE	Finland	145
NRK	Norway	124
SVT	Sweden	116
DR	Denmark	104
RÚV	Iceland	41
UR	Sweden	40
Total		570

Source: Nordvision, 2010.

Programme Hours Generated by Co-productions, by Genre 2009 (%)

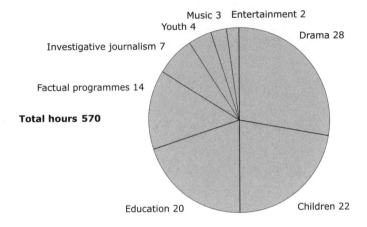

Music 3 Entertainment 2
Youth 4

Investigative journalism 7

Factual programmes 14

Total hours 570

Drama 28

Education 20

Children 22

Note: In total among Nordvision broadcasters DR, YLE, RÚV, NRK, SVT and UR.

Source: Nordvision, 2010.

Number of Offered and Received Programmes per Broadcaster 2008

		Programmes offered	Programmes received
DR	Denmark	351	174
NRK	Norway	136	563
RÚV	Iceland	175	382
SVT	Sweden	7	182
UR	Sweden	115	112
YLE	Finland	228	510
Number of programmes in total		1 012	1 923

Source: Nordvision, 2010.

Video/DVD

Penetration of VCRs and DVD-players 2000-2009 (%)

	Year	Denmark[1]	Finland[1]	Iceland[2]	Norway[3]	Sweden[3]
VCR	2000	77	71	89	79	85
	2003	80	72	84	77	87
	2006	70	65	78	68	81
	2008	..	52	74	62	57
	2009	..	40	67	55	53
DVD-player	2000	..	..	9	..	7
	2003	32	20 [4]	54	43	37
	2006	74	54 [4]	81	80	78
	2008	84	59 [4]	83	87	85
	2009	..	59 [4]	82	86	86
PVR	2006	..	2	..	..	2
	2008	..	33	..	26	12
	2009	..	37	..	29	15

.. Data not available.

[1] Share of households.
[2] The figures come from different surveys and are not wholly comparable between years. In a few cases data are based on households, otherwise on population.
[3] Share of population 9-79 years.
[4] Separate DVD-players.

Source: Nordicom, 2010 (processed), see www.nordicom.gu.se/eng.php?portal=mt

Video and DVD Viewing the Average Day in Finland, Norway and Sweden 2000-2009 (%)

	Finland		Norway			Sweden		
Year	Age: 10+	10-24	Age: 9-79	9-15	16-24	Age: 9-79	9-14	15-24
2000	19	20	10	19	19	15	37	26
2003	..	..	9	21	19	14	36	23
2006	14	22	10	20	21	14	25	21
2009	10	19	13	16	29	12	24	18

Note: Including both VHS- DVD and PVR-viewing (from 2007 in Sweden).
Sources: Statistics Finland, Statistics Norway, Nordicom-Sweden, 2010.

Radio

Number of Radio Channels[1] 2009

			2009
Denmark	Public	Nationwide	4
		Regional	9
		Digital (DAB)	12
	Private	Nationwide[2]	2
		Local	341
		Digital (DAB)	1
Finland	Public	Nationwide	6
		Regional	26
		Digital (DVB)	2
	Private	Nationwide	1
		Near-nationwide	9
		Other private	44
Iceland	Public	Nationwide	2
		Regional	3
		Digital (DAB)	1
	Private	Nationwide	2
		Regional/Quasi-national/local	15
		Total	17
Norway	Public	Nationwide	3
		Regional	16
		Digital (DAB) Nationwide	8
		Digital (DAB) Regional	1
	Private	Nationwide	2
		Local	249
		Digital (DAB)	–
Sweden	Public	Nationwide (FM)	4
		Regional	27
		Digital (DAB)	7
	Private	Local	89
		Community radio	ca 900

[1] Most channels are transmitted via several platforms. Channels not stated as 'digital' are principally FM channels, most of which are also transmitted on digital platforms. The table's 'Digital' includes principally digital channels (DAB/DVB); even though some also offer limited analogue transmissions. Channels/stations transmitted exclusively via web, cable or satellite are not included in this table.

[2] The nationwide private channels with concessions from the state are also transmitted via DAB since 2005.

Source: Nordicom, 2010 (processed), see www.nordicom.gu.se/eng.php?portal=mt

Public Service Radio Market Shares[1] 2000-2009 (%)

		2000	2003	2006	2009
DR	Denmark	66	70	72	..
YLE	Finland	60	50	52	52
RÚV	Iceland	56	52	51	55
NRK	Norway	59	59	62	62
SR	Sweden	66	66	63	66

.. Data not available.

[1] Average daily listening Monday-Sunday.

Note: Different methods have been used, which impairs comparability between countries and years. Data should be taken as indicators of the trend and level of listening. Data include listening to radio, irrespective of platform.

Source: Nordicom, 2010 (processed), see www.nordicom.gu.se/eng.php?portal=mt

Radio Listening: Daily Reach 2000-2009 (%)

Year	Denmark (Age: 12+)	Finland (Age: 9+)	Iceland (Age 12-80)	Norway (Age: 9+/12+)	Sweden (Age: 9-79)
2000	86	81	..	66	79
2003	83	82	88	69	77
2006	80	79	83	69	79
2007	81	79	88	67	74
2008	70	78	..	78	75
2009	78	78	..	75	75

.. Data not available.

Note: Different methods have been used, which impairs comparability between countries and years. Data should be taken as indicators of the trend and level of listening. Data include listening to radio, irrespective of platform.

Source: Nordicom, 2010 (processed), see www.nordicom.gu.se/eng.php?portal=mt

Radio Listening: Daily Reach by Sex and Age[1] 2006/2007-2009 (%)

Denmark: All radio	2006
All	82
Sex	
Men	83
Women	82
Age	
12-24	75
25-39	79
40-59	85
60+	88

Finland: All radio	2009
All	78
Sex	
Men	78
Women	78
Age	
9-14	60
15-24	69
25-34	74
35-44	77
45-54	82
55-64	86
65+	87

Norway: All radio	2009
All	75
Sex	
Men	76
Women	74
Age	
12-19	63
20-34	68
35-44	76
45-54	82
55-64	81
65+	83

Sweden: All radio	2009
All	75
Sex	
Men	76
Women	74
Age	
9-19	68
20-34	68
35-49	78
50-64	80
65-79	82

Iceland 2007 (three largest channels)	RÚV/Rás 1	RÚV/Rás 2	Bylgjan
All	30	42	38
Sex			
Men	29	49	40
Women	30	35	36
Age			
12-19	4	18	28
20-29	11	39	34
30-39	17	33	52
40-49	27	55	49
50-59	48	58	37
60-80	70	50	28

[1] Monday-Sunday, except for Iceland: Monday-Friday.

Note: Different methods have been used, which impairs comparability between countries. Data should be taken as indicators of the trend and level of listening. Data include listening to radio, irrespective of platform.

Source: Nordicom, 2010 (processed), see www.nordicom.gu.se/eng.php?portal=mt

Radio Listening: Daily Listening Time[1] 2000-2009 (minutes)

Year	Denmark (Age: 12+)	Finland (Age: 9+)	Iceland (Age 12-80)	Norway[2] (Age: 9+/12+)	Sweden (Age: 9-79)
2000	197	201	204	135	174
2003	189	206	236	145	163
2006	179	194	237	137	174
2009	127	191	117	98	151

[1] Average daily listening Monday-Sunday.
[2] 2000-2006: age 9+, 2009: age 12+.

Note: Different methods have been used, which impairs comparability between countries and years. Data should be taken as indicators of the trend and level of listening. Data include listening to radio, irrespective of platform.

Source: Nordicom, 2010 (processed), see www.nordicom.gu.se/eng.php?portal=mt

Newspapers

Number of Newspapers 2009

	Denmark 2009	Finland 2008	Iceland 2008/2009[1]	Norway 2009	Sweden 2009
Paid-for newspapers total	32	201	12	225	160
of which dailies[2]	31	51	1	75	78
of which non-dailies[3]	1	150	11	150	82
Free papers total[4]	..	..	13	26	..
of which dailies[2]	3	2	2	0	4
of which non-dailies[3]	232	144	11	26	82

.. Data not available.

[1] Iceland: Paid-for newspapers in 2009, free papers in 2008.
[2] Published 4-7 days/week.
[3] Published 1-3 days/week.
[4] A wide variety of papers that fill two minimum criteria: they contain editorial material and appear at least once a week.

Source: Nordicom, 2010 (processed), see www.nordicom.gu.se/eng.php?portal=mt

Total Newspaper Circulation in the Nordic Countries 2008/2009 ('000)

	Denmark 2009	Finland 2008	Iceland 2008	Norway 2009	Sweden 2009
Paid-for newspapers total	1 093	3 066	81	2 659	3 610
of which dailies[1]	1 040	2 127	67	1 943	3 229
of which non-dailies[2]	53	939	14	716	382
Free papers total[3]	..	6 800	270	902	..
of which dailies[1]	476	..	211	–	932
of which non-dailies[2]	8 837	..	59	902	2 807

.. Data not available.

[1] Published 4-7 days/week.
[2] Published 1-3 days/week.
[3] A wide variety of papers that fill two minimum criteria: they contain editorial material and appear at least once a week. Data are based on total print and distribution, instead of circulation.

Source: Nordicom, 2010 (processed), see www.nordicom.gu.se/eng.php?portal=mt

Newspaper Readership: Daily Reach 2000-2009 (%)

	Readers of paper version (%)					All readers, paper and/or online (%)	
Year	Denmark[1,2] Age: 12+	Finland[3] Age: 12+/10+	Iceland Age: 12-80	Norway Age: 9-79	Sweden[4] Age: 9-79	Norway Age: 9-79	Sweden[4] Age: 9-79
2000	75	86	74	77	81	77	85
2003	75	..	..	77	74	80	81
2006	74	81	..	74	..	82	81
2009	67	75	..	65	71	78	77

.. Data not available.

[1] Weekdays only. Including free papers.
[2] Changes in method in 2006 and 2009. Figures from these years are not comparable with previous years.
[3] 10+ from 2006. Figures from 2006 onward are not comparable with previous years.
[4] Including free daily newspapers.

Source: Nordicom, 2010 (processed), see www.nordicom.gu.se/eng.php?portal=mt

Newspaper Readership in Finland, Norway and Sweden: Daily Reach by Sex and Age 2009 (%)

Readers of paper version (%)

Finland	Reach	Norway	Reach	Sweden[1]	Reach
All	75	*All*	65	*All*	71
Sex		*Sex*		*Sex*	
Men	75	Men	66	Men	70
Women	76	Women	64	Women	71
Age		*Age*		*Age*	
10-24	**53**	**9-15**	**38**	**9-14**	**39**
25-44	**72**	**16-24**	**46**	**15-24**	**50**
45-59	85	25-44	63	25-44	65
60+	88	45-66	81	45-64	83

All readers, paper and/or online (%)

Norway	Reach	Sweden[1]	Reach
All	78	*All*	77
Sex		*Sex*	
Men	81	Men	77
Women	75	Women	76
Age		*Age*	
9-15	**43**	**9-14**	**41**
16-24	**73**	**15-24**	**58**
25-44	84	25-44	76
45-66	86	45-64	88
67-79	83	65-79	89

[1] Including free daily newspapers.

Source: Nordicom, 2010 (processed), see www.nordicom.gu.se/eng.php?portal=mt

Books

Books Published for Children and Youth 2000-2009 (number of titles)

Year	Denmark	Finland[1]	Iceland[1]	Norway[2]	Sweden[1]
2000	1 924	993	156	833	946
2003	1 543	896	151	921	1 016
2006	1 782	1 118	217	1 245	1 556
2007	1 992	890	276	1 302	1 677
2008	1 937	1 138	269	1 259	1 977
2009	2 010	..	..	1 116 [2]	1 744

.. Data not available.

[1] Includes both fiction and non-fiction, but not text books.
[2] The most recent figures are generally low, as not all data have been registered.

Note: Books and booklets (less than 49 pages).

Source: Nordicom, 2010 (processed), see www.nordicom.gu.se/eng.php?portal=mt

Daily Book Reading in Finland, Norway and Sweden 2000-2009 (%)

	Finland[1]		Norway[3]			Sweden[4]		
Year	Age: 12+/10+[2]	Age: 10-24	Age: 9-79	Age: 9-15	Age: 16-24	Age: 9-79	Age: 9-14	Age: 15-24
2000	36	..	20	18	19	39	66	44
2003	..	..	23	31	18	35	55	40
2006	..	..	24	31	16	38	61	39
2009	32	42	27	32	16	36	59	40

.. Data not available.

[1] Figures for 2003 and onwards are not fully comparable with the figures of 2000.
[2] 10+ from 2006.
[3] Occupation- and school related reading and reading aloud to children not included.
[4] Included is all reading/book use. From 2006 and onwards also listening to audio-books.

Sources: Statistics Finland, Statistics Norway, Nordicom-Sweden, 2010.

Norway: Book Reading Among Children 9-15 Years by Genre 2009 (%)

9-15 years

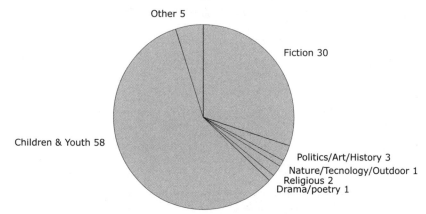

Other 5

Fiction 30

Children & Youth 58

Politics/Art/History 3
Nature/Tecnology/Outdoor 1
Religious 2
Drama/poetry 1

16-24 years

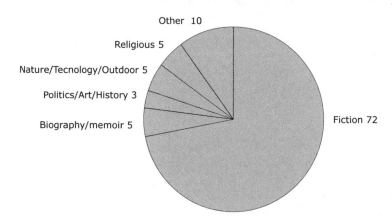

Other 10

Religious 5

Nature/Tecnology/Outdoor 5

Politics/Art/History 3

Biography/memoir 5

Fiction 72

Note: Book reading an average day.
Source: Statistics Norway, 2010.

Sweden: Book Reading Among Children and Youth by Genre 2009 (%)

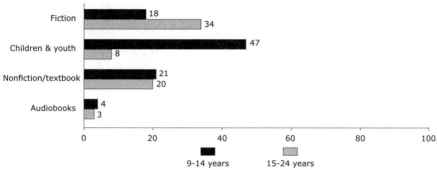

Note: Book reading an average week.

Source: Nordicom-Sweden, 2010.

Sweden: Different Ways of Obtaining Books 2009

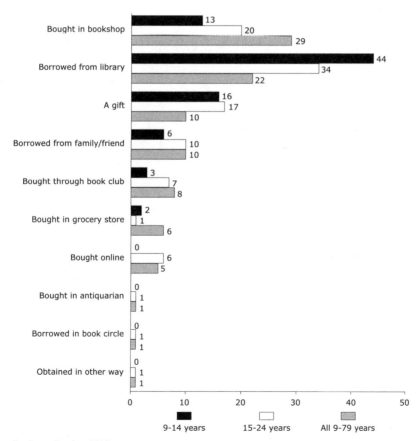

Source: Nordicom-Sweden, 2010.

249

Basic Indicators

Country	Total Population ('000) 2007	under 18	under 5	Life expectancy at birth (years) 2007	HIV prevalence (%) among young people (15-24) 2007 male	female	Youth Literacy Rate (%) 2000-2007 male	female
Denmark	5 442	1 210	318	78	0.2	0.1	100	100
Finland	5 277	1 093	287	79	0.1	<0.1	100	100
Iceland	301	78	21	82	0.2	<0.1	100	100
Norway	4 698	1 092	284	80	0.1	0.1	100	100
Sweden	9 119	1 912	505	81	0.1	0.1	100	100
Summary Indicators								
Sub-Saharan Africa	767 218	383 988	127 624	50	1.1	3.2	77	68
Eastern and Southern Africa	378 926	186 875	61 296	50	1.5	4.5	78	69
West and Central Africa	388 292	197 113	66 328	50	0.7	1.9	77	66
Middle East and North Africa	389 176	153 178	44 789	69	0.1	0.2	93	85
South Asia	1 567 187	614 747	175 250	64	0.3	0.2	84	74
East Asia and Pacific	1 984 273	559 872	144 441	72	0.2	0.1	98	98
Latin America and Caribbean	566 646	197 226	55 622	72	0.5	0.4	97	97
CEE/CIS	405 992	100 110	26 458	68	0.8	0.5	99	99
Industrialized countries[1]	974 913	204 334	54 922	79	0.4	0.2	..	..
Developing Countries[1]	5 432 873	1 962 419	562 128	67	0.4	0.7	90	84
Least Developed Countries[1]	804 450	383 853	124 237	55	0.6	1.4	75	65
World	**6 655 406**	**2 213 456**	**629 106**	**68**	**0.4**	**0.6**	**90**	**85**

.. Data not available

[1] Also includes territories within each country category or regional group.

Source: UNICEF, 2010: www.unicef.org/sowc09, Youth literacy in the Nordic countries: UNESCO 2004.

Sources (Statistics)

Danish Media Council & Zapera.com A/S, 2009: *Digitalt Børne og Ungdomsliv anno 2009* [Digital childhood and youth in the year 2009], København, 2009. www.medieraadet.dk

European Audiovisual Observatory, 2010: *European Audiovisual Observatory Yearbook 2009: Volume 2*, 'Trends in European Television', Strasbourg, 2010. www.obs.coe.int

European Commission, 2008: *Flash Eurobarometer 248 'Towards a Safer Use of the Internet for Children in the EU: A Parents Perspective'*, Luxembourg, 2008. http://ec.europa.eu/information_society/activities/sip/surveys/index_en.htm (retrieved May 2010).

Finnish Communications Regulatory Authority, 2009: Tiina Aaltonen; *Mediakasvatus suomalaisperheissä 2009* [Media education in families in Finland 2009], Helsinki, 2009. www.ficora.fi

Nordicom, 2010: Nordic Media Trends and Media Statistics, University of Gothenburg. http://www.nordicom.gu.se/eng.php?portal=mt (Retrieved May 2010).

Nordicom-Sweden, 2010: Mediebarometern [The Media Barometer], annual survey, Nordicom-Sweden, University of Gothenburg. www.nordicom.gu.se

Nordvision, 2010: Nordvision Annual Report 2008 and 2009. www.nordvision.org (Retrieved May 2010).

Norwegian Media Authority, 2010: *Barn og Digitale Medier 2010* [Children and digital media 2010], Fredrikstad, 2010. www.medietilsynet.no

Statistics Finland, 2010: *Joukkoviestimet 2009/Finnish Mass Media 2009,* Helsinki 2010. www.stat.fi

Statistics Norway, 2010: Norsk Mediebarometer [Norwegian Media Barometer], annual survey, Oslo-Kongsvinger, 2010. www.ssb.no

Swedish Games Industry, 2010: *Speltoppen 2009* [Games top sales list 2009], Stockholm, 2010. www.dataspelsbranschen.se

TNS Gallup TV-Meter/DR, 2009: *Udfordringer for danske medier og public service i en global medieverden* [Challenges for Danish media and public service in a global media world], København, 2009. www.dr.dk

UNESCO, 2004: *EFA Global Monitoring Report 2005: Education for All, the Quality Imperative.* Statistical Annex, Table 2. Paris: UNESCO.

UNICEF, 2009: *The State of the World's Children 2009*, www.unicef.org/sowc09 (Retrieved April 2010).